# Mexicans in Alaska

Anthropology of Contemporary North America

**SERIES EDITORS**

James Bielo, *Miami University*

Carrie Lane, *California State University, Fullerton*

**ADVISORY BOARD**

Peter Benson, *Washington University in St. Louis*

John L. Caughey, *University of Maryland*

Alyshia Gálvez, *Lehman College*

Carol Greenhouse, *Princeton University*

John Hartigan, *University of Texas*

John Jackson Jr., *University of Pennsylvania*

Ellen Lewin, *University of Iowa*

Bonnie McElhinny, *University of Toronto*

Shalini Shankar, *Northwestern University*

Carol Stack, *University of California, Berkeley*

# Mexicans in Alaska

An Ethnography of Mobility,
Place, and Transnational Life

*Sara V. Komarnisky*

University of Nebraska Press
Lincoln and London

© 2018 by the Board of Regents of the University of Nebraska

Parts of chapter 5 were originally published in "Suitcases Full of *Mole*: Traveling Foods and the Connections between Mexico and Alaska," *Alaska Journal of Anthropology* 7, no. 1 (2009): 41–56. Reprinted by permission of the Alaska Anthropological Association.

All rights reserved. Manufactured in the United States of America. ♾

Library of Congress Cataloging-in-Publication Data
Names: Komarnisky, Sara V., author.
Title: Mexicans in Alaska: an ethnography of mobility, place, and transnational life / Sara V. Komarnisky.
Description: Lincoln: University of Nebraska Press, 2018. | Series: Anthropology of contemporary North America | Includes bibliographical references and index.
Identifiers: LCCN 2017038779 |
ISBN 9781496203649 (cloth: alk. paper)
ISBN 9781496205636 (pbk.: alk. paper)
ISBN 9781496206466 (epub)
ISBN 9781496206473 (mobi)
ISBN 9781496206480 (pdf)
Subjects: LCSH: Mexicans—Alaska—History. | Mexican Americans—Alaska—History. | Mexicans—Alaska—Social conditions. | Mexican Americans—Alaska—Social conditions. | Foreign workers, Mexican—Alaska—History. | Foreign workers, Mexican—Alaska—Social conditions. | Migrant labor—Alaska—History.
Classification: LCC F915.M5 K66 2018 |
DDC 305.868/720798—dc23
LC record available at https://lccn.loc.gov/2017038779

Set in Charter ITC by E. Cuddy.

Para la próxima generación de Acuitzences en Alaska:
que no se olviden de sus raíces

Echarle vueltas y vueltas y vueltas
(Going back and forth and back and forth).
LUIS BRAVO SR., describing his working life

## Contents

| | |
|---|---|
| List of Illustrations | xi |
| List of Tables | xiii |
| Acknowledgments | xv |
| Acuitzences in Alaska | xix |
| Introduction: Yes, There Are Mexicans in Alaska | 1 |
| 1. Tracing Mexican Alaska: A Transnational Social Space | 19 |
| 2. The Annual Migration of the Traveling Swallows: Shared Experiences of Mobility across North America | 45 |
| 3. "My Grandfather Worked Here": Three Generations of the Bravo Family in Alaska and Michoacán | 75 |
| 4. "You Have to Get Used to It": Living the North American Dream | 107 |
| 5. The Stuff of Transnational Life: Suitcases Full of *Mole*, T-Shirts, Roosters, and Other Things That Move | 135 |
| 6. "It Freezes the People Together": Producing a Mexican Alaska | 165 |
| Conclusion: Freedom to Move | 197 |
| Notes | 215 |
| Bibliography | 241 |
| Index | 251 |

# Illustrations

### FIGURES

1. Air crossroads of the world, 2013 — 50
2. Canadian-U.S. border along the Alaska Highway, 2011 — 60
3. Road between Tiripetio and Acuitzio, 1967 — 67
4. The Bravo family, 2012 — 78
5. "Oscar" and his rooster, 2012 — 136
6. Xochiquetzal-Tiqun at the Anchorage Museum, 2011 — 174
7. Chichén Itzá—Chugach — 184
8. Chichén Itzá—North Slope — 184
9. Zitácuaro—Chugach — 184

### MAPS

1. Interior Michoacán, Mexico — 29
2. Alaska — 36
3. Routes between Mexico and Anchorage, Alaska — 49

# Tables

1. Acuitzences in Alaska as of 2011–12    xx
2. North American economics, 2012    111
3. Things that travel, 2011–12    140

## Acknowledgments

Gracias a todos los Acuitzences en Alaska y en México. Les valoro la oportunidad que se dieron de compartir parte de sus experencias como migrantes e inmigrantes en los Estados Unidos. Agradezco especialmente a mis amigos de ambos países: Mariano y Lupe Villaseñor, Mariano Villaseñor Jr., Andrea Villaseñor, Ady Villaseñor, Ricardo y Tere Villaseñor, Natali Villaseñor, Cirila Sánchez, Vicente Sánchez, Gardenia Sánchez, Maria Elena y Daniel Calderón, Rosa Altamirano Dorantes, Daniela Villa, Jose Sánchez, Gonzalo y Eugenia Calderón, Taide y Esperanza Calvillo, Edgardo Calvillo López, Carlos Arjon, Brenda Calvillo López, y Ken and Imelda Cox. Gracias también a Martha, Adriana, Paulina, Luci, y Rosalía: nos divertimos mucho!

In Anchorage, thank you to Maria Elena Ball and Bart Roberts for talking about the *Mexico in Alaska* postcards with me and allowing me to reproduce them here. I am indebted to Ana Gutiérrez-Scholl, Ana Del Real, and everyone in Xochiquetzal-Tiqun for inviting me to practices and performances and for teaching me how to dance. I have learned a lot from Dayra Velázquez and Brooke Binkowski; both have their own fascinating projects about *mexicanos* in Alaska. Thank you to Sarah Hazell and Cameron Welch, who were fellow Canadian anthropologists in Alaska. Thank you to Kerry Feldman for your support over the years. And finally, thank you to the archivists who worked at the U.S. National Archives in Anchorage (especially Robyn!) and to Alea Oien, who did research for me at the Alaska State Archives in Juneau.

At the Department of Anthropology at the University of British Columbia, Vancouver, I want to especially acknowledge Gastón Gordillo, who gave me guidance and mentorship when I needed it, and the space to make this project my own. Thank you, Gastón. I am grateful to Alexia

Bloch, Juanita Sundberg, Pilar Riaño-Alcalá, Jon Beasley-Murray, and Lynn Stephen for their invaluable insights and suggestions. Thank you all. Felice Wyndham also contributed important ideas to the development of this project. As I struggled with writing, I read Shaylih Muehlmann's book *When I Wear My Alligator Boots*, which encouraged me to try to write like the ethnographies I love to read. For reading and engaging with earlier drafts of this work, thank you especially to Marlee McGuire, Natalie Baloy, Ana Vivaldi, Solen Roth, Tamar Scoggin-McKee, and Molly Malone. Thank you to Wade Tymchak and Tony Calvillo for your help with table 2. This work has also benefited immensely from conversations with my friends and colleagues who work in the Canadian North: thank you to Zoe Todd, Crystal Fraser, and Lindsay Bell. I also acknowledge Julie Cruikshank for her encouragement and interest in my work and Raymond Wiest for taking me on as a student and introducing me to Acuitzio, and for his support and mentorship since then.

I completed the book manuscript while a postdoctoral fellow at the University of Alberta. This has been an incredibly supportive environment in which to write and start new research, especially thanks to my mentor, Beverly Lemire, the whole Object Lives and Global Histories of Northern North America research group, and my colleagues in the Department of History and Classics—Sarah Carter, Crystal Fraser, Jaymie Heilman, Liza Piper, Susan Smith, and Shannon Stunden-Bower. Thank you to Colleen Skidmore for publishing advice!

Carrie Lane and James Bielo, editors for the Anthropology of Contemporary North America series, were enthusiastic about this project from start to finish. Thanks to you both! I also thank Alicia Christensen, American studies editor at the University of Nebraska Press, who has been a patient and supportive guide through the process. Thank you to reviewers Ruth Gomberg-Muñoz and Leigh Binford: your insightful critiques, comments, and suggestions have made this a better book.

Research for this project was funded by the Vanier Canada Graduate Scholarships program, the University of British Columbia, and the Liu Institute for Global Issues at UBC. For institutional support during fieldwork, I would like to extend my sincere thank-you to the Colegio de Michoacán and Dra. Gail Mummert Fulmer for arranging an *alumna visitante* position for me during fieldwork in Mexico, and to the Institute for Social and Economic Research (ISER) and Dr. Marie Lowe for a visiting student position at the University of Alaska, Anchorage.

Finally, thank you to Chris Shapka, the very best person I can imagine to travel through life with. As I prepared the final draft of this manuscript we welcomed our sweet daughter, Ingrid. I wish her, too, deep roots and the freedom to move.

Acuitzences in Alaska

This is an ethnography of people from Acutizio del Canje, Michoacán, Mexico, who live and work in Anchorage, Alaska. Most of these people have dual U.S.-Mexican citizenship or U.S. permanent residency (Green Card) and are able to move between Mexico and the United States, between Acuitzio and Anchorage. Everyone in this book is a real person (not a composite), but I have used pseudonyms and changed identifying details about them. Many of these people are part of interconnected multigenerational networks, families, *compadres*, and friends who have lived between Acuitzio and Anchorage for generations now. Those with last names (Bravo and Cárdenas) are part of families analyzed as multigenerational networks in the book. Here, I introduce you to the Acuitzences in Alaska who appear in this book:

Table 1. Acuitzences in Alaska as of 2011–12

| PSEUDONYM | AGE | ALASKA CONNECTION | MAIN RESIDENCE | "PAPERS" | RELATIONSHIPS | WORK |
|---|---|---|---|---|---|---|
| **Bravo family** | | | | | | |
| Ana Bravo | 42 | Moved to Alaska in 1992 after marrying Miguel Bravo. | Anchorage | Dual citizen (-) | Married to Miguel Bravo. Araceli Bravo is their daughter. Ana's brother Tomás also lives and works in Anchorage. Her sister Rosa lives in Acuitzio. | Industrial food preparation |
| Araceli Bravo | 18 | Born in Alaska. | Anchorage | U.S. citizen | Miguel and Ana's daughter, and Luis Sr.'s granddaughter. | Restaurant hostess |
| Gloria Bravo | 48 | Visited Anchorage from July to September 1980, and moved there with her husband in 1995. | Anchorage | Dual citizen (1998) | Luis Sr.'s daughter and Renata's mother. Her siblings, Luis Jr. and Miguel also live in Anchorage. | Industrial food preparation |
| Humberto Bravo (deceased) | - | Worked in Alaska in the 1960s. | - | - | Luis Sr.'s brother. | - |
| Juana Bravo* | 44 | Moved to Anchorage with her husband and children in 1996. | Anchorage | Dual citizen (2005) | Married to Luis Bravo Jr. They have three children: Toño, Verónica, and Sophia. Lupe's cousin Eduardo also works in Anchorage. | Industrial food preparation |

| Name | Age | | | | | Occupation |
|---|---|---|---|---|---|---|
| Luis Bravo Sr. | 78 | Worked in Alaska for twenty-five years, from 1960 to 1985. | Acuitzio | Mexican citizen | All of his children except for one currently live and work in Anchorage. | Retired |
| Luis Bravo Jr. | 46 | Came to Anchorage to work in 1983. | Anchorage | Dual citizen (1995) | Luis Sr.'s son, married to Juana Bravo. They have three children: Toño, Verónica, and Sophia. | Restaurant cook |
| Luis Antonio (Toño) Bravo | 20 | Born in Mexico and moved to Anchorage with his family as a small child in 1996. | Anchorage | Dual citizen (2004) | Luis and Juana's son, and Luis Sr.'s grandson. His sisters are Verónica and Sophia Bravo. | Restaurant dishwasher |
| Miguel Bravo | 43 | Went to Anchorage to work in 1986. | Anchorage | Dual citizen (1990) | Luis Sr.'s son, married to Ana Bravo. Araceli Bravo is their daughter. | Restaurant owner |
| Renata Bravo | 19 | Born in Mexico but moved to Anchorage with her parents as a small child in 1995. | Anchorage | Dual citizen (1999) | Gloria's daughter and Luis Sr.'s granddaughter. | Waitress |
| Sophia Bravo | 16 | Born in Mexico and moved to Anchorage with her family as a small child in 1996. | Anchorage | Dual citizen (2004) | Luis and Juana's youngest daughter, and Luis Sr.'s granddaughter. Her siblings are Toño and Verónica Bravo. | Restaurant office administration |
| Verónica Bravo | 18 | Born in Mexico and moved to Anchorage with her family as a small child in 1996. | Anchorage | Dual citizen (2004) | Luis and Juana's daughter, and Luis Sr.'s granddaughter. Her siblings are Toño and Sophia Bravo. | Restaurant hostess |

| PSEUDONYM | AGE | ALASKA CONNECTION | MAIN RESIDENCE | "PAPERS" | RELATIONSHIPS | WORK |
|---|---|---|---|---|---|---|
| **Cárdenas family** | | | | | | |
| Alina Cárdenas* | 50 | Lived in Anchorage from 1989 to 1991 and then moved back to Acuitzio with her children while Ernesto kept working in Alaska. The family moved back to Anchorage in 2000. | Anchorage | Mexican citizen; U.S. permanent resident | Married to Ernesto Sr. Claudia is their second-oldest daughter. | Restaurant kitchen manager |
| Bernardo Cárdenas | – | – | Anchorage | – | Married to Ernesto Jr.'s sister. He co-owns a restaurant with Miguel Bravo. | Restaurant owner |
| Claudia Cárdenas* | 30 | Born in Mexico and lived in Alaska as a child from 1989 to 1991. Moved back to Acuitzio with her family. Spent a short time in Anchorage from May to October 2001 and moved to Anchorage again in 2002. | Anchorage | Dual citizen (2007) | Ernesto Sr.'s granddaughter and Ernesto Jr. and Alina's daughter. Married to Iván. | Tax preparation |
| Ernesto Cárdenas Sr. | 78 | Lived and worked in Alaska for eleven years from 1966 to 1977. | Morelia | – | All of his children and most of his grandchildren live and work in Alaska. His wife was born in the United States but not in Alaska. | Retired |

| Name | Age | History | Location | Citizenship | Family | Occupation |
|---|---|---|---|---|---|---|
| Ernesto Cárdenas Jr. | 54 | Went to Alaska to work in 1987. | Anchorage | Dual citizen (1999 or 2000) | Ernesto Sr.'s son. Married to Alina. Claudia is their second-oldest daughter. | Costco |
| Iván Cárdenas | 30 | Has lived and worked in Alaska since 2001. | Anchorage | Mexican citizen; U.S. permanent resident | Married to Claudia. His uncle worked in Alaska from the 1950s to 1970s. | Merchant (buy/sell) |
| Adán | 28 | Has never been to Alaska but would like to work there someday. Has worked elsewhere in the United States. | Acuitzio | Mexican citizen | Luis Jr., Miguel, and Gloria Bravo are his tíos (uncle/aunt). | — |
| César* | 49 | Has been in Anchorage off and on since 1996. Said he was there from 1996 to 1997; 2002 to 2003; 2003 to present, a total of nine years. | Anchorage | Mexican citizen | César's wife and children live in Acuitzio. | Restaurant sous-chef |
| Diego | 28 | In Alaska from 2002 to 2009. Left because he feared deportation. | Acuitzio | Mexican citizen | Has a child who still lives in Anchorage. | Store owner |
| Eduardo* | 64 | Has worked in the United States for most of his adult life, and in Alaska since 2003. | Acuitzio | Mexican citizen; U.S. permanent resident (1992) | Wife, children, and grandchildren all live in or near Acuitzio. His cousin is Juana Bravo. His sister and her family also live in Anchorage. | Costco |

| PSEUDONYM | AGE | ALASKA CONNECTION | MAIN RESIDENCE | "PAPERS" | RELATIONSHIPS | WORK |
|---|---|---|---|---|---|---|
| Efrén | 39 | Born in the United States, and has lived and worked in Alaska since 1990. Started out working in a remote fish cannery. | Anchorage | U.S. citizen | Married to Soledad. Efrén and Serefina's husband are brothers. | Janitorial services manager and business owner |
| Esteban | 53 | First went to Anchorage in 1989. Stayed until 1991 and then went back to Mexico. Went back to Anchorage in 1992 and has been there since. | Anchorage | Dual citizen (1996) | Married to Laura. Went to school with many of the men from Acuitzio in his age group and works with many Acuitzenzes at Costco. | Costco |
| Fernando | - | Went to Alaska in 1992 *por buscar trabajo*, to find work. | Anchorage | Dual citizen | Married to Ivonne; they met in Alaska. Salvador is his brother. | Costco |
| Gilberto* | - | Went to Anchorage in 1986 after working in vegetable and fruit fields in California for many years. | Anchorage | - | Lola's brother-in-law. Married to Mónica. His godfather was one of the first Acuitzences to go to Alaska. His father was also a migrant, a *bracero*. | Restaurant waiter |
| Gonzalo Calderon | 80 | One of the first Acuitzences to go to Alaska. Lived and worked there from 1952 to 1973, with visits back to Acuitzio. | Long Beach | Dual citizen (1959?) | None of Gonzalo's close family members live in Alaska. Some of his extended family does, including a nephew. | Retired |

| Name | Age | Residence | Place | Citizenship | Family | Occupation |
|---|---|---|---|---|---|---|
| Inés | 39 | Has lived in Anchorage since 2008. | Anchorage | Mexican citizen; U.S. permanent resident | Married to Salvador. | Fast food restaurant employee |
| Ivonne | - | Born in the United States but not in Anchorage. Went to Anchorage to join her parents there in 1992. | Anchorage | U.S. citizen | Married to Fernando. | Office administration |
| Jaime | 75 | Lived and worked in Alaska from 1960 to 1968. Was deported in 1968. Never went back to work in the United States. | Acuitzio | Mexican citizen | None of his close family lives in Alaska. | Retired |
| Laura | 43 | Has lived in Anchorage since 1996. | Anchorage | Dual citizen (2001) | Married to Esteban. | Library employee |
| Leonardo | 46 | Has lived in Anchorage since 1989. Before that, worked elsewhere in the United States. | Anchorage | Dual citizen (2000) | President of the Migrant Club. | Construction worker |
| Lola | 41 | Lived in Anchorage for eleven years from 1990 to 2001. | Acuitzio | - | Married to Gilberto's brother. Both Gilberto and Lola's husband work in restaurants. | Councilor of migrant issues |
| Mónica* | - | Has lived in Anchorage since 1994. | Anchorage | - | Married to Gilberto. They met and got married in Alaska. | Fast food restaurant employee |

| PSEUDONYM | AGE | ALASKA CONNECTION | MAIN RESIDENCE | "PAPERS" | RELATIONSHIPS | WORK |
|---|---|---|---|---|---|---|
| Octavio | 66 | Has lived and worked in Alaska since 1968. | Anchorage | Dual citizen (1995) | Uncle to Luis Jr., Miguel, and Gloria Bravo. Both Luis Jr. and Miguel worked at his restaurant. | Restaurant owner and bartender |
| Oscar | 36 | Has lived in Alaska since 1992, with annual trips back to Acuitzio. | Anchorage | Dual citizen (1995) | Oscar's parents also live between Alaska and Acuitzio, and most of his siblings live in Anchorage. His son lives in Acuitzio. | Taxi driver; rooster breeder |
| Pascual | 37 | Lived in Alaska for six years, from 1991 to 1997. | Morelia | Mexican citizen | His father also worked in Alaska in the 1960s. | Ecotourism business owner/operator; photographer |
| Rosa | 44 | Has never been to Alaska. | Acuitzio | Mexican citizen | Many of her siblings live and work in the United States, including Ana Bravo and Tomás, who both live in Alaska. | - |

| Serefina | 30 | Has lived in Anchorage since 2002. | Anchorage | Dual citizen (2007) | Serefina's husband is Efrén's brother. He has been living and working in Anchorage for much longer. | Hairdresser |
| --- | --- | --- | --- | --- | --- | --- |
| Salvador* | 47 | Has lived and worked in Anchorage since 1992. | Anchorage | Dual citizen (2002) | Married to Inés. He and Fernando are brothers. | Costco; janitor |
| Soledad | 39 | Has lived in Anchorage since 1999. | Anchorage | Dual citizen (2009) | Married to Efrén. | Nonprofit manager; janitorial services business owner |
| Tomás | 46 | Has been living and working in Anchorage since 2003. | Anchorage | Dual citizen (2000) | Ana Bravo's brother. | Costco |

*Also interviewed in 2005.

# Mexicans in Alaska

# Introduction

YES, THERE ARE MEXICANS IN ALASKA

On a visit to Anchorage in 2010 I took the bus downtown to see the Mexican consulate, which had opened in 2008. A lot had changed since the last time I was in town almost five years earlier. The Anchorage Museum had a new glass facade and landscaping, and across C street was the consulate itself, a yellow two-story building with the words "Consulado de México" spelled out in black and a large Mexican flag waving in the wind. Walking on the museum grounds across from the consulate, I stopped to take a photograph and overheard the comments of a middle-aged white couple, walking past slowly, with cameras slung around their necks. Tourists. Indeed, summertime in downtown Anchorage means tourists, lots of them, arriving on buses from cruise ships, spending a few hours in the city before taking the bus or train for sightseeing elsewhere. Others might fly in and spend a couple of days in Anchorage before gearing up and leaving town for a backcountry adventure. I suspected these two were of the cruise ship variety.

"Honey," the woman said, "Consulado de México—now what do you suppose that is?"

"Not sure, looks like some kind of Mexican government office," the man said.

"Well, what the heck is it doing *here*?"

On a cool, cloudy summer day in Anchorage, the Mexican dance and culture group Xochiquetzal-Tiqun had been asked to perform along the route for a five-kilometer fun run. They thought there would at least be a stage! Or a sound system! There was neither, only an empty parking lot. I stood with the dancers as the adults deliberated about what to do. After a quick vote, the group decided to go ahead and dance anyway, "After all, we're already in costume." As the dancers got to their places, someone backed up a Chevrolet Suburban, opened all of the doors, and turned up the speakers so that the dancers and runners could hear the music playing from the automobile's CD player. Someone hit play, and the young dancers—girls in colorful dresses and boys in black pants, white shirts, and a red sash—danced to a *jarabe* in the Jalisco style. As they danced, parents and supporters chatted on the sidelines. One woman joked about how the runners would be confused by the scene as they jogged past: "They'll think that they've run all the way to Tijuana!" The group erupted with laughter as the adult dancers took to the parking lot—women dressed in white lace dresses, dancing to a song from Veracruz.

Almost every evening when I lived in Vancouver, I went to the dog park at the end of the block. While there, the dog owners inevitably struck up conversation with each other. One of them, the owner of a labradoodle tumbling around with my golden retriever, asked me, "So what do you do?"

"I'm an anthropologist. I'm working on my PhD in anthropology."

"Oh yeah, so what do you study?"

I replied, "I work with people from a small town in central Mexico who live and work in Anchorage, Alaska."

"What? There are Mexicans in Alaska? What do they do there? How do they get there? Isn't it too cold for them?"

I sat with Renata in her living room in Anchorage, my digital tape recorder running to capture her responses in an audio file.[1] I asked her, "When you're in Mexico and you say you live in Alaska, what do people say about that?"

She replied, "Their first expression usually is something like, 'Oh my gosh, don't you, like, freeze up there?' Because they think it's always snowing. I'm like, 'No, it doesn't just always snow. It's actually snowing less and less as the years go by." She paused and glanced out the window. "I'm really surprised that it hasn't snowed yet this year."

"I know!" I exclaimed. "I thought it would have snowed by now for sure."

Renata continued, "Yeah. But anyway, that's their first impression. 'It's so cold over there in Alaska,' 'Do you live in igloos?' stuff like that, you know? People from the *pueblo* know that there are a lot of people living in Anchorage who are from Acuitzio, but once I went to Mexico City I realized that people there were surprised. Like, 'Oh my gosh, there's Mexicans up there in Alaska? Like, there's *Latinos*?' And I'm like, 'Yeah, there's not just Mexicans—there are Colombian people, people from Venezuela, there's so many of us in Alaska.'"

This book is about the transnational lives of three generations of people from Acuitzio del Canje, Michoacán, Mexico, who have been living and working in Anchorage, Alaska, since the 1950s. Since I began working with Acuitzences (people from Acuitzio) who move regularly between Michoacán and Alaska, the most common questions I am asked about my work are as follows: "There are Mexicans in Alaska?" "How do they get there?" and "What do they do there?" Each of the vignettes above, snapshots of moments during my research, hints at a sense of anomaly and dissonance when "Mexico" and "Alaska" are brought together. Alaska is thought of as a separate, isolated, wild place where people of Mexican background are not supposed to belong. Racial and spatial perceptions that have become mainstream within the United States about Mexican migrant-immigrants place them closer to the U.S.-Mexican border. The joke among Mexican dancers in Anchorage that people will think they've run "all the way to Tijuana" evokes how there is something unexpected about the materialization of a Mexican dance performance in Alaska. Similarly, the Mexican consulate building in downtown Anchorage is perceived by tourists who arrived on a cruise ship as something anomalous or out of place. Finally, in my own everyday life in Canada the most common reaction to my work is similar to that of the man at the dog park: surprise. Elsewhere in Mexico, people are surprised to hear of their *paisanos* living so far north.[2]

That these questions are asked at all illustrates how effectively Alaska and Mexico have been produced as separate in the popular imagination. Not just separate but distant and fundamentally different from one another, far away both geographically and socially. As well, Mexican migrant-immigrants are perceived as spatially located closer to the physical border with Mexico, and "out of place" so far north. Alaska and Mexico are produced as spatially and racially distant spaces, located at either end of the North American continent. Conventional wilderness narratives and adventure tales about Alaska do not leave much room for diversity in what it means to be Alaskan, aside from the White Settler European–Alaska Native dichotomy.[3] Spatial terminology that marks distance is also widely used within the state of Alaska to demarcate it from other locations. Many people refer to the rest of the United States as "the Lower 48," for example, emphasizing Alaska's location as both north of and separate from the contiguous forty-eight states. People also refer to locations "Outside."[4] Capitalized, the term indicates "everywhere else." This spatially demarcates Alaska as separate from everywhere else Outside of its territorial boundaries. A similar linguistic spatial demarcation divides Mexico from the United States: *el otro lado* or "the other side" (of the border) is used in Mexico to refer to the United States in general. In so many ways, Mexicans in Alaska are interpreted as unexpected, odd, as people out of place.

*Mexicans in Unexpected Places*

Philip J. Deloria wrote about expectation and anomaly in his book *Indians in Unexpected Places*. In it he described the broad cultural expectations in the United States relating to Native Americans and how events that do not fit within the norm are considered anomalous. Even as anomaly defines the event as unnatural and odd, the naming of an anomaly re-creates and re-empowers the same categories it escapes.[5] Mary Douglas's classic work *Purity and Danger* shows that when people or objects cross categories, they are considered "matter out of place" and even dangerous or polluting. Such anomalies reinforce the categories they cross.[6] There are spatial expectations as well. Akhil Gupta and James Ferguson argue that representations of space in dominant discourses and also in the social sciences are dependent on images of break, rupture, and disjunction so that each society, nation, or culture is presented as occupying its own discontinuous space.[7] Nation-states are also formed based on the idea of territorial separation and boundedness and a sedentarist metaphysics where "people are often thought of, and think of themselves, as being rooted in place and as deriving their identity from that rootedness."[8] Indeed, in this framework a migrant or a refugee would be considered "uprooted" and anomalous, signaling a loss of moral and emotional bearings and threatening to spoil cultural and national identities.[9]

In the work of philosopher Henri Lefebvre, the official and normative expectations that structure how we understand places like Alaska, Mexico, and North America are "representations of space" that exist in dialectical tension with spatial practices or "representational spaces," which include lived, everyday spatial symbols and meanings.[10] One particularly powerful representation of space in the United States is the Immigration and Nationality Act (INA).[11] When the INA was created in 1952, it brought together a variety of statutes that governed immigration law. The act has been amended many times since then, but it makes up the basic body of immigration law in the United States. As a legal document, the INA is profoundly about spatial relationships. Words such as "in" or "out," "entry" or "deportation," and so on evoke movement between places outside of the United States into the nation-state itself. And it is abundantly clear that the law also allows the state to control, regulate, and limit that movement by legally defining who may cross the border into the United States and who may not. In this formulation, borders are presented as unproblematic delineations that separate nation-states and cultures. This is a representation of national space that is dependent on images of break, rupture, and disjunction where the distinctiveness of societies, nations, and cultures is based upon the idea that they occupy their own "naturally" discontinuous spaces. As argued by Gupta and Ferguson, discontinuity forms the starting point from which contact, conflict, and contradiction between cultures and societies has been traditionally theorized.[12] A legal representation of the world as a collection of discrete nation-states fragments space into diverse national societies, each rooted in its own proper place. "Space itself becomes a kind of neutral grid on which cultural difference, historical memory, and societal organization are inscribed. It is in this way that space functions as a central organizing principle in the social sciences at the same time that it disappears from analytical purview."[13]

This idea of space also functions as a central organizing principle in U.S. immigration law.

It is important to note that this vision of space is *produced* by the state and by the many politicians who have written, debated, voted on, passed, and later amended this body of laws. Analyzing the INA can "supply clues to, and testimony about, this productive process."[14] As a representation of space, the INA is "tied to the relations of production and to the 'order' which those relations impose, and hence to knowledge, to signs, to codes, and to 'frontal' relations."[15] The INA could also be seen as what Michel De Certeau calls "spatial legislation" that determines rights and divides up lands by "acts" or discourses about actions. In so doing, a spatial legislation story like the INA "has distributive power and performative force."[16] This allows the state to create and *enforce* its spatial vision of the United States. Through mechanisms of surveillance, many of which are outlined in Title II of the INA, state discipline, in the words of Michel Foucault, "fixes; it arrests and regulates movements; it clears up confusion; it dissipates compact groupings of individuals wandering about the country in unpredictable ways; it establishes calculated distributions."[17] This idea that state discipline seeks to "fix" bodies in space is also taken up by Gilles Deleuze and Felix Guattari, who argue that one of the fundamental tasks of the state is to striate the space over which it reigns.[18] "It is a vital concern of every State not only to vanquish nomadism but to control migrations and, more generally, to establish a zone of rights over an entire exterior, over all of the flows traversing the ecumenon."[19] The state tries to capture all flows, restricting movement to clearly defined, carefully measured, and heavily regulated paths.[20]

It would follow then, that stories and practices about places that are excluded, that do not fit with expectations, that *interrupt* would be perceived as anomalous, such as the practice of Mexican dancers in an Anchorage parking lot.[21] Michel-Rolph Trouillot describes how anomaly arises out of a process whereby dominant narratives of globalization silence the past on a massive scale, systematically erasing the long-distance encounters that have marked human history across time and space: "For sushi in Chicago to amaze us, we need to silence the fact that the Franciscans were in Japan as early as the fifteenth century. For Muslim veils in France to seem out of place, we need to forget that

Charles Martel stopped Abd-al-Raman only three hundred miles south of Paris two reigns before Charlemagne. To talk of a global culture today as a new phenomenon, we need to forget that Chinese chili paste comes from Mexico, French fries from Peru, and Jamaican Blue Mountain coffee from Yemen."[22]

This is why many scholars have instead emphasized the contingent, entangled, interconnected, and coproduced nature of places. Such a focus undermines the apparent stability, boundedness, and timelessness of place.[23] For example, Audra Simpson writes about how Mohawk/Haudenosaunee nationhood continues to interrupt the nation-state.[24] Philip Deloria advocates "unexpectedness" as a framework to rethink those moments when places get entangled in ways that may strike some people as "anomalous." The unexpected resists categorization and questions expectation itself.[25] Along similar lines, Liisa Malkki writes there is no such thing as "matter out of place" and shows how Hutu refugees and migrants created their own categories. Indeed, "people categorize back."[26]

*People Who Categorize Back*

This book, then, is about people who categorize back. Specifically, it is about the lives, mobilities, family networks, and livelihoods of three generations of Acuitzences who have been living and working in Anchorage, Alaska, since at least the 1950s.[27] In the pages that follow, I show how over time (chapter 3) and based on mobility (chapter 2) they build a way of life in both Alaska and Michoacán that transcends the continent (chapters 4, 5, and 6). They regularly go back and forth, *echarle vueltas*, between their hometowns of Acuitzio and Anchorage. Rather than understanding this way of life as "neither here nor there,"[28] I argue that their way of life requires *both* locations to feel at home. Their transnational lives interrupt the idea that Alaska is an exceptionally separate wilderness frontier, as it also contributes a different story to the anthropology on U.S.-Mexican migration. In contrast to the estimated 5.8 million undocumented migrants from Mexico in the United States, these Acuitzences occupy a significantly different class position based on access to dual citizenship or U.S. permanent residency that allows them to travel regularly between Mexico and Alaska and successfully take advantage of the inequality between economies and the peso and the dollar across generations.[29] Since upward class mobility has been seen as difficult to achieve in Mexico for many decades now, people go to the United States to get ahead, with plans to return to Mexico and live comfortably someday. However, class, citizenship, race, and gender are mutually constructed and part of larger systems of inequality that extend across the continent. Migrants are therefore positioned in terms of race, gender, and class in two interrelated and intersectional national systems of inequality—Mexico and the United States.[30] Moreover, Alaska has a somewhat different racial, class, and gender structure than elsewhere in the United States, due to its location as an explicitly Indigenous space and its ongoing construction and exploitation as a (resource) frontier.

Even so, the Acuitzences in this book have been able to achieve a position as dual citizens or permanent residents who travel back and forth annually, and who own property and businesses in both locations. This is a very different structural position from the undocumented Indigenous or mestizo migrant in California, North Carolina, or Washington State. Even so, these different groups of migrants may share similar goals. Anthropologist Deborah Boehm asked people in both the United States and Mexico where they would choose to live, if anywhere. They told her that they wished for the freedom to come and go, to build their lives from both sides of the border.[31] She analyzed the multiple barriers to flexible mobility that undocumented or mixed-status families face, including the presence of the U.S. state in everyday lives, and its imposition of categories that define and exclude, border controls, and deportations. These processes limit movement and can result in long periods between coming and going.[32] Other factors that prevent fluid, unrestricted movement include different subjectivities, experiences, and circumstances based on legal status, age, gender, sexuality, socioeconomic class, access to resources, race/ethnicity, marital status, and family ties. These intersect with political-economic realities shaping who migrates, if, when, and how often, the character of their border crossings, and their length of stay in the United States.[33]

In spite of these barriers, Boehm shows that people still want the freedom to come and go between the United States and Mexico, to make lives from both sides of the border, to live here *and* there.³⁴ The dream of achieving a class position and ability to move back and forth, to come and go, is what I call the North American Dream. Here, I explore transnational life among people who *are* able to come and go. This has important implications for immigration policy, since many people want to be able to live across the border, to move around more freely, and, ultimately, to exploit the structural inequality of the North American economy, building their lives across the U.S.-Mexican border and in more than one place. Unfortunately, only very few are able to.

Acuitzences who have built a life across North America form "multiplicities of attachments" in both Anchorage and Acuitzio.³⁵ Through mobility and a transnational way of life, they challenge and test the territorial boundedness of the nation-state.³⁶ For people who have been moving back and forth between Mexico and Alaska for several decades, the old anthropological assumption that there was a neat correlation between a "culture" and a "place" becomes more problematic than ever. Instead of people who live in Mexico and Alaska looking for roots, their everyday lives demonstrate how places are continually produced through connection with other geographies. Specifically, their lives illustrate that rather than extremely separate spaces at either end of the continent, Mexico and Alaska are profoundly entangled places and part of the everyday lives and livelihoods of people in Acuitzio and Anchorage.

*To Come and Go*

Many Acuitzences in Alaska are living the North American Dream due to relative privilege and expertise with mobility and living across borders. These people hold dual U.S.-Mexican citizenship or U.S. permanent residency and are able to move across the continent in a way that many Mexican migrants cannot. They regularly come and go and have been successful at maintaining connections and building identities in both Anchorage and Acuitzio. Although people experience being "neither here nor there" like the immigrant workers that anthropologist Steve Striffler describes, through mobility and other spatial practices Acuitzences in Alaska also work to be here *and* there, to come and go, orienting themselves to a transnational social field that extends between both places.³⁷ To feel at home in the world, these people rely on their fraught and uneven spatial attachments to each place and on the common experience of mobility between them.

To do this, they have developed a "transnational habitus." This concept builds on the work of sociologists Pierre Bourdieu and Henri Lefebvre, both of whom theorize "practice," the things people *do* to make and transform their social world. Neither Bourdieu or Lefebvre theorized migration and mobility, however.[38] Developing a transnational habitus is therefore a process of placemaking and of territorialization whereby getting used to living between Anchorage and Acuitzio means the development of a habitus and set of dispositions that can accommodate the contradictory, paradoxical, and tension-filled experience of living across the continent.[39]

Roger Rouse wrote about this process for Aguilillan migrants based on research between the years 1982 and 1984 in both Aguililla, Michoacán, and Redwood City, California. In his doctoral dissertation, he argued that migrants orient their lives to the transnational migrant circuit as a whole, rather than to a single locale in it. By living transnationally, and balancing fundamentally different class experiences, "Aguilillans broadened their repertoire of attitudes and standards to include both ways of life. Yet they did so without achieving any synthesis. The two cultures remained tensely juxtaposed, their incompatibilities often hidden but always capable of coming to the surface in the course of events."[40]

But rather than extending a *rancho* habitus to an expanded field, as Rouse proposed elsewhere in his dissertation,[41] I argue for the development of a new set of dispositions, practices, strategies, and goals—especially those related to mobility—that are oriented toward a transnational habitus. The Acuitzences in Alaska that I write about here are oriented to both locations, a way of life defined by constant tension between here and there, and a common experience of mobility across the continent.[42] In *Mexicans in Alaska* I show that the development of a transnational habitus has been a process based on mobility (chapter 2) that happens over generations (chapter 3) and that entails a process of "getting used to it," building lives, livelihoods, and communities over time (chapters 4, 5, and 6). The transnational habitus is therefore not an extension of "home" to the Last Frontier; it has shifted to fit the whole social field between Alaska and Mexico. *Both* locations, and mobility between them, are necessary to feel at home.

For example, in interviews and conversations I asked migrant dual-citizen Acuitzences where they felt most at home and where they say they are from. For many people, these were difficult questions, and they told me as much. Their responses reveal the uneven attachments to place of Acuitzences in Alaska. For example, Serefina said, "What a question! That's very difficult to answer. I've never even asked myself that. Ay, I don't know." Like others to whom I spoke, she explained that she says that she lives in Alaska but is from Mexico. "*Vives en Alaska . . . pero eres pues, de México.*" When it comes to feeling at home, Serefina says,

> I go to Mexico. I spend my time there feeling really content, really happy with my family, with my parents, with everything. But after four or five weeks I am desperate to come back to my house in Anchorage! And my husband says, but why? I don't know. You tell me, because I can't tell you! It's something about how you are already accustomed to your routine, your work, your things. And so I say, *mi amor*, let's go! I don't know. Maybe I prefer it more in Alaska already? I go to Mexico, I'm happy there, content for four weeks. But after four weeks I want to go back to *mi casa* [in Anchorage].

I also asked Juana, "When someone asks you where you're from, what do you say?" She replied, "That I'm from Mexico but I live in Alaska. Or like, I'm from Mexico with U.S. nationality, and I feel like I have both. But more Mexico," and then she burst into laughter.

I asked Juana's niece, Renata, what she says if someone asks where she is from. She said, "Mexico" without hesitation but then went on to explain: "But people say to me, yeah you were born there, but your homeland is here [Alaska]. And I tell them no, my homeland is Mexico. And they just don't understand that, they're like no, you're wrong, you're from here. And I was like, okay, yeah, I might be a citizen and I have my house here, but I also have my house in Mexico, and my culture and everything *is* from Mexico."

"Where do you think your future will be?" I asked.

"My hope is that I finish school here and get my degree and everything, but I don't see myself living in Mexico, I'd rather just go visit and everything."

For Renata, although she feels like her home is in Mexico, she says she cannot see herself living there. Instead, she sees herself living between Anchorage and Acuitzio, moving back and forth. Indeed, once Renata finished her studies as a massage therapist in Alaska, she went to Mexico for additional training there. She since moved back to Anchorage and opened her own massage studio, featuring techniques she learned in Mexico along with those she learned during her training in Alaska.

On the other hand, Renata's mother, Gloria, spoke with painful nostalgia about Mexico and about the difficulty of the winters in Alaska. She said that in Mexico life is very different, but there is no work. "There isn't money there, but here there's work and we've *adapted*. The United States has given us everything, *verdad*? It's given us food, it's given us work, but our roots, our heart is in Mexico. *Así es nuestra vida*. That is our life." Like Renata and many other Acuitzences, Gloria went on to explain how she doesn't really feel at home in either place.

> I go to Mexico and for a few days with all the family I am *a gusto*, happy. But time passes, and I want to leave, like I am not *a gusto* anymore, I am no longer content. I've gotten used to the routine here in Alaska, and I want to leave. Or maybe it's the security that it gives you here, the *tranquilidad*, more than anything. In Acuitzio, even though the family is there and you know everywhere because you have lived all your life there, you still want to leave. So, it's really difficult. *No te puedes adaptar ya ni allá ni acá. Estás en la mitad.* You can't adapt to it here or there anymore, you're in the middle.

Laura talks about how part of her is always in Mexico. "This is where we live, and we have adapted. But we can't deny that we live here only 75 percent, and the other 25 percent of the mind is there in Mexico. That's how we are. *Así nos tocó*." Pascual described how most Acuitzences in Anchorage live: "They live and talk about what happened in Acuitzio yesterday. About the wedding of who knows who. Did you know so-and-so died? Or like they still live in *el pueblo*, like they don't really live in Anchorage. Or like, they're there physically, but their mind is in Acuitzio."

Watching soccer games, especially matches between Mexico and the United States, often brings out these contradictions.[43] In 2005 when I was in Anchorage for the first time, my MA supervisor and I were invited to watch a World Cup qualifying match between Mexico and the United States. We were watching it at a house in south Anchorage where some single, male Acuitzences lived together at the time. During that game my supervisor asked one of the men who he was cheering for. The man explained, in a perfect expression of transnational class status, that he was cheering for both: "My heart is in Mexico, but my money is in the United States." Similarly, while I was in Acuitzio in 2011, the United States played Mexico in the finals of the Gold Cup, which determines the regional champion of North America, South America, and the Caribbean. Juana, Luis, Toño, and Juana's brother were there, and we sat in Toño's room because he had the biggest television and a couch to sit on. Toño wore a Mexican national team jersey while we watched the game. Luis asked me which team I hoped would win, and I said, "Mexico."

Luis was surprised. "I thought you would go for the USA."

"No," I said, "Canada and the USA are very competitive with each other in sports." I paused. "Who are you cheering for Luis?"

He said, "*Yo soy mitad-mitad*, I'm half and half." At the time, the game was tied, and Luis's brother-in-law said, "Oh, then this is perfect for you!" In the end, Mexico won. Toño yelled, "We're champions!" raising his fist in the air.

People therefore express the fraught contradictions of transnational life in a variety of ways. Serefina feels at home in both places, but in Alaska she feels at home in terms of her daily routine, whereas in Mexico she feels at home in terms of her roots. Renata feels more at home in Mexico, but she would never live there, and her mother feels somewhat "stuck in the middle." Laura's mind is divided between "here" and "there." Luis's wallet and his heart are in different locations. All of these expressions imply that people rely on *both* locations for a sense of identity and belonging—Acuitzences in Alaska do not feel completely at home in either location, but they have built lives and livelihoods that require both locations.

Their transnational habitus is thus built on uneven attachments to both places, expressed by Acuitzences in contradictory statements: "I feel like my home is Mexico, but I would never live there"; or, "First I dreamed of coming to Alaska, and after that I dreamed of going back";

or, "My heart is in Mexico, but my money is in the United States." These quotes are important because they reveal that many people do not feel entirely at home in Alaska and maintain their hometown in Mexico as an important spatial and affective point of reference. And when your heart is in Mexico but your money is in the United States, there is an explicit focus on *work*. Yet some people no longer feel entirely at home in Mexico either.

Alongside the uneven attachments to place expressed by Acuitzences is the finding that as they become more mobile, they also work to establish more roots. Or, in some cases, the process of putting down roots *requires* mobility. Processes and events that tie Acuitzences to place in Acuitzio, such as owning property, celebrating major life events, and having income-generating businesses there, end up *facilitating* mobility, making it easier to come and go. In Anchorage too, as people spend more time there, become more established socially and financially, own property, and advance in their careers, it becomes *easier* to travel back and forth. Long-term settlement and ongoing mobility between Anchorage and Acuitzio thus *complement* each other.[44] For example, consider the relationship between citizenship and mobility. Citizenship is intended to tie individuals to a specific nation-state, as evident in the language and procedures of becoming a citizen. Through the process of becoming a citizen, you "become" American, tied to the nation-state as you receive the rights and obligations of a citizen. However, the process of obtaining citizenship also facilitates mobility or even requires it as a matter of process.

*Organization of the Book*

In analyzing the everyday lives of Acuitzences who move between Acuitzio and Anchorage, I start from their words, insights, and actions along with my own participant observation in this transnational social field as a Canadian anthropologist. In the following chapter, I introduce the transnational space of "Mexican Alaska" and the specific locations within it: Acuitzio and Anchorage. I also write about the process of doing fieldwork across North America in two communities and along routes between them. The following two chapters analyze mobilities between Mexico and Alaska, specifically the spatial practice of Acuitzences in terms of mobility, the physical and material flows, transfers, and interactions that occur in and across space and assure production and social reproduction. Chapter 2, "The Annual Migration of the Traveling Swallows," is about the materiality of mobility across the long distance between Mexico and Alaska. Studies of mobility between Mexico and the United States typically focus on the U.S.-Mexican border region and particularly on the vast stretches of desert that most illegal migrants cross by foot. However, the lines of mobility that connect the United States and Mexico also include ports of entry along highways, airline routes, and even ferry crossings at points on corridors that stretch all the way to Alaska. As well, the border itself and practices of boundary enforcement have been spatially dispersed to airports, checkpoints, and workplaces throughout the United States.[45] In this chapter, I trace the mobilities of Acuitzences along corridors that extend well past the physical geography of the Mexican-U.S. border, to include airports and highways at different locations between Acuitzio and Anchorage, some of them located in Canada. I use the concept of friction to show how mobility of people is never smooth, for they encounter challenges and obstacles along the way. This chapter shows how part of developing a transnational habitus is this common experience of mobility, as well as the development of practices that make Acuitzences expert at travel and at navigating these frictions. It also illustrates that taking the continent as a frame of analysis is important for understanding their social world. I illustrate this with analysis of two trips: one by airplane from Mexico to Alaska with a family traveling back to Anchorage after a summer in their hometown, and one by automobile from Alaska to Mexico with a man who was driving back to Acuitzio after working in Alaska in the 1950s. Mobility therefore plays an important role in the production of transnational space. Travel back and forth of people and other agents is key for maintaining a connection between Anchorage and Acuitzio. Indeed, for some people the very "state of movement" is being "at home."[46] Over time, Acuitzences orient themselves to a social world that encompasses both Anchorage and Acuitzio, and the common experience of mobility between them. Even when people settle more permanently at a site within the transnational social field, as I describe in more detail in the conclusion, the possibility of movement is always there.

I continue the focus on mobility through time within a multigenerational family unit in chapter 3, "'My Grandfather Worked Here.'" I continue to analyze the mobilities of Acuitzences who move between Mexico and Alaska, but rather than focusing on the materiality of mobility through space, I explore mobility through time and across generations. I show how multigenerational family networks have spatially expanded from Acuitzio to Alaska, and how this connection has gained traction over time. The history of movement between Acuitzio and Anchorage takes place within this multigenerational family I call the Bravo family.[47] Depending on the generational and gendered position of individual family members, Bravo family members established footholds in Alaska in the 1950s and 1960s and have gained ground since. They have gained ground in terms of spatial mobility, as well as class mobility and immigration status, moving from undocumented laborers to working-class dual citizens with middle-class aspirations today. The initial trajectories of Acuitzences have developed into more resilient mobility patterns and a transnational way of life. Their story shows that migration is not a linear or unidirectional movement between distinct, bounded nation-states, nor is it a progression from Mexican to U.S.-American over time. Instead, people orient their lives to the circuit as a whole where the shared experience of mobility produces a translocal social field across the continent. By translocal social field, I mean the field of social relations that extends between points in different locales,[48] but not necessarily between nation-states (i.e., United States and Mexico)—specific social relations that extend between localities (Acuitzio and Anchorage). Here the translocal social field is produced through the shared experience of mobility and the maintenance of familial, economic, social, organizational, religious, and political relations between Anchorage and Acuitzio. A multigenerational focus on mobility and transnational migration is important because it illustrates that the connections between Alaska and Michoacán are not especially "new," and that the development of such a way of life and of a transnational habitus occurs over generations.

The next two chapters shift the analysis away from mobility per se to other forms of spatial practices within transnational spaces. In chapter 4, "'You Have to Get Used to It,'" I write about a common expression used by people who live in Anchorage and Acuitzio. They often say, when talking about their experience, *"uno tiene que acostumbrarse,"* or "you have to get used to it." I analyze the practices that people draw upon to "get used to" transnational life to show how developing a transnational habitus and way of life across the continent takes time and work. This is an embodied process, a social process, and also an institutional one that depends on gaining immigration and other statuses. This fraught process of getting used to it happens in both Mexico and Alaska, and not in one direction or in one location only. Transnational life then, is a constant process of getting used to two very different places, ways of life, and affective experiences. As I argue throughout, both are necessary for people to feel at home in the world.

Chapter 5, "The Stuff of Transnational Life," focuses on transnational material culture, specifically the things people travel with. The movement of foods, like *mole*, cheese, bread, and candy, as well as other objects, are wrapped up in configurations of power that attempt to facilitate, constrain, or limit the movement of people, commodities, technology, ideas, finance capital, and the media (among other things) in extremely complex ways.[49] Things that people travel with are a material reality of people's daily lives but also a symbolic marker of those lives.[50] Things that move, then, are both a marker and material reality of transnationality, a symbol of mobility as well as an item that has literally traveled between Mexico and Alaska.[51] I argue that traveling with things is an important part of transnational lives, as well as transnational livelihoods. People not only travel with things to feel at home, connect distant places in their everyday lives, and build social relationships in Acuitzio and Anchorage; they also sometimes travel with things to buy, sell, or trade in another location in the transnational social field.

In chapter 6, "'It Freezes the People Together,'" I write about groups that re-categorize space to produce a Mexican Alaska. I describe institutions and groups that "freeze the people together" in Anchorage and Mexico, such as the Mexican consulate in Anchorage, the dance and culture group Xochiquetzal-Tiqun, the restaurant Mexico in Alaska, and the Acuitzio del Canje Migrant Club in Alaska to explore how each of these groups produces representations of Mexican Alaska through image and collective action. These groups each bring Mexico and Alaska together into new representations of space, re-categorizing and expanding the borders of Latin America.

I conclude by analyzing where Acuitzences in Alaska see their future. People orient their lives and mobilities to the transnational space that extends between Mexico and Alaska, but as circumstances change along the life course, within Acuitzio and Anchorage, in North America, or globally, people are able to be flexible and expand or contract the network as necessary. In fact, some Acuitzences are reorienting their primary residence to Mexico but decide to keep a house in Alaska for future visits. Again, the possibility of mobility is always there. The ideal transnational life is lived in both Anchorage and Acuitzio and along routes between them, and identities are built that draw on these multiple spatial points of reference. Moreover, by *echandole vueltas* and going back and forth, Acuitzences also rework expectations about the North, Alaska, and Mexicans in the United States.

# 1 Tracing Mexican Alaska

A TRANSNATIONAL SOCIAL SPACE

Mexican migration to the United States has been ongoing at least since the Treaty of Guadalupe ended the Mexican-American war in 1848 and created the spatial boundary of these two nation-states in its current form. Since that time, the United States has been dependent on Mexican labor first to build railroads, later to supplement the workforce during a world war, and now to provide low-cost labor for agricultural work and service industry positions. The United States endures as a primary destination for Mexican labor migrants, as generations of *mexicanos* continue to seek a better life in *el norte* even as xenophobic opinion and policy in the United States make immigration reform an ongoing issue.[1] Labor migration between Mexico and the United States has been the topic of much anthropological research.[2]

Migration between Mexico and Alaska is not typically included in the scholarly literature on Mexican migration in the United States, and existing research and news coverage frames the connection between Mexico and Alaska as "new."[3] But the connections between Alaska and Acuitzio are long-running, and links between what is now Alaska and Mexico have even deeper historical roots. Spanish explorers departing from Mexico in the eighteenth century explored the Pacific Northwest and what is today Alaska, leaving their names behind on Valdez, Cordova, and Revillagigedo Island, Alaska.[4] Labor migration between Mexico and Alaska has been ongoing since at least 1901 but likely started earlier.[5] To draw attention to the historical and contemporary links between Mexico and Alaska, I instead conceptualize "Mexican Alaska" as a transnational field site, a spatial formation that extends across the continent. Acuitzences live and work in a translocal social space between Anchorage and Acuitzio, and here I describe Mexican Alaska, retell the history of Alaska through Mexican migration, introduce Acuitzio and Anchorage as important points in the transnational social field, and outline my methodology.

*Mexican Alaska*

"Mexican Alaska" is the term I use to refer to the spatial formation where Mexico and Alaska are connected through transnational and transgenerational mobility, which I analyze in more detail in chapters 2 and 3. Here I draw on the idea of "Greater Mexico" proposed by Américo Paredes as all areas inhabited by people of a Mexican culture.[6] I extend Greater Mexico all the way to Alaska, both drawing upon and defying the geopolitical boundaries along the way. I also envision a spatial formation like De Genova's Mexican Chicago, whereby Alaska is practically and materially implicated in Mexico and belongs meaningfully to Latin America.[7] Specifically, I trace the extension of "Greater Acuitzio" within a larger Greater Mexico that extends throughout the continent. People even talk about Anchorage this way, calling it "Anchorage del Canje," because there are so many people from Acuitzio who live there.

There are spatial implications to how the history of labor migration from Mexico to the United States is told by researchers. Some scholars have argued that the "traditional sending regions" of migrants have diversified over time.[8] Others argue this is not the case, that most migrants continue to be from the historic "heartland" for migration from Mexico: the states of Aguascalientes, Colima, Durango, Guanajuato, Jalisco, Michoacán, Nayarit, San Luis Potosí, and Zacatecas.[9] Researchers also show that migrants are being "pushed" out of traditional receiving areas such as California and the U.S. Southwest and "pulled" into other areas such as small-town Pennsylvania, rural Montana, and Arkansas and other southern states.[10] This creates a relatively coherent temporal and spatial trajectory of migration from Mexico to the United States where migration historically is between the traditional sending region in west-central Mexico and traditional receiving areas in the United States. For example, Douglas S. Massey, Jacob S. Rugh, and Karen A. Pren write that "historically, the vast majority of Mexican immigrants went to just five states: the border states of California, Arizona, New Mexico, and Texas, and the industrial hub of Illinois. From 1910 to 1960, 90 percent of all Mexican immigrants lived in one of these states."[11] Over time, the geography of Mexican migration concentrated in California, so that "by 1980, 57 percent of all Mexican immigrants lived in California alone, with 23 percent in Texas and 8 percent in Illinois, so that 88 percent of all Mexican immigrants lived in just three states."[12]

The authors attributed the expansion of Mexican migrant-immigrants to other "new" destination points in the United States to increased frictions at the border and in border regions.[13] The increasing militarization of the border and the construction of actual walls and fences diverted flows away from traditional destinations in California toward new locations elsewhere in the United States.[14] Steve Striffler writes that migrants are increasingly settling in the U.S. heartland, where economic conditions in small towns make settlement financially possible but require longer stays. People follow family and community members to new locations so that "once a few pioneers determine the viability and desirability of a new location in the United States, the circuit can shift quickly from California to, say, Arkansas."[15] This is more than a shift in location. Striffler argues that the transnational migrant circuit is being totally disrupted as people approach permanent settlement in places such as Arkansas. Similarly, Debra Lattanzi-Shutika frames Mexican migration-immigration to Pennsylvania as a "new destination settlement," part of a larger trend since the mid-1980s, "the phenomenon of Mexicans settling permanently in communities outside the border region."[16] In her study of Mexicans in rural Montana, Leah Schmalzbauer shows how increased militarization of the border, a shifting economic landscape, the draw of agricultural and construction work, and the appeal of an idealized rural lifestyle has led increasing numbers of Mexicans to establish roots in the Mountain West.[17]

Alaska has not been included in these studies about geographical diversification in migrant-immigrant origins and destinations, likely because the numbers in Alaska are, and always have been, comparatively small. For example, the percentage of the Alaska population who are of Mexican origin was only 0.26 percent in 1960, 1.7 percent in 1990, and 3.0 percent in 2010.[18] My research could add Alaska as a "new destination settlement" in this way, but I problematize such a linear trajectory for Mexican migrant-immigrants in Alaska. For one thing, such a conceptualization of a migrant heartland confines "the Mexican United States" to the Southwest and Chicago. However, this renders *mexicanos* in other parts of the country as invisible or newly "out of place," *golondrinas* outside of their "habitat." Migration-immigration from Mexico to Alaska has been ongoing for decades, and although there have been changes over time, I hesitate to add Alaska as "new." Alaska is a *different* destination from elsewhere in the United States, but it is not especially new. As well, rather than approaching permanent settlement in Alaska, this book shows how, over time, people orient themselves more to the transnational social field as a whole and require *both* locations and the common experience of mobility between them to feel "at home." In this book Anchorage becomes a site for the negotiation of the U.S.-Mexican border despite its physical distance from the actual border, a site for the contingency of boundaries, for the ongoing social production of the boundaries between Alaska and the rest of the United States, between the United States and Mexico, and between Latin America and elsewhere. Families of Mexican background in Alaska are not people out of place; they are part of a conjectural space with repercussions in all directions.[19] Indeed, Latin America does not end at the U.S. border.[20] By conceptually extending the influence of the U.S.-Mexican border across the entire continent, it is possible to envision links between south and north in producing larger systems and the fundamental total influence of the border and its inequalities across all of North America, not just along the border zone itself.

Preconquest America was characterized by the flow of social life across the continent. Moreover, Western expansion and U.S. imperialism in Latin America went hand in hand. The same American imperialist project that produced Alaska as a "Last Frontier" also produced "the West" and Latin America as spaces for resource exploitation. Central to this process was the production of the U.S.-Mexican and U.S.-Canadian borders to delineate the limits of the imperial frontier. The border with Mexico was required for western expansion, including Alaska.[21] Spanish explorers who went to Alaska left from the shores of what later became Mexico means that the history of connection and exchange between what is now Alaska and Mexico is potentially very long and very rich. Southwestern United States was once Mexico, leaving behind Spanish-speaking residents who say, "the border crossed us." Alaska could have been Mexico, with a history of Spanish exploration, Spanish names inscribed on the landscape all over the state.[22] What if, before the American presence there, the Spanish had settled? What if they never left?

More recently, North America has been produced as a profoundly unequal economic and political unit, institutionally congealed within the North American Free Trade Agreement (NAFTA), which produces its own crossings and disjunctures, potentially drawing together Alaska and Mexico under the rubric of "free trade" but ending up institutionalizing difference and capitalizing on social and economic inequality. Migrations in North America today are produced by inequality and reflect the profound imbalance of power playing out in everyday lives.[23] As Deborah Boehm writes, "the intimacy of transnationality has been and continues to be characterized by both continuity and fragmentation: flows, connections, and linkages characterize transnational lives as do breaks, shifts, dislocations, and disruptions."[24] U.S. immigration policies and practices have profoundly shaped Mexican migrant family life.[25]

But the reterritorialization of people of Mexican background in Alaska can unsettle and interrupt hegemonic assumptions about the racial-spatial order of the United States.[26] After all, Alaska is the furthest North American point from the U.S.-Mexican border. Mexicans are not supposed to be here, far away from Los Angeles, San Jose, Texas, and other geographies where their presence is taken for granted. But they are. As I have argued elsewhere, Alaska needs to be conceptually "reconnected."[27] Although northern spaces occupy a unique position geographically and historically, they have always been produced through their interconnections with elsewhere. Alaska is the product of translocal imaginative, historical, and political economic processes.[28] Translocal spatial formations that have produced Alaskan landscapes as a place for either extractive resource development or of bountiful pristine nature were constituted and defined from afar, through legislative acts and imaginative representations made by southern outsiders.[29] Viewing the North through its connections serves to contest stereotypes of Alaska and the Circumpolar North as distant wilderness frontiers and bring the North and the South together as coproduced geographies. Alaska has been a homeland and a crossroad for Indigenous people on both sides of the Bering Strait since time immemorial. It has also been a crossroad between different territories on the mainland, Spanish and British explorers, Russian fur traders and missionaries, American colonists, and people from all over the world who seek their fortunes in gold, fish, and oil, or look to find themselves as tourists in sublime wilderness landscapes.[30]

While in Anchorage, I visited the federal archives to look for traces of *mexicanos* in Alaska in federal court records, including declarations of intent and petitions for citizenship that were submitted and reviewed within the territory, and later the state of Alaska. I spent many days there leafing through the pages of heavy, hardbound volumes of naturalization records from district courts across the territory of Alaska.[31] One of the earliest was a Declaration of Intention to apply for U.S. citizenship for a Mexican citizen living in Ketchikan, Alaska, in the 1910s. From the information on the form, this person was born in 1890 in Santa Rosalía, Mexico.[32] At the age of sixteen, he walked across the border to El Paso, Texas, in 1906 and by 1917 was residing in the then-territory of Alaska. He served in the U.S. Army and was honorably discharged in 1918; for this, the $4.00 fee to apply for U.S. citizenship was waived. By 1919, when he filed his declaration of intent and petition for citizenship, he was living in Ketchikan and working as a laborer. The declaration of intent says: "I am not an anarchist; I am not a polygamist nor a believer in the practice of polygamy and it is my intention in good faith to become a citizen of the United States of America and to permanently reside therein. So help me god, Signed Simón Vega. Jan 18, 1919." Court records contained cases that involved Mexican nationals in southeast Alaska back to the 1910s, describing men who worked in canneries or as miners. Indeed, it is likely that Mexican stampeders and muleteers, who went to California in pursuit of gold followed the rushes north, to British Columbia, the Klondike, and later to Nome, reached Alaska in the late 1800s.[33] Many early twentieth-century mining company employment records from southeast Alaska list the birth country of their foreign-born employees. One of these from 1916 is for John M. Baltazar, who worked in a Juneau mine as a mucker.[34] Before that, he worked for a cannery on Excursion Inlet, "pitching fish." He wrote that he does not live with family, and that he sends remittances to his mother, who lived in Purépero, Michoacán. Mexicans were also recruited to work in fish canneries in Alaska, with documentation indicating that this work began as early as 1905 and continued during wartime labor shortages until the late 1920s.[35]

As military presence grew in Alaska during World War II, citizenship records show that many Mexican nationals applied for citizenship while stationed there. My ethnography begins after the war, when Acuitzences first began traveling to Alaska in the early 1950s, seeking higher wages than they had been earning in California. These young men were likely seeking adventure, too. But the links to Mexico are historically deeper.[36]

The Consulate of Mexico in Anchorage hosted an exhibit called "First Mexican and Spanish Explorers of Alaska" from September 15 to October 15, 2012, to celebrate both Mexican Independence Day and U.S. Hispanic Heritage Month.[37] The exhibit represented "the historic relationships between Alaska and Hispanic cultures, beginning with Spain's exploration and emphasizing Alaska's connection with Mexico through rarely-seen maps and illustrations depicting six voyages that took place from San Blas, Nayarit, Mexico in the late eighteenth century." These maps were displayed alongside "vibrant and colourful Hispanic traditions in textiles," including a dress from Nayarit. The press release notes "the original content of this exhibition is based on a publication about Spanish voyages to Alaska by the anthropologist M. Wallace Olson."[38] What is interesting is how these voyages are reframed from *Spanish* voyages of exploration to *Mexican* ones. After all, the point of departure for the Spaniards is now the Republic of Mexico. Consul Javier Abud Osuna gave a presentation at the University of Alaska, Anchorage, titled "Historical and Social Links between Mexico and Alaska," where he introduced the Spanish voyages of exploration and then moved directly to speaking about present-day Hispanics in the United States, and then the Mexican population in Alaska, ending with a review of Mexican cultural activities and events in Anchorage.[39] I write more about the Spanish-speaking population in Anchorage below and about the Consulado de México en Alaska in chapter 6, but here it is important to note how a historical connection between Mexico and Alaska is produced, and a line of continuity is made between eighteenth-century Spanish explorers and today's Spanish-speaking population in Alaska. Especially in southeast Alaska, Filipino, Mexican, and other immigrants intermarried with the local Tlingit residents.[40] Indeed, interrogating the history of the connection between Mexico and Alaska questions the line between newcomer and native and sometimes between Indigenous and immigrant.

In spite of a deep and ongoing history of continental connection, Mexicans in Alaska have been viewed as unexpected, as people out of place. However, people "categorize back," and throughout this book I analyze the "crossings" that draw together Alaska and Mexico in the everyday lives of people who move between these places.[41]

In Anchorage itself, Hispanic/Latinos comprise approximately 7.6 percent of the population.[42] Estimates about the number of people from Acuitzio currently living and working in Alaska vary. But of the roughly 11,526 individuals living in Anchorage who were of Mexican origin at the time of research (3.9 percent of the city's population), participants estimated that about 1,000 men, women, and children in Anchorage are from Acuitzio, a number that fluctuates depending on the season.[43] By asking interviewees about their network of family, friends, and acquaintances from Acuitzio in Alaska, I estimated during 2011–12 fieldwork that there were about 400 Acuitzences in Anchorage. However, this does not include certain groups of individuals such as, for example, a group from town who worked at a greenhouse in south Anchorage every summer. I understand that they work under a temporary foreign worker program and are provided with room and board at the greenhouse site. For my purposes here, the exact number of Acuitzences in Alaska doesn't matter as much as the way Anchorage is experienced. The social world of Acuitzences in Anchorage is made up of other Acuitzences, both in Anchorage and in Acuitzio itself.

Some characteristics of the Mexican population in Alaska seem to be different from that of Mexican migrants elsewhere in the United States. My colleague Dayra Velázquez certainly found this to be true when she arrived in Anchorage for her graduate research in 2006.[44] Arriving with questionnaires developed for use with low-skill laborer and farm worker migrants in Southern California, she found that the questions were totally inappropriate in Alaska, where Mexican migrants and immigrants have very high levels of social and economic capital that could not be accounted for in the survey, which was developed for use with low-skill laborers and farm workers. These people owned their own homes and businesses and were not working in fields or as dishwashers, struggling to make ends meet. This surprised her, and she frames migration to Alaska as different in terms of both destination and the kind of work that people do, so that rather than working in farms and fields as in California, newcomers from Mexico work in fish canneries and restaurant kitchens.[45]

In a 2013 report about Alaskan economic trends, drawing on data from the 2010 U.S. census, the authors found that the Hispanic population in Alaska has grown by 52 percent between 2000 and 2010.[46] Although Hispanic residents in Alaska make up a smaller segment of the population compared to the nation as a whole (5.5 percent in Alaska, 16.3 percent nationwide), the increase over the 2000–2010 census period is higher for Alaska (52 percent increase, whereas it was 43 percent nationwide). The authors of the report attribute this growth both to migration/immigration and "natural increase," meaning that there were more births than deaths in this population. Like the nationwide Hispanic/Latino population, Alaskan Hispanics tend to be younger than the general population. Most Hispanic Alaskans live in Anchorage (home to 56.2 percent of all Hispanic Alaskans), and within the Anchorage Bowl, Hispanic people are not concentrated in any particular neighborhood. Outside of Anchorage, U.S. census data shows higher shares of Hispanic residents in the Aleutian census areas, Kodiak Island, and Fairbanks borough. Different from the Hispanic population in the Lower 48, most Hispanic Alaskans were born in the United States (77.5 percent in Alaska, 61.9 percent nationwide), more report speaking English well (88.0 percent in Alaska, 77.2 percent nationwide), and they have a higher educational attainment than Hispanic people in the Lower 48 (76.7 percent in Alaska have received a high school diploma, compared to 61.5 percent nationwide). Finally, "substantially fewer Hispanics were below the poverty level in Alaska than in the nation as a whole" (11.6 percent in Alaska, 22.4 percent nationally).[47] In another report, "New Americans in Alaska," new immigrants and their children are characterized as "growing shares of Alaska's population and electorate."[48] They report a growth of the Latino population in Alaska from 3.2 percent in 1990 to 5.8 percent in 2011.[49] Of these, so-called unauthorized immigrants made up less than 1.5 percent of the state's workforce in 2011.[50]

Although the categories of Hispanic or Latino as a category are much broader than my study group of Acuitzences in Alaska, many of the findings in these reports are verifiable ethnographically. For example, I did fieldwork in Anchorage because I knew from previous research that most Acuitzences live in Alaska. In my research I did not find any geographic clustering of people of Mexican background within Anchorage. The people I met, talked to, and interviewed were dual-citizen or U.S. permanent resident Acuitzences who are able to move back and forth between Acuitzio and Alaska. They received good wages at work, and many own businesses and property in Mexico and the United States.

In terms of migration and immigration and the composition of the Spanish-speaking community in the state, Alaska is unique. I believe the history of migration between Mexico and Alaska is also novel compared to elsewhere on the continent. Thus, transnational life in Alaska cannot be easily compared with transnational life in Southern California, or Oregon or Montana, or other points "Outside."

*Acuitzio, Michoacán, Mexico*

Specific locations within the transnational social field also inflect it with particularities. Thus in some ways this is a translocal social field, based on a way of life that extends between two specific locations. Acuitzio del Canje is the *cabecera*, or head of the municipality of Acuitzio, which encompasses forty population centers, most of which are small *ranchos* or hamlets with fewer than 100 residents each.[51] It is located in a beautiful setting in the cool uplands of the state of Michoacán, near the capital city of Morelia.[52] In the 2010 census, the population of the municipality was reported as 10,987, with over half of the population (6,333) residing in Acuitzio del Canje.[53] Of course, this does not include the entire population of Acuitzences who claim the municipality as their home, and to my knowledge there are no numbers currently available to calculate how many Acuitzences live elsewhere yet travel back regularly and maintain homes and social relationships there.

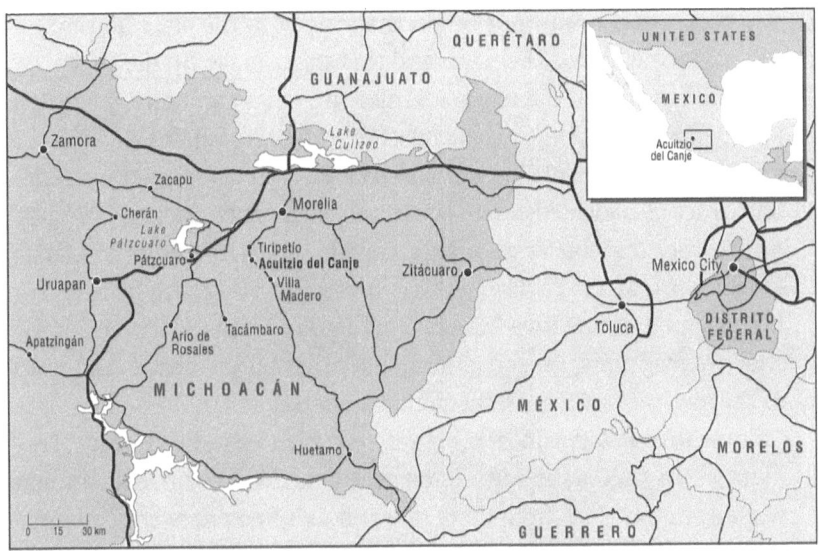

MAP 1. Interior Michoacán, Mexico. Map by Erin Greb Cartography.

From Morelia, located in the Guayangareo valley surrounded by hills, one takes Highway 14, the Morelia-Uruapan highway, in the direction of Tiripetio. The highway winds up into the hills, gaining elevation. The road then levels out, and at Tiripetio one turns left onto the *libramiento* that leads from Tiripetio, through Acuitzio, and on to Villa Madero and the Tierra Caliente. Acuitzences proudly state that one of the first universities in the Americas was established in Tiripetio, and now an *escuela normal rural* is located there.[54] After Tiripetio, the road now follows a valley bordered by *milpas* and then begins to gain elevation again, onto the shoulders of the Cerro Viejo overlooking the town, also known as the Cerro de la Cruz for the cross mounted at the summit. At the Colonia of Las Peñas, so named for its location among the rocky cliffs and hills of the Cerro Viejo, is a large sign that reads, "Welcome to Acuitzio del Canje: Place of the Exchange of French and Belgian Prisoners for Mexicans 1865,"[55] highlighting the historical significance of this exchange of prisoners and adding *del Canje* to the town's name, becoming Acuitzio of the Exchange.

To enter the town itself, a driver would make a left-hand turn off of this highway, driving down a street that starts out fairly wide, narrows and becomes one-way as it bends, then passes by the plaza and continues on Riva Palacio. The plaza and this street make up the social and economic hearts of the town. It is also the religious center, since Riva Palacio is bookended by two churches, the Parroquia de San Nicolás and the Santuario del Sagrado Corazón. The municipal administration offices are also located at one end of the plaza, opposite the Parroquia. Adobe brick and concrete houses sit snugly against the sidewalks, many of which are painted a deep red and white, following a traditional style in the region. Along Riva Palacio hand-lettered signs advertise butcher shops, restaurants, grocery stores, and other businesses. To the south of the town center just off the highway that leads to Villa Madero is La Colonia Riva Palacio, most often referred to as La Colonia by local residents.[56] La Colonia is considered pretty far from town, even though walking to the plaza from there takes about fifteen to twenty minutes.

The plaza itself is rectangular in shape, with the town administration at one end and the Parroquia at the other. It has low walls around all sides, a *kiosco* and a fountain, carefully tended grass and manicured shrubs, and benches to sit on. The plaza is the center of social relations for Acuitzences who live in town and the focus of much nostalgia for those who live and work abroad. The *portales* run along both sides of the plaza with the small library, the only ATM in town, a restaurant, an ice cream shop, and a veterinarian, as well as several stores. In the plaza itself are vendors in carts who sell tacos, hamburgers and hot dogs, and fresh juice, among other things. Going to the plaza for tacos, ice cream, or hamburgers is a popular and delicious pastime. Major celebrations also happen in the plaza, or in the *plazuela*, just off to one side near the Parroquia. When I stayed in Acuitzio during the summer of 2011, there was a basketball tournament in the *plazuela*, and every evening a crowd would gather to watch local teams compete against each other. Just "going to the plaza" is a social event in and of itself. I remember sitting on a plaza bench, listening to the sounds of birds in the trees, murmurs of conversation, the sounds of streets and sidewalks being swept, and recorded advertisements or loud banda music played from car speakers. Acuitzences describe their town as *tranquilo*, quiet or peaceful and very beautiful. As Luis Bravo Jr. said, "It's the most beautiful town in Mexico. No, *cabrón*, in the world!"

Acuitzio is described as peaceful even as Michoacán in general is known as the home of drug cartels La Familia and Los Caballeros Templarios. The attempts of these groups to control space and mobility can make it more difficult to travel within the region. After buses were hijacked and set on fire along local highways, residents became wary of traveling by bus, and especially at night. My friend Alina would ask friends and family to update her by text if there were any problems on the highway when driving her own car on day trips within the region to Uruapan, Pátzcuaro, or local water parks.[57] Local residents cautioned me about hiking in the mountains, taking the bus or driving at night, or visiting more dangerous towns and regions in Michoacán. When I started fieldwork in 2011, twenty-one corpses were found at the freeway entrances and exits to the capital city of Morelia, effectively closing the city until the police completed their investigation. More recently, *fuerzas autodefensas*, or self-defense groups, were formed in some communities in Michoacán to fight back against organized crime and corruption. In spite of staggering levels of violence and crime in Michoacán associated with cartel control over territory, government corruption, and the U.S.-led War on Drugs, many people continue to describe Acuitzio as *tranquilo* and go home to visit regularly. Others who live in the United States are not so sure and wonder how safe it is to travel back.

The town is also known for its natural beauty and its abundance of water. In Morelia, when I told taxi drivers or shop clerks or others that I was staying in Acuitzio, a common response was: "Ah, Acuitzio, hay mucha agua allá." And so there is: one important landmark for town residents is the *ojo de agua*, or spring. At higher elevations farmland gives way to pine forests. In the past an important industry in the region was forestry and, related to that, furniture production. Today, many of the pine forests in the area have been cleared to farm avocados in the highlands. Avocados are called *oro verde*, or green gold, in this region, and they require a large investment and huge pools of water for irrigation.

Local narratives are rich, and town residents share histories of the *pueblo*, and how Acuitzio is a crossroads, a meeting point for many trajectories. For example, I met with Pascual for an interview in the plaza in Acuitzio in 2011. Pascual was born and raised in Acuitzio but lived and worked in Alaska in the 1990s. His father also worked in Alaska before that. During our interview I asked him to describe Acuitzio for me. He said, "Well, it's a *pueblo tradicionalista*, and the most important part of Acuitzio is the history, no? Acuitzio is marked by historic events." Among the first is its location at the borderlands between the Aztec and P'urhépecha territories.[58] Aztecs called the area "Coatepec," which was translated by the P'urhépecha into their own language as Acuitzio, both of which mean "place of snakes."[59] Later, Augustinian priests moved into the area, founding a convent in Tiripetio, as well as a university, the Casa de Estudios Mayores in 1540. The Augustinians gave Acuitzio San Nicolás de Tolentino as its patron saint, and for many centuries the town was indeed known as San Nicolás Acuitzio.[60]

The most important historical crossing of all was the exchange of French and Belgian prisoners for Mexican ones on December 5, 1865, an act that historians say led to the end of the Franco-Mexican war, created by the brief attempt by the Second French Empire under Napoleon III to conquer Mexico. Orchestrated by General Vicente Riva Palacio, whose name graces Acuitzio's main street, this exchange is celebrated annually with day-long celebrations featuring a reenactment of the exchange itself. In 1901 the town's name was changed to Acuitzio del Canje, or in English, Acuitzio of the Exchange, to commemorate this event.

Pascual said that even though the exchange of prisoners in Acuitzio eventually led to the end of the war, it has had a lasting impact on the area: "Certainly, some French people stayed here, living in the fringes, in the mountains, because they were people who had already spent many years here, decades even, fighting for a king and country they have lost. They couldn't cross the Atlantic back to France so they stayed here."

The last names of many people in Acuitzio reflect this, Pascual's included. He said, "My name isn't Mexican, it isn't Gómez or López, it isn't Spanish, right? The French who stayed were persecuted, and they sought refuge in the mountains near Tacámbaro, and they changed their last names." Moreover, Pascual thinks his grandfather looked phenotypically French. "My grandfather was tall, really tall. He was also *güero*, not very Indigenous looking at all, more French, no?" It's true that many people from Acuitzio have light skin, eyes, and hair. Another Acuitzence in Alaska told me that many people don't believe that he's Mexican, with his blue eyes, light skin, and brown hair.

Pascual also inherited his grandfather's *güero* complexion and told me, "Every December 5 when I was a child I always dressed up as a French soldier for the parade. Anyway, the exchange was the most important historical event for the town."

Carlos Arenas García characterized Acuitzio as the access point to the mountains and the natural way to the southern part of the state, which allows for regional products from a large area to be distributed to other areas of the state and even outside of it.[61] The town is near the path of the Camino Real, which was once used by colonists, missionaries, and supply caravans to travel between Mexico City and Santa Fe during the Spanish colonial period. Gonzalo Calderón says that portions of that road still remain, buried under the dirt. In his dissertation, Raymond E. Wiest notes that the most memorable events in town history occurred during periods of conflict, due to the town's strategic location between the Tierra Caliente and the railroad, which was completed in 1901.[62] Since the town was in a strategic place for the control of goods, Acuitzio was caught up in the independence movement, the French intervention, the Mexican Revolution of 1910–20, and the Cristero rebellion of the 1920s.[63] The town was also an important commercial center and stopover point in the trade route of agricultural products from the Tierra Caliente.[64] In fact, the main route went straight through town, right along Riva Palacio. The town was once well known for wagon wheel building and repair, as well as *huarache* and shoe making.[65] Shoe making remained important well into the 1970s.[66] In the 1930s the heavy traffic of goods from the lowlands to the railway and Morelia was diverted when the government constructed roads into Tacámbaro through Pátzcuaro, and into Huetamo from the highway leading to Mexico City. Wiest wrote, "a town that once relied on income from trade, in the form of night lodging, services, small businesses, and crafts, suddenly was caught with an excessive number of retailers and services. This change has had a marked effect on the entire municipality and is the single most important factor underlying the continuous rate of out-migration."[67] As the route shifted, then, Acuitzio lost its position as an important waypoint, and many people left, seeking work elsewhere in Mexico and across the border in the United States.

All of these things show how Acuitzio has long been a place spatially connected to elsewhere, and that this is vital for the town's sense of itself. Then, as now, "Acuitzio must be seen as a town within a region relating to national Mexico and even to parts of the rest of the world," including Alaska.[68] The town, then, has been configured as outward-reaching and, indeed, as a collective, and it has been successful at extending its residents to points elsewhere, while keeping them engaged in the community.

An important part of the contemporary connection to elsewhere is labor mobility. Acuitzio has a long history of labor migration to many destinations in the United States and elsewhere in Mexico.[69] In 1970 Wiest wrote: "There has been a heavy emigration out of the rural areas into the *cabecera*, while at the same time townspeople have left the *cabecera* and migrated to urban centres, primarily Mexico City. This changeover of town residents is continuing."[70] Today there are sizable populations of Acuitzences in Chicago, in the Los Angeles region, in agricultural towns of the San Joaquin Valley in California, and in Anchorage.[71] Acuitzio is a town of migrants and has been for generations now, and this is visible on license plates on vehicles in town, in currency exchange businesses along the main street, and in the annual celebration of the Día de los Norteños, or Day of the Northerners, on January 2, which celebrates town residents who work in the United States with a *jaripeo* and dance.[72]

### Anchorage, Alaska, United States

Over 7,800 kilometers north and west of Acuitzio is the city of Anchorage, located at about 61 degrees north, nestled between Cook Inlet and the Chugach Mountains. The Dena'ina people had settlements along Knik Arm for centuries before English explorer Captain James Cook explored and described the area in 1778. Russian traders and missionaries likely frequented the area as well, at least until Russian America was sold to the United States in 1867. The city of Anchorage itself was originally established as a tent city for workers building the Alaska railroad beginning in 1914. Anchorage is now the largest city in Alaska, with a population of approximately 291,826 in 2010, about half of the population of the entire state.[73]

On the way into Anchorage along the Alaska Highway and the Glenn Highway from Tok there are only smaller settlements and towns, forests, mountains, rivers, and lakes. On the outskirts of Anchorage, however, the population density grows as you pass through the Matanuska Valley and the towns of Wasilla, Palmer, and Eagle River. Wasilla is now famous as the home of ex-governor and one-time vice presidential candidate Sarah Palin, but it is also known as the start of the Iditarod dogsled race. The freeway widens, and on one side you pass a large American flag and a sign welcoming you to Joint Base Elmendorf-Richardson. Construction of Alaska's military facilities began during World War II, due to Alaska's proximity to Japan. These facilities assumed an increasing role during the Cold War, then because of proximity to the Soviet Union. Military bases such as Elmendorf-Richardson have had a huge impact on the city of Anchorage. Today they employ over five thousand soldiers and civilians, many of whom come from outside Alaska.[74] After the entrance to Elmendorf-Richardson, one passes Tikahtnu Commons with its expansive parking lot, movie theater, nationwide chain stores and restaurants like Target, Kohl's, and Olive Garden, and more local businesses such as the Firetap Alehouse and Alaska Communications.

The city stretches out in all directions. It has one of the lowest population densities of any city in the United States, and its nearly three hundred thousand residents live in an urban area roughly the size of the state of Rhode Island. The city of Anchorage fills the whole plain between Turnagain Arm to the south and Knik Arm to the north, extending from the mudflats of Cook Inlet to the east up into the shoulders of the Chugach Mountains to the west. This spread-out arrangement of the city means that there are many parks and areas of open forest here and there. It also means that most people drive to and from home, work, school, shopping, and other activities. In contrast to Acuitzio, it is difficult to get around by bus, and walking long distances is challenging. I found walking also to be considered odd by most people I knew in Anchorage, who would offer me a ride rather than let me walk.[75]

Driving through the city one might notice that the tallest buildings are either hotels or oil company offices, reflecting two of the main industries in the state: tourism and oil. Wildlife is frequently spotted in the city, especially moose, and it is very common to see them ambling down a busy street or sleeping outside of a doorway, even in more densely populated areas. When the salmon are running, residents and tourists

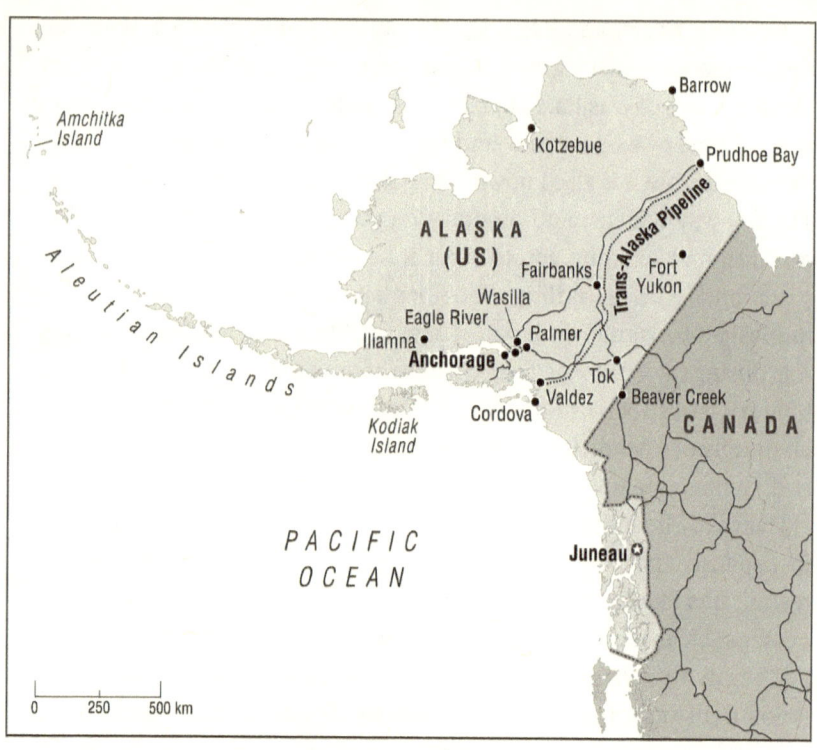

MAP 2. Alaska. Map by Erin Greb Cartography.

can fish downtown at Ship Creek or watch the fish running in Chester or Campbell Creeks. On a clear day, looking north, Denali Mountain looms over the horizon, even though it is located about 214 kilometers away. Also on a clear day, looking west, you can see the Tordrillo Range, snow-covered and jagged peaks across the sea.[76] Mount Susitna, or Sleeping Lady Mountain, so named because the mountain looks like a prone person, sits directly across Knik Arm, and is a notable landmark in the area.

Running through Anchorage from north to south is the Seward Highway, so named because it goes to Seward, about two and a half hours away on the Kenai Peninsula, the town itself a namesake of William H. Seward, the governor who initially purchased Alaska from Russia in 1867. In addition to the highway, Anchorage also has a large port, located near downtown, rail service, Ted Stevens International Airport, and multiple smaller airports, as well as Joint Base Elmendorf-Richardson to the north of town. For the state of Alaska, Anchorage is where things move in, and through, to other destinations around the state, or to locations within the city. Anchorage is also a hub for international shipping, and the sounds of airplanes taking off, landing, or flying overhead are commonly heard, as is the constant hum of traffic and the clicks, calls, and echoes made by city-dwelling ravens.

Alaska is uniquely ethnically diverse, and Anchorage is no exception.[77] For one, Anchorage is the largest "native village" in the state, with many people of Iñupiat, Yupik, Aleut, Eyak, Tlingit, Haida, Tsimshian, and Northern Athabaskan backgrounds who live, work, or study in the area.[78] As well, people who live in rural villages travel to Anchorage to access health and social services, for cultural gatherings, to shop, to visit family, for leisure, or en route to other destinations. Students in the Anchorage School District speak at least ninety-three different languages at home.[79] As well, the Alaskan Institute for Justice has trained over two hundred bilingual interpreters in forty languages through their Language Interpreter Center.[80] The three census tracts with the highest diversity in the United States in 2010 were in Anchorage, encompassing the neighborhood of Mountain View and parts of Airport Heights and Muldoon.[81] Finally, the top three highest-diversity high schools in the United States are East, Bartlett, and West High Schools, all located in Anchorage.[82]

Anchorage can thus be seen as a crossroads of cargo, cultures, and humans and animals. In fact, in downtown Anchorage in front of the Log Cabin Visit Anchorage Information Center, there is a sign that proclaims Anchorage as the "Air Crossroads of the World," with arrows pointing from all sides listing distances to major global cities. People from all over North America and other continents have passed through Anchorage or other points in Alaska, entry points to the gold rush, the oil boom, or fishing camps or fishing boats. Perhaps, then, Anchorage *gathers*. It is a place that people go toward and seek out, whether for work, adventure, or access to wilderness.

Perhaps unexpectedly, there are many similarities between Acuitzio and Anchorage. The network of Acuitzences who regularly move between Acuitzio and Anchorage means encountering the same people in each place. People that I met in Anchorage who are part of the Spanish-speaking community there often said, "There are many people from Acuitzio here," or, "Almost everyone from Acuitzio is in Anchorage." As described earlier, people in Anchorage know of Acuitzio because there are so many Acuitzences there.[83] In Acuitzio as well, people know about Anchorage. When I talked to Pascual in the plaza in Acuitzio, he said, "Anchorage, we call it Anchorage del Canje," and laughed. "Just, among ourselves, no? Anchorage del Canje, that's how we know it."

Indeed, Tomás talked about his decision to move to Alaska after working in California for many years, "My sister was here, and she suggested that I come here, so I did. And I also have many friends here, I know many people from *el pueblo* here. People who have lived in Acuitzio and have lived here for many years. So I said, well, there will be people I know in Anchorage, and it won't be so difficult to live there, like it is when you don't know anyone."

This made it easy for him to adapt to life in Alaska: "It wasn't difficult for me because I could adapt to whatever. I could accommodate whatever climatic, social, logistical change, everything."

Laura talked about how much she likes it that there are so many people from Acuitzio: "Anchorage has many people from *el pueblo* living here. Wherever you go, you run into people you know from Acuitzio, I think that is what we like about it here." After she said that, I talked about how people use the same words to talk about both places, that Anchorage and Acuitzio are both *tranquilo* and *seguro*, with lots of nature, mountains, and forests. Laura agreed, "Yes, yes, it's true. Maybe because of that we like it here because in one way we feel in the same place because all of Michoacán looks like Alaska!"

The emphasis on nature, especially mountains and water, in both places, is another similarity that people mention. In Acuitzio in 2011 someone told me that the things that people appreciate most about Acuitzio are "the natural spring, the ice cream in the plaza, and the *naturaleza*." Jaime, one of the first men to go to Anchorage, and Pascual, who went there much later in the 2000s, also drew similarities between Michoacán and Alaska in terms of their love of outdoor pursuits and their own adventurous personalities. Both of them climbed mountains and worked in natural areas in Mexico: Jaime worked in forestry, and Pascual has an ecotourism business. In Alaska, as well, they continued these interests. Jaime worked as a field assistant for an Alaska Fish and Game biologist. Pascual said, "I am one of those who went to Alaska and found my truth in its landscapes and mountains." He even gave his daughter a name that reflected his love for the state. A photo of Jaime and other first-generation Acuitzences in Alaska cooking food after a hike sometime in the 1960s shows that they, too, engaged in outdoor pursuits.

My friend Ana said that life in Alaska became more enjoyable once her family took up Alaskan activities like camping, mountain biking, and fishing. She said, "Until we got the motor home, Sarita, summer was so boring!" They go camping every summer with a large group of Acuitzences and other friends, and Ana looks forward to grilling *gorditas* over the campfire. Many Acuitzences have taken up quintessentially Alaskan activities like salmon fishing, camping, mountain biking, and cross-country skiing, as well as snowboarding and hiking.

People draw comparisons between Anchorage and Acuitzio all the time, describing both places as tranquil and natural. This is ironic because Alaska's status as extremely separate and disconnected from elsewhere is partly due to its image as a wilderness state. For Acuitzences, this wilderness status makes it *more like* the uplands of Michoacán where Acuitzio is located, an area that is also highly valued for its forests, rivers, and mountains. Acuitzio is known for having lots of water and is the source of natural springs. The forests around Acuitzio, though managed for forestry and increasingly logged and replaced with avocado orchards, are also part of this natural environment. Describing Acuitzio as "tranquil" is also interesting, considering the fact that Michoacán in general is associated with violence related to the drug cartels and the *autodefensa* groups that have proliferated in the state. In fact, the forests are said to have helped the cartels, hiding their activities from authorities. As well, Alaska is only tranquil for some. Federal immigration agents in the state work to arrest and deport Mexican workers, just like elsewhere in the United States.[84] Nevertheless, people draw comparisons between Anchorage and Acuitzio in these terms, collapsing the sense of spatial and social distance between them.

Indeed, another one of my interviewees told me that when he first arrived in Alaska, it seemed "almost like Mexico because of the vegetation. Because of the vegetation it was like the countryside in Mexico. Different kinds of trees, but the pines are really similar. And the city of Anchorage was small." The fact that Acuitzio and Anchorage are both experienced as relatively small also makes the experience of these two places more similar. For some people, Mexico City was experienced as more different and sociospatially distant than Anchorage. Consider as well that Acuitzio is not tropical. Since it is located at a higher altitude in the highlands, during the winter months it can be cold. It is possible to feel colder in Acuitzio with no central heating than in Anchorage, where residents often traverse between heated homes, heated cars, and heated workplaces.

The location within the United States matters as well, so that Mexican Alaska is qualitatively different from Mexican Chicago, from southern California, or from other destinations where Acuitzences live. Acuitzences in particular organize differently in each place and therefore experience each U.S. location differently. For example, in Chicago Acuitzences are very involved in politics, including national-level immigration protests and labor rights as well as Acuitzio-focused fund-raising and action. In Anchorage they are less involved with these kinds of organized activities, which fits more with Alaska's libertarian political climate. Alaska is also unique as a destination because of the large number, unique status, and diversity of Alaska Native people, the distinctive ethnic diversity in Anchorage, and a widespread culture of hunting, fishing, and living from the land.

*North American Fieldwork*

At the end of twelve months of fieldwork in July 2012, ten of which I spent in Anchorage, I found myself left behind in Alaska. It was late June, and the sun only set for a couple of hours each night, leaving the city in twilight until the very early dawn. I spent my time visiting fieldwork contacts who were leaving for Mexico, packing up my own small apartment in Fairview, and planning the long drive back to Canada. As more of my main contacts and friends in Anchorage left, I soon realized that I wasn't an anthropologist preparing to leave the field; I was an anthropologist whose field had already left.

Similarly, since I first went to Acuitzio for fieldwork in 2005, I had returned at times when my Alaskan contacts were visiting and other times when they were absent, and found it a very different experience. The town was quieter, there were fewer events with no migrants visiting their hometown, and houses where I had been welcomed were closed up and empty for the season. My field site hadn't arrived yet; I was visiting at the wrong time.

This is only possible because I had designed my project to focus on *Acuitzences* in Alaska, and not Acuitzio or Anchorage in general. Or, more specifically, the goal of my research was to examine the historical and ongoing connections created between Alaska and Mexico by multigenerational families of Mexican background. In particular, I focused on the spatial practices of families living in Anchorage and Acuitzio, and how their constructions of a new sense of belonging in Alaska are entangled with ongoing patterns of mobility, practices, and imaginings that connect them with Acuitzio, their town of origin in Michoacán. Through ethnographic fieldwork in both Anchorage and Acuitzio, I planned to explore the potential tensions that may emerge between these people's patterns of transnational mobility and the more rigid spatial imaginings of North America, like that of U.S. immigration law, the dominant media representations about Mexican migrants in the United States, and the widespread image of Alaska as a space of wilderness seemingly removed from the impact of Mexican migration, due to its location in the far north of North America. I was interested in how people from Acuitzio produce these spaces as connected even as political, economic, and imaginative processes produced them as extremely separate. My research intended to focus on how transnational connections are constructed through family and kinship ties and how these family ties take social form within specific networks of social relations. My field site was a transnational space that extends between Mexico and Alaska, which, although not clearly delineated on a map, could be found among the people who live transnationally. Although North America became the structural frame for my ethnography, I chose a methodology that would allow me to zoom in on the everyday lives of people who move across the continent.

To do this, I engaged in multisited ethnography, a mobile ethnography that traces a cultural formation across and within multiple sites of activity. "Multi-sited research is designed around chains, paths, threads, conjunctions, or juxtapositions of locations in which the ethnographer establishes some form of literal, physical presence, with an explicit, posited logic of association or connection among sites that in fact defines the argument of the ethnography."[85] This method has been taken up by anthropologists in general but has been particularly important for the study of transnational processes, enabling the researcher to ethnographically trace processes as they play out in daily life in different sites. For studies of Mexican migration and immigration to the United States, multisited research usually implies ethnography in communities in both Mexico and the United States.[86]

I ethnographically "followed the people" from Acuitzio to Anchorage, spending summer in Acuitzio, and the fall, winter, and spring in Anchorage, like they do. As I followed the people and focused on the connections they make to produce transnational space, I also became one of those connections between places, someone who, along with my research participants, lived in the same transnational social field. As such, I also documented my own travel to and from Acuitzio and Anchorage along airplane and highway routes. In conducting fieldwork along routes between Acuitzio and Anchorage, I conceptualize cultures as sites of both dwelling *and* travel.[87] Throughout my fieldwork, I sought informal and formal tape-recorded descriptions of travel between Anchorage and Mexico in an attempt to "take travel knowledges seriously."[88] Inspired by Steve Striffler's trip from Arkansas to Santo Domingo, Guanajuato, with his research participants,[89] I also traveled with the Bravo family by car, bus, and airplane, documenting our trip in field notes and learning about how they experienced the trip. I drove from Vancouver to Anchorage and from Anchorage to Edmonton with my partner Chris, our pets, and our 1997 Jeep Cherokee on the Glenn, Alaska, Cassiar, and Yellowhead Highways, documenting our experience of travel with photographs and field notes.

Is research conducted this way best conceived of as multiple field sites or as one site extended across the continent? I believe there are methodological implications of each. By defining transnational space as a spatial formation produced by and extended from Acuitzio to Anchorage by the people I worked with, then my field site represents one single spatial formation, with key points at either end. In the following chapters, by examining the lives and travels of Acuitzences to, within, and from Alaska, Acuitzio and Anchorage are understood as a single transnational social field. This is different than two places linked through migration, a conceptualization of space that reinforces the sedentarist metaphysics of nation-states as distinct and bounded spaces.

## 2 The Annual Migration of the Traveling Swallows

SHARED EXPERIENCES OF MOBILITY
ACROSS NORTH AMERICA

During the summer of 2011 I lived with Juana, Luis, and their children in their Acuitzio home, a two-story yellow house located about three blocks away from the plaza. Juana and the kids lived there when Luis was commuting back and forth to Alaska. Now the whole family lives in Anchorage for most of the year and travels to Mexico every summer. I was with them on one of those summer trips.

The walls in the kitchen and sitting area in their home in Acuitzio are decorated with framed photos from Alaska: Denali mountain, the northern lights illuminating the Anchorage cityscape, sled dogs running the Iditarod Race, and a poster commemorating the fiftieth anniversary of Alaska statehood in 2009. One day I returned to the house after an interview to find that a television, benches, and chairs had been moved onto the patio to watch the Mexico soccer team play in the Under-17 World Cup. Juana and Luis, Juana's parents, and two of Juana's brothers and their families were all there to watch the game. I sat next to Luis, and he handed me a cold beer. I took a sip and then noticed that my chair was under a bird's nest. I moved over a little. Living in a house arranged around an open-air patio, typical of many homes in Mexico, means that birds frequently fly in and out of the living area, and some build nests around the patio. Luis saw me move my chair over and glanced up at the bird's nest. The nest was small, made of a clay-like substance molded onto the wall just where it meets the ceiling, and small birds flew frequently to and from these nests.

Luis said, gesturing toward the nest, "I don't want to kick them out because they come from so far away."

He went on to tell me that they are called *golondrinas*, or swallows, and they come to Mexico for the winter from as far away as Alaska. He said they come every year at the beginning of the rainy season: *"Vienen a criar y se van."* They come to raise their children, and then they go.

"Do the same ones come back every year?" I asked.

He said, "I think one of them is the same, but who knows."

Juana pointed out the other nests around the house. There was a nest upstairs, and another one in the back, and another over the truck, in addition to the one right over our heads. She said "other houses don't have them because many people break their nests and kick them out, even though they use a special soil so their nests are really durable."

Luis said, "They say if a child doesn't want to talk, you take a swallow and get it to kiss the child. With Juana, they did this with ten swallows!" Everyone laughed, knowing that Juana is a bit of a chatterbox, while she gave her husband a sideways look and a loving swat on the arm.

Juana's mother said, "They used to say that in the old days, but who knows."

Luis said, "Sarita, there's even a song called 'Golondrinas Viajeras,' from a TV show."

Later, I looked up the song "Golondrinas Viajeras," or "Traveling Swallows." It was performed as a duet by Lucero and Joan Sebastián for the title sequence of a telenovela called *Soy Tu Dueña*. The television show is not about labor migration or immigration to the United States, but rather it is a soap opera that centers on the dramatic love life of a wealthy and beautiful woman from Mexico City. In that sense, the song may be read as overcoming adversity to find true love. However, the lyrics also highlight the mobility of the swallow, its crossing of borders and seas and storms over long distances looking for a place to nest, to rest. Indeed, the chorus goes:

Traveling swallows
We will not rest
Longing for an illusion
But always looking for somewhere to nest[1]

Like Luis, Juana and their family, many Acuitzences move regularly across the continent, from their hometown in Acuitzio del Canje, Michoacán, to their current home in Anchorage, Alaska. Like swallows, their movement transcends geopolitical borders, creating a social space that connects these two distant locales. For the swallows, we tend to call the spatial formation within which they move a "habitat." For the migrant-immigrant, scholars have called the transnational social space produced through movement "the transnational migrant circuit," a "transnational community," the "articulatory migrant network," a "transnational conjectural space," or "transborder lives."[2] These are social spaces produced through mobility. Roger Rouse, for instance, argues that the *circulation* of people, money, goods, and information between places across the globe creates settlements that become so closely woven together that they constitute a single community spread across a variety of sites.[3]

That Juana and Luis felt an affective connection with the *golondrinas* that, like them, move back and forth across vast distances and international borders reveals how mobility has become essential to their way of being in the world. For Luis, Juana, and other migrant-immigrants I met in Alaska and Acuitzio, part of developing a transnational habitus and way of life across the continent is becoming expert at travel and traveling often between homes. Transnational lives and communities are constructed and sustained, not only at the end points or "nodes" in the networks but along the lines, routes, trajectories, or corridors that connect them. The back and forth trip, *la vuelta*, is essential for the production of a social space extending from Mexico to Alaska, and the shared experience of travel along these routes is important for a sense of belonging in transnational space. Infrastructure such as roads and airline travel reconfigures social relationships across the continent, making mobility between Mexico and Alaska possible. A focus on mobility also explores the relationship between citizenship and mobility for Acuitzences who live in both Mexico and Alaska. Citizenship allows for the freedom to move, and as a result people become more mobile even as they are "rooted" as nation-state citizens. At the same time, the process of obtaining citizenship also requires mobility as a matter of bureaucratic process.

This chapter follows Acuitzences along corridors that extend well past the physical geography of the Mexican-U.S. border, to include airports and highways at different locations between Acuitzio and Anchorage, some of them located in Canada. Ethnographic attention to these long-distance mobilities illustrates that taking the continent as a frame of analysis is important for understanding the social world of Acuitzences in Alaska, which includes experiences of travel all across North America. After all, this is a way of life that depends on mobility and a group of people who collectively draw a sense of belonging from hometowns of Acuitzio and Anchorage as well as a common experience of mobility between these places. Along snow-covered highways in Alaska and Canada, in airports and airplane cabins, and up steep roads into the mountains of rural Mexico, Acuitzences move back and forth across the continent.

### Air Crossroads of the World

On Fourth Avenue in downtown Anchorage, amid hot dog vendors and souvenir stores, sits the Old Log Cabin, one of Anchorage's oldest buildings, now converted into a visitors center. In front stands a post with arrows pointing in all directions, noting distances to cities such as New York, London, San Francisco, and Seattle, in addition to points within Alaska such as Nome, Fairbanks, and Valdez. On the top, a sign proclaims: "Anchorage: Air Crossroads of the World." Indeed, air travel has been essential for traveling to and within Alaska, opening up the state to new residents, workers, and capital. Located within or very near to the city are Ted Stevens International Airport, Lake Hood float plane airport, and Joint Base Elmendorf-Richardson, as well as two smaller airfields, Merrill Field and Campbell Airstrip. By air, Anchorage is roughly equidistant from Europe and Asia, making it a strategic location for international air commerce. In fact, its airport is one of the busiest in the world, not from commercial passenger flights but due to freight traffic to and from Asia.[4] When the weather cooperates, the sky buzzes with smaller airplanes that service vast parts of Alaska that are not easily accessible by road or water, locations that can be reached faster by air.

Late one night in 2011 an Alaska Airlines Boeing 737 landed at Ted Stevens International Airport in Anchorage. Juana, Verónica, and Sophia woke up as the wheels hit the runway and prepared to disembark. I had

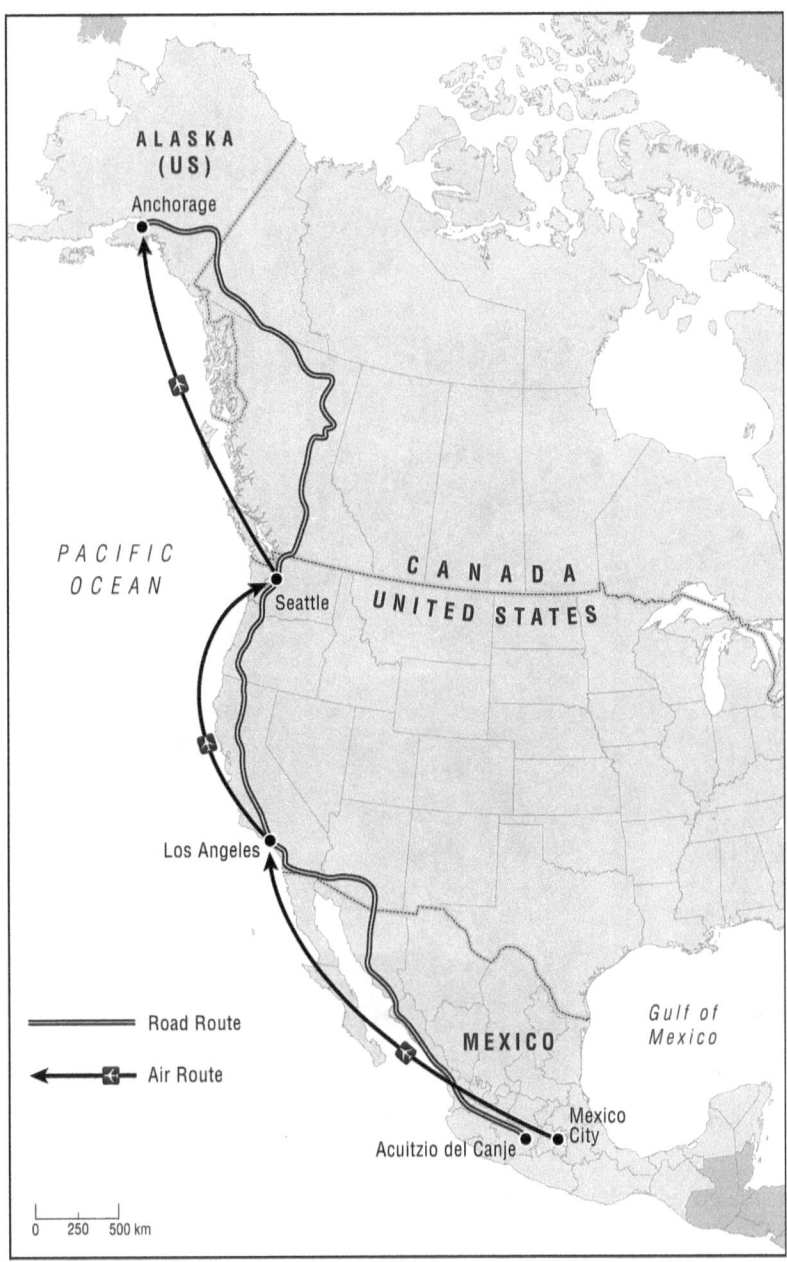

MAP 3. Air and road routes between Mexico and Anchorage, Alaska. Map by Erin Greb Cartography.

FIG. 1. Air crossroads of the world, downtown Anchorage, 2013. Photo by author.

traveled with the Bravo family from Acuitzio to Morelia by car, from Morelia to Mexico City by bus, and from Mexico City to Los Angeles and Seattle by airplane. From Seattle, the Bravo women boarded a flight to Anchorage, and I boarded my flight home to Vancouver, Canada. While traveling together, I documented the family's experience of mobility between Acuitzio and Anchorage. This is a trip repeated annually by the Bravo family and others like them.

Earlier that morning, in Mexico City, Juana was repacking her suitcase, arranging clothing, food, and souvenirs so that each bag would not be too heavy, and so that fragile items like bread wouldn't get squished. She called her sister who lives across the street to ask if she knew anyone who could give us a ride to the airport. Her sister wasn't able to give us a ride and did not know anyone else who could, so Juana called the airport taxi and made a reservation for it to pick us up at one p.m. The van was cheaper than she had expected, plus it would be safe and have ample space for the four of us and our luggage.

Suitcases packed, we left the house for a street vendor near the market to purchase tamales, prepared Oaxacan style, with the corn dough and filling wrapped in banana leaves instead of the cornhusks usually used to make tamales in Acuitzio. Juana said, "Sarita, we will make these in Alaska!"[5] After returning to the house and eating the tamales, washing them down with glasses of Coca-Cola, Vero and Sophia repacked their suitcases, and Juana's sister brought a scale so we could weigh them. Verónica and Sophia wanted to go on a last-minute shopping trip to a nearby market to buy some candy to take back to Alaska. Their cousins took us to buy candy ice cream cones filled with marshmallows, chili-flavored cigarette-shaped candies, and some gummy sticks.

The taxi van that Juana booked rolled up outside the house just after one p.m. Hugs all around, kisses on cheeks, promises to keep in touch, waves goodbye from the windows of the van. After saying goodbye, we were all pretty quiet in the taxi. We drove past streets lined with low concrete houses, painted in a rainbow of colors. We passed grocery stores, restaurants, soccer fields, and auto repair shops. Verónica said, "I don't like coming to Mexico City, there's too much traffic, everything looks the same, and it's smelly with pollution." Sophia agreed. They prefer smaller towns and cities like Acuitzio and Anchorage and value the slower pace of life and the natural beauty that both towns share. As we got closer to the airport, we entered the freeway and sped up to keep pace with the traffic around us.

We slowed down as we exited the freeway and turned onto the road that accesses the passenger terminals at Benito Juárez International

Airport.[6] The taxi driver broke the silence to ask what airline we were traveling on. "Alaska Airlines," Juana said. The taxi stopped, and Juana handed him the money as the rest of us got out of the van. When a valet came to ask if he could carry our luggage, Juana told him to go ahead, and then she leaned over to say, "I have too many suitcases!" Indeed, between the four of us we were traveling with seven large suitcases, plus carry-on bags. Verónica and Sophia had even left clothes behind in Acuitzio, either giving them away to friends and family, or leaving them hung in the closet in their house to wear when they return the following summer.

In the lineup at the baggage counter, Juana said she felt nervous. She said her husband, Luis, usually handles all the passports, tickets, and documents when they travel. But, like his daughters, Luis dislikes Mexico City; he prefers to fly into Guadalajara or Ixtapa. Juana likes traveling through Mexico City because her family lives there. While we waited in line to check in, Vero and Sophia put luggage tags on the checked luggage and carry-on bags. After checking in, we lined up for the security review and went through a procedure familiar to anyone who has traveled by air in North America: place your bag on the conveyor belt to be scanned, make sure your laptop is out if you have one, hand your boarding pass and passport to the officer, wait to be waved through the metal detection device, and wait as another officer reviews an image of the inside of your suitcase.

Once in the waiting area, we found a place to sit, and Juana propped her legs up on her wheeled carry-on suitcase. She told me earlier that she purchased that suitcase in particular because she could put her feet up like that. Juana said she felt happy to be going to Alaska with her kids and excited to see her husband. Even though she felt sad to be leaving her family in Acuitzio, she said that being away makes her want to return to Anchorage even more. In an interview in Anchorage later that year, Juana talked about when she first arrived in Alaska, and how she felt very far away from her family in Acuitzio: "When we arrived, my children were happy, but I felt somewhere between happy and sad. Sad because I left my family and *I didn't know when I would be able to go back there*. And then, it's so far away. So far away." This experience of emotional in-betweenness is part of transnational life, and an important reason why people like Juana are more mobile as they develop stronger connections to places, as discussed below.

The announcement was made to board our plane, and we waited until our rows were called. In the meantime Juana helped some of the other people in the airport lounge who approached her for help to decipher their tickets. Some of them seemed like they had not traveled by air before, and some could not read their ticket, but Juana spoke with authority. Indeed, she is an experienced traveler who makes this trip every year. It is possible to take for granted the knowledge required to travel back and forth—moving to and through airports, navigating customs and immigration, booking flights, securing the appropriate paperwork—but all of this requires knowledge that is typically gained through practice. Migrant Acuitzences have been socialized to be mobile and are well acquainted with the practice of air travel, but this is not the case for everyone.

The airline employee finally called our rows, and we stood in line, boarded the aircraft, and located our seats. The flight attendants handed out the customs and immigration cards early on, a document that everyone will have to present to U.S. customs agents upon landing in Los Angeles. Juana filled it out for her family and then read the in-flight magazine. We were served tamales and churros in-flight, and I wrote field notes as the sound of voices in Spanish and English chattered around me and the drone of the engines hummed in the background. The girls brought out their pillows and blankets. My travel companions fell asleep, and I changed my watch to Pacific Time, two hours earlier.

We landed in LA early, disembarked, and entered the terminal. LAX is a hub for many national and international airlines, including Alaska Airlines. The hub system of air travel organizes air traffic connections so that all routes are connected to hubs like spokes on a wheel. Alaska Airlines has hubs in Anchorage, Seattle, Portland, and Los Angeles, which means that anyone flying to destinations besides these will need to switch airplanes at the hub.

Verónica turned on her U.S. phone to check text messages and Facebook updates, meaning that she quickly activated the networks of connectivity grounded in U.S. territory. She had been using a different phone in Mexico, one with an Acuitzio number. She takes that Mexican cell phone back to Anchorage so that friends and family can text her from Mexico without paying extra. To get extra cell phone credit while in Anchorage, she asks an aunt in Acuitzio to buy it and then pays her back later. Some people leave money with a friend or family member when they head back to the United States to buy cell credit on their behalf while they are away. This is one way that people can easily stay connected to close friends and family in Acuitzio without those in Acuitzio having to pay the long-distance charges.[7] At the time of my fieldwork it was very common among migrant-immigrants to have multiple phones. And by the end of my fieldwork I had three cellphones—a Canadian one with a Vancouver number, a Mexican one with an Acuitzio number, and a U.S. one with an Anchorage number.

We passed through the U.S. Customs and Border Protection review checkpoint in the airport. Juana, Verónica, and Sophia, who hold both Mexican and U.S. citizenship and who were traveling with U.S. passports, went through the line for citizens, while I, a Canadian citizen traveling with a Canadian passport, went through the line for visitors, or "aliens" in the terminology of U.S. Homeland Security. Afterward I asked Juana if they question her in English or in Spanish. She said, "Always in English." I later asked her if they travel with Mexican or U.S. passports, and she said that they always travel with the U.S. ones: "it's easier that way."

We met up in a large, spacious baggage claim area after being admitted to the United States, and I noticed that Juana seemed both stressed and rushed as we hurried to the baggage carousel. All of the suitcases arrived promptly except one. Meanwhile, Verónica was stacking the suitcases on a cart, placing a particularly large one on the bottom. Her mom said, "No *hija*, there's bread in that one." Many people travel with food from Mexico to Alaska (discussed further in chapter 5), and one of Juana's large suitcases was stuffed with not only bread but also with two large blocks of cheese wrapped in foil, plastic bags full of rich dark *mole* paste, *pinole*, candy of all kinds, crispy churros, chamoy chile sauce, handicrafts with which to decorate their home, and souvenirs for friends in Alaska.[8] Verónica rolled her eyes and moved it from the bottom of the cart as Juana watched anxiously for the last bag. After a few minutes she spotted it as it rolled down the chute and onto the conveyor belt, and she immediately ran to grab it off of the carousel.

After collecting our bags, we left the international terminal and transferred to Terminal 3. My flight to Vancouver was due to depart from gate 31 and theirs to Anchorage from gate 30, with a difference of about five minutes between the departure times listed on our boarding passes. I said, "Well, I'll walk to your gate and then say goodbye."

Juana said, "Oh, how I dislike goodbyes. No one likes them, do they?"

Even though Juana regularly travels back and forth between Mexico and Alaska, or perhaps because of it, she hates saying goodbye. She always says "See you soon." I hugged Juana, then Verónica, then Sophia. Juana said, "Take care of yourself; we'll see you in Alaska soon." I walked to my gate, boarded, and settled into my window seat, where I watched their airplane slowly back away and depart. They arrived in Anchorage late that night, and I knew they had made it home when I saw Vero's updated Facebook status.

It is important to place this one example of air travel into a broader temporal and social context. This is only one trip of many that the Bravo family has made between Acuitzio and Anchorage, and they plan to continue to make in the future. Indeed, most Acuitzences with dual citizenship travel once per year between Anchorage and Acuitzio with additional trips for special occasions or family emergencies. Travel opportunities, by which I mean the number of trips taken per year, increase for many people the longer they are in Alaska.

For instance, the Bravo family was not able to travel very often during their early years in Alaska, due to financial constraints and lack of U.S. citizenship, which restricted the amount of time they could spend outside of the United States.[9] Previously, they went every two years, in the winter, for the fiestas that happen throughout December.[10] The switch from winter travel to summer was one that worked better with the school schedule, as the children grew up and could not miss as many weeks of school during the winter holiday. The switch from travel once every two years to every year represents the family's increased income over time: Juana, Luis, and the children all worked in the service industry during my fieldwork. They have attained a level of financial security that allows them to travel annually, and they all have U.S. citizenship and U.S. passports. Many Acuitzences who live in Anchorage hold Alaska Airlines credit cards, which allow travelers to collect points and receive an annual companion fare: the first ticket is full price, but a companion ticket in 2011 was $99.00 USD, plus taxes. For the Bravo family, it means that they can all travel to Mexico for the cost of three full-price tickets, and two companion fare tickets. Acuitzences like the Bravo family may also use the annual Alaska Permanent Fund Dividend (PFD) check to pay for travel to Mexico. The PFD is paid to all Alaska residents on an annual basis. The amount varies each year since the money comes from investment earnings of state mineral royalties.[11] Luis works at the same restaurant as his brother, but they arrange their trips with each other so they are not both gone at the same time. With work and school they are skilled at finding a time to leave that works for everyone. People tend to describe these trips as "a vacation." The trip I took with the Bravo women in 2011 is therefore part of a pattern of increasing mobility between Mexico and Alaska. This is why the Bravos are so expert at travel, and why travel was such a popular topic of conversation during my fieldwork.

Air travel is certainly the main means by which Acuitzences move back and forth between Alaska and Mexico. Air travel is also the travel technology most associated with time-space compression and the acceleration of the global flow of people, things, and ideas.[12] In the 1990s, globalization theory focused on flows and frictionless motion and implied that everyone would soon have the freedom to travel everywhere.[13] But time-space compression is not evenly experienced. Not all points on the globe are experienced as uniformly "close" or "distant" to one another.[14] For this reason, distance is essential to a continental analysis of transnational mobility.

Distance is a fact of the terrain across the eight thousand kilometers between Anchorage and Acuitzio. The materiality of this distance over mountains, across rivers, through cities, along highways, and between airports cannot be exhausted by how it is socially appropriated or politically controlled.[15] Even though corridors of travel, roads and airline routes, have been built to facilitate more rapid mobility between them, Alaska and Mexico are still experienced as spatially and socially distant from one another. These two forms of distance are entangled with one another, so that people experience distance as both social and spatial. Even in a global world, sociospatial distance remains important when considering the experience of people who regularly cross the continent.

For example, Juana's sister-in-law Gloria also related how hard it is to be so far away from family and that sometimes her family talks about moving closer to Mexico, "Sometimes we want to move a little closer to Mexico, to the Lower 48." She continued explaining some of the difficulties involved in traveling between Acuitzio and Anchorage by air:

> It's frustrating because we're so far away and there are only one or two departures per day. From Anchorage you go to Seattle or Dallas or another airport like Houston or Los Angeles, and then to Mexico, to Guadalajara. But now that we fly a lot with Alaska Airlines it's Seattle, Los Angeles, and then Guadalajara. Or to Ixtapa-Zihuatenejo, Guerrero, which is a beach resort on the Pacific Ocean. It's four hours from Acuitzio now that they've opened the toll highway. It's easy, but also it's a little complicated because you can bring fewer suitcases with you when you leave from Ixtapa-Zihuatenejo. You can only bring one suitcase or something like that. From Guadalajara, since it isn't the beach, you can bring two suitcases.

First, it is worth noting that the distance involved in air travel evokes a whole constellation of towns and airports scattered along several regions of the United States and Mexico. But Gloria also explained that when there is a family emergency, such as when her parents in Mexico were very ill, this distance is felt as especially frustrating: "Among families who are very close, if something happens, or someone passes away, you are so far away, and all you want to do is fly there right then. But if it happens over spring break, or over Christmas or any holiday, there are no flights out of Anchorage. *No puedes trasladarte como tu quisieras*, you cannot move as you want to. There are good things here in Alaska, but we have suffered too."

Geographical, economic, institutional, and seasonal factors make it so that Gloria cannot move as freely she wants to, potentially spatially disconnecting her from important events across the life course and creating the sense that she is, indeed, "very far" from loved ones in Mexico. There are no direct passenger flights between Alaska and Mexico, and flights are usually expensive and always time-consuming. Travel between Anchorage and Acuitzio by plane generally takes all day, since you have to stop in Seattle or Los Angeles (or both) and then arrange a ride with family or friends or take a bus or taxi from Guadalajara or Mexico City or, less preferably, Morelia.

Mobility also involves more than just the infrastructure of travel: "How we run depends on what shoes we have to run in."[16] Due to the power geometry of mobility, some social groups and things move much more easily between Alaska and Mexico than others.[17] Among Acuitzences moving between Michoacán and Alaska, immigration status as defined by U.S. Citizenship and Immigration is something that can smooth out the trip, making it easier to move. This is especially the case when crossing international borders on back-and-forth trips between Mexico and Alaska.

*Transcending the Border*

Most academic analyses of the materiality of mobility between the United States and Mexico focus on the U.S.-Mexican border itself, where people cross at one of forty-five designated checkpoints or surreptitiously along the more than three-thousand-kilometer line. The border traverses a variety of terrains, from dense urban areas to inhospitable deserts. From the Gulf of Mexico, the border follows the course of the Rio Grande to the crossing between El Paso, Texas, and Ciudad Juárez, Chihuahua, before heading west to cross vast tracts of the Sonoran, Chihuahuan, and Colorado deserts to another urban crossing between San Diego, California, and Tijuana, Baja California, finally reaching the Pacific Ocean. Much popular and academic coverage of border mobility focuses on undocumented crossings made by Mexican migrants, many assisted by "coyotes," the middlemen who are paid to guide potential crossers through the border region on foot across mountains and deserts to finally arrive in the United States.[18]

The trajectories of border crossers extend well past the border region itself, and practices of boundary enforcement have been spatially dispersed to airports, checkpoints, and workplaces throughout the United States.[19] Juana, Vero, Sophia, and I crossed the border at the Los Angeles International Airport in 2011. Traveling by road requires that Acuitzences cross at two Canadian-U.S. border crossings as well as at the Mexican-U.S. border, meaning that the experience of land travel involves three different border crossings. Migrations across international borders are one of the processes of mobility whose flow the state tries to code and regulate, but not always successfully.[20] Borders split and maintain territorial imperatives through nation-state politics while at the same time regulating, constricting, and allowing for the movement of people and things across them.[21] In other words, although nations are divided along borders, they are also points of connection. This is true in terms of state action as well as individual experience. While my travel companions in 2011 were moving across vast distances as dual U.S.-Mexican citizens and therefore without challenging the state territorializations, they were at the same time deterritorializing their bodies, food, and objects to points outside of Mexico. They were able to transcend the border and expand past it.

But what about Acuitzences without U.S. citizenship or permanent residency? Claudia's family—the Cárdenas family—has made a complicated series of moves between Mexico and Alaska, beginning with her grandfather's trip north to work on the Alaska pipeline in 1966 through 1977, followed by her father's move north in 1987 to pay off his debts. After a few years of living apart, Claudia's mother wanted to reunite the family in Alaska, so she and her four children crossed the Mexican-U.S. border as undocumented immigrants in 1989. Claudia remembers the day they crossed the border and traveled to Alaska for the first time.

"I remember that we traveled by bus from Acuitzio to Tijuana, which took forever because the bus was stopping in every little town. It was not like a direct bus. I remember that there were lot of people, some of them had seats and some of them were just standing in the middle so the bus was full at all times. And then I remember, my grandpa's friend—she's from Nicaragua, and she went to Tijuana with her sister, and she crossed the border with us." Her grandpa's friend was someone that he met while he was working in Alaska in the 1970s.

Claudia and her family then crossed the border in two cars. Claudia was in the back seat with her aunt, who was so nervous that she put lemons under her arms for luck, "for protection or whatever she was calling it." Her aunt needed protection because they were all crossing the border "illegally," without U.S. visas or Green Cards. Their immigration status and the fact of the border slowed and could have stopped

FIG. 2. Canadian-U.S. border along the Alaska Highway, 2011. Photo by author.

Claudia and her family in Tijuana. The immigration status of Claudia and her family also affected their speed of movement. They did not fly directly to Anchorage; they took a bus to the border and crossed by car. That is, they moved through longer, slower, and more roundabout corridors, and in addition the experience of the border crossing required both luck and protection, at least for Claudia's aunt. Even so, their mobility extended well past the border, since after crossing the border they traveled by airplane from California to Anchorage.

Crossing the border without citizenship or permanent residency also affects the frequency of travel back and forth. I met people in Anchorage who are undocumented and not able to return home. I also met people in Acuitzio who are unable to return to their families in Anchorage because they have been deported. They perceive the risk of travel back and forth across the border to be too great. Distance also limits the ability to travel home regularly since the trip back is long and expensive. So, as migrants gain legal status and capital in Alaska, they are able to travel back and forth more often than previously. Indeed, among the Acuitzences I worked with in Anchorage, there is a pattern of increasing trips home. With more time spent living in Alaska, people are able to travel back to Acuitzio *more* often. With more time spent living transnationally, people are able to develop the skills, statuses, and capital that enable them to travel more freely.[22] Citizenship thus makes it possible to move more freely as it also ties people to a particular nation-state.[23]

My discussion with Octavio exemplifies these dynamics. Octavio now owns a restaurant in Anchorage and has dual citizenship. However, he came to Alaska without papers and told me about how he had trouble with U.S. immigration officials more than once during his early years in Anchorage. I asked him, "Before you got your Green Card, did you go back and forth between Acuitzio and Alaska many times?"

> No, not many times because I couldn't leave the country. Every time I traveled I had to travel without documents. So when I traveled, I traveled by plane. Like nowadays they won't let someone get on if they don't have documents. But back then there weren't the same problems like there are now. If I arrived in Los Angeles, for example, they would ask me where I was going, and I would tell them I was going to Mexico. Someone who didn't have a passport could show an ID proving they were *mexicano*, and they would let them go.

Octavio points out that getting back into Mexico wasn't easy either: "When I arrived in Mexico City, I always had to save some money to give them to let me into Mexico." Octavio explained that he had to pay because he did not have any documents, and until he paid the border guards, they would tell him to go and talk to Mexican immigration since he could not prove where he was from.[24] "I didn't want to travel very often because it was a lot of trouble. It was better to stay here in Anchorage, *ya*. Because every time I went, it was just all immigration problems."

I asked Octavio about how he felt once he got a Green Card: "And so it was a total difference once you got your papers?"

Octavio replied, "Yes, it ended the feeling that . . . they'll surprise you, and take you away." He continued, "Finally the day arrived where I felt free. *Estuviera libre*. After that, I came back to Alaska, and I started to work again because I could work and I wouldn't have any problems." Octavio was free to *travel*, and he could go to Alaska again to work.

Obtaining permanent residency also involves a lot of travel. Citizenship often *requires* mobility as a matter of process. For example, Green Card or permanent residency applicants who have previously entered the country illegally and who are currently living in the United States need to exit the United States and file their paperwork from Mexico before they reenter as U.S. residents.[25] This is called consular processing and is usually used for applications of family members who are living in their country of origin. Those who have "never left," according to the immigration system, and are resident in the United States without a Green Card or visa are also required to leave the country for consular processing of their applications. Ruth Gomberg-Muñoz writes about consular processing as part of understanding processes by which "unlawful entrants" become U.S. permanent residents and citizens, including the long-term separation that this requirement causes for mixed-status families.[26]

Many Acuitzences also talked about having to travel to Mexico for consular processing for U.S. permanent residency applications for themselves or their family members. They did not experience separation as a result, but it did require a lot of mobility. In 2012 I met with Salvador and Inés at their townhouse apartment in south Anchorage for dinner and an interview. We had not spoken in depth since the last time I was in Acuitzio in 2005. At that time, Inés and their son lived in Mexico, while Salvador lived in Anchorage, working in landscaping during the summer months and returning to Acuitzio over the winter. Salvador and Inés had to travel a lot to arrange papers for the family. He got his residency in 2002, and in 2005 he became a naturalized U.S. citizen so that he could apply for his family to join him in Anchorage. People had told him that once he was a citizen it would be easy and in six months his wife and child would be with him in Anchorage. Six months became six years as they waited for a decision. They waited and wrote letters to Alaska's governor, to a senator, and even to then-president George W. Bush. Meanwhile, Salvador continued to travel back and forth between Anchorage and Acuitzio. During this time, his daughter was born.

After six years, a letter finally arrived, directing them to be present for an appointment at the American consulate in Ciudad Juárez so that their son could obtain his Green Card. Salvador flew to Mexico, and then the whole family traveled from Acuitzio to Ciudad Juárez together for the appointment. Acuitzio and Ciudad Juarez are about 1,700 kilometers apart, a drive that takes at least eighteen hours by automobile and much longer by bus. At the consulate they found out that because Salvador was a U.S. citizen, his daughter was also already a U.S. citizen, even though she was born outside of the United States. So they had to go to Mexico City to the U.S. Embassy to get a passport for their daughter. They went from Ciudad Juárez, to Acuitzio, and then to Mexico City a few days later. Acuitzio del Canje is located about 325 kilometers from Mexico City, along toll highways from Morelia. Salvador and Inés were in a rush to arrange their papers because, as Salvador put it, "As we say in Mexico, *la cosa era calientita*, we had to strike while the iron was hot." They couldn't get an appointment until three days later, so they went to Acuitzio, and then to Mexico City again, and then returned to Acuitzio to wait. "We were wondering *when* she would get an appointment," Salvador said. Again they waited and wrote letters. The time came for Salvador to return to Alaska to go back to work, and he once again left Acuitzio for Anchorage.

Exactly one year after the letter arrived for his son, his wife's letter arrived, and they went back to Ciudad Juarez for another interview. By this time his daughter's U.S. passport had also arrived, and the whole family was finally able to relocate to Anchorage to live together in 2008. Because they all have either U.S. citizenship or residency, now they are all able to travel together to Acuitzio as well. Citizenship, then, facilitates mobility between Mexico and the United States, but the process of becoming a U.S. citizen *requires* long-distance mobility between multiple locations. An applicant not only has to leave the spatial boundaries of the United States to reenter as a resident but also might have to file paperwork in U.S. immigration offices based in very different places within Mexico and very far from each other, such as Mexico City, in the center of the country, and Ciudad Juárez, on the northern border.

*Highways of North America*

Anchorage and Acuitzio are connected by the vast network of roads that stretches across the continent, producing a web of lines that directs traffic along particular corridors. Building a road in North America is usually the domain of the government, as it requires engineering and a high level of investment and organization.[27] Moreover, existing roads not only need to be planned and engineered but also maintained: potholes need to be filled, cracks repaired, snow or debris cleared in order to keep the way smooth and the traffic flowing. Roads, whether they are gravel trails, city streets, or multilane highways, reorient social relations along them because they change how people move to, through, and beyond places, and how and where people encounter one another.

Driving means engaging with the terrain through the technology of the automobile.[28] The characteristics of one's car (weight, aerodynamics, tires) interact with the materiality of the road as the car slows to ascend or maneuver around corners, accelerate on descents, or pass a slower automobile. Weather has an effect on the speed because ice, snow, wind, and rain affect mobility by road and potentially increase risks. Frost heaves along the Alaska Highway result in bumpy ride for those traveling along the border of Kluane National Park in Yukon Territory. Wet lowlands on the road from Morelia to Acuitzio near Tiripetio mean the road could flood. As well, drivers follow the formal and informal rules of the road. In Mexico, travel on many highways requires paying a toll. Traveling along northern highways might mean traveling with extra gasoline and tires just in case you cannot reach a service station or repair shop. All of these things affect the experience of travel between Anchorage and Acuitzio.

Gonzalo Calderón began working in Alaska in 1952. When we first spoke by telephone, he told me about the first time he went back to his hometown in Michoacán in 1957. He had saved some money while working in Alaska, and his plan was to return to Mexico to keep studying, even though it had been five years since he left medical school in Morelia to go to Alaska. He had been working in a Distant Early Warning (DEW) Line construction camp along the Yukon River, cooking for the workers in the camp kitchen.[29] When he decided to go back to Mexico, he left the camp and drove to Fairbanks in his car. Then he drove to Anchorage, where he boarded a plane to fly to Los Angeles, where two of his sisters lived. When he arrived in LA, he purchased a brand new car and left for Mexico with plans to continue his medical school training.[30] He said, "crossing the border I started to see the differences. I had already forgotten the poverty of Mexico. I saw the poverty, and I started to feel a lot of compassion for the people."

He arrived in Morelia, "*llegué a mi tierra*," as he puts it, "I arrived in my homeland." Since at that time there was no highway to Acuitzio, he said to himself, "Well, how am I going to get this car into town?" He explained how only half of the highway up into the mountains was paved, and the rest was basically a dirt road, where driving conditions were inhospitable to vehicles that were not big trucks or buses. His new car was fast, brand new, and low to the ground, but it could not drive on dirt roads like that. "I thought about it and I drove through the cultivated fields [instead of on the road]. I don't know how I did it, but I made it to town with my car."

In Acuitzio at that time, only the main street was paved, and it was paved with cobblestones that had been laid by hand. "And that's where I arrived in my town, on Riva Palacio Street," Gonzalo said.

When I arrived I saw the poverty there, and it embarrassed me, right? No one there had ever seen a new car; there were no cars because there was no highway. And a brand new car, nobody had seen one like that in the *pueblito*. I was embarrassed by my new car, the clothes I wore, and the money I brought. I felt *fuera de lugar*, out of place. And I started to think: should I stay here to study, or should I go back to Alaska to keep working, back to where I had been developing?

Gonzalo felt out of place in Mexico and especially in Acuitzio. His car and clothing exemplified the differences between life in Mexico and

Alaska and the sociospatial distance between those locations. He felt embarrassed and uncomfortable, like he no longer fit in in his hometown. He wondered if he should return to Alaska to continue working there.

The terrain was also difficult, especially the road up the mountain to Acuitzio along a highway that today is known as Federal Highway 14 (Michoacán), or the Morelia-Uruapan highway. The highway begins at the bottom of the Guayangareo Valley where Morelia, the capital city of Michoacán, sprawls out. Almost immediately after leaving Morelia, the four lanes of Highway 14 gain elevation rapidly, leveling off before passing the Cointzeo Dam. The road between Morelia and the dam was paved during the Cárdenas administration (1934–40), but the road from Cointzeo to Villa Madero through Acuitzio was only opened and graded between 1952 and 1954.[31] In Gonzalo's day, this road was little more than a dirt trail, difficult to navigate, especially in the rainy season. Raymond Wiest describes his experience driving on the same road in the 1960s:

> We had considerable difficulty driving through the very wet section south of Tiripetio, but also had difficulty getting up the rise to Acuitzio due to exposed rocks and boulders, which made it difficult to maneuver between and around the changing obstacles. . . . The 25 kilometres would take between 2 and 3 hours to traverse. Often in those days, buses got stuck in the lower wet section and/or on that relatively steep incline. And beyond Acuitzio it was often impossible for buses to reach Villa Madero since the road was barely graded.[32]

Travel to Morelia therefore used to take hours along an ungraded dirt road. The entire route between Acuitzio and Morelia was paved sometime between 1970 and 1972, making travel faster and easier by personal automobile or bus.[33] Although road construction greatly improved travel for local residents moving into, out of, and through Acuitzio, the road was likely improved to facilitate resource extraction and manufacturing, specifically timber extraction and processing.[34] When I first traveled to Acuitzio in 2005, the road was paved the entire way from Morelia to Acuitzio and beyond. The distance from Acuitzio to Morelia is now easily traversed by car or bus in about half an hour.

So far in this section I have written about Gonzalo's trip from Los Angeles to Acuitzio in 1957, focusing on the counterpoints that he encoun-

FIG. 3. Road between Tiripetio and Acuitzio, 1967. © Raymond E. Wiest.

tered due to the difference he felt upon crossing the border into Mexico and the difficult terrain on the road from Morelia to Acuitzio. But a few years later, once he was back in Alaska, Gonzalo also drove between Alaska and Acuitzio and therefore traveled through what he described as vast sections of northern wilderness, which added a different dimension to his experience of mobility and distance. We talked about his trip when I visited him at his home in Long Beach, California, in 2012. He is retired and lives with his wife in a tidy trailer home. I visited Long Beach specifically to learn more from him about his time in Alaska, and he showed me photographs and newspaper clippings as he reminisced about his time in the North. He also told me about driving from Anchorage to Acuitzio in the winter of 1964. As he spoke, he was standing, motioning out the narrative, animating everything with his voice, his hands, and the movement of his whole body. I later asked him to write the story down for me, and he sent it as a letter a few months later, describing his trip as both "tragic and beautiful."[35]

Gonzalo decided to visit Mexico to visit his young son, who was living with his mother and sister in Morelia at the time. Before leaving, he readied his Chevy 1500 and offered a free ride to anyone who wanted to join him. He ended up traveling with a man who had driven from Los Angeles to Anchorage in the summer but had difficulty finding work; now that it was winter, he did not have any way to get home. Gonzalo agreed to take him since he would appreciate the company.

Gonzalo said he knew that driving in the winter was risky due to the possibility of dangers like blizzards or ice on the highway, but he felt confident that his vehicle was in good condition. Besides that, he had studded tires so he would not need to carry tire chains for steep icy sections. And so he got together some provisions for the trip, and, he said, "on December 10 at 4 in the morning, we left towards Palmer on the Glenn Highway. The morning was dark and cold at -38 F below zero and a terrible freezing blizzard was blowing." At Eklutna they rescued a man whose car had broken down, dropping him off in Palmer before carrying on to Glenallen, "where it was much colder and I felt like maybe we should turn back, but we carried on along a narrow and mountainous road that looked untouched."

"Finally," Gonzalo writes, "we crossed a metal landmark that said on one side 'Alaska, USA' and on the other 'Yukon Territory, Canada.' I thought that we were still far from there, and the old man I was traveling with yelled 'So long Alaska, we're in Canada now!'" In his telling of the story, and in the written version he sent me later, Gonzalo did not mention this border crossing in any more detail than this. His lack of emphasis on the border and the apparent ease of crossing indicate that it was not experienced as an obstacle for him and his travel partner. In fact, he does not even mention slowing down for any review of his passport or other documents, nor those of his travel companion. At this time, Gonzalo was already a U.S. citizen, presumably traveling with a U.S. passport. For him, the obstacles involved in his drive from Alaska to Morelia were not of a geopolitical nature but produced by weather, fatigue, and distance across difficult terrain. Gonzalo continued, "Driving was very stressful because it was night and the highway was deserted and icy and full of snow. The old man noticed the danger that we were in and began to sing. We had coffee and sandwiches with us and we only stopped when we needed to refill our gasoline and coffee. And so we went in this white and lonely darkness, without encountering a single vehicle."

They arrived in Whitehorse, the largest city and capital of Yukon Territory, late at night but decided to carry on. On the way out of town, the police stopped them, asking, "Where are you going?"

"To Los Angeles, sir."

"Very good. But no one is heading that direction because up ahead there's a blizzard that's covering the highway with packed snow. It's like sand, you know."

"Yes sir, I've been through blizzards like that, but I have studded tires, and two extra just in case. I've made it through blizzards without too much trouble, so if it's alright with you, could I drive a few more miles and if it looks bad, I'll come back here to stay the night."

"Okay, it's up to you!"

Gonzalo continued the story, describing what it was like to drive through the blizzard: driving uphill and feeling afraid because of the snow and ice, and how the tires kept sliding, making him more nervous. His travel companion was nervous too: "My companion was afraid, and he started to sing a song that my father liked, 'La Pajarera.'[36] The song brought back memories, and I wanted to be in my *rancho*."[37]

He arrived at a curve in the road, and there that the pickup truck slid off the road and into the ditch. Panicking, Gonzalo got out of the truck and onto the road: "I looked up, and between the pines I saw the northern lights. I looked down, and noticed that the road was winding downhill. I felt a terrible fear and desperation, and I wanted to cry. I thought of God, knowing that death was certain. What a shame, so far from *mi tierra*, my homeland, and knowing that my body would surely be torn apart by wolves and coyotes before anyone found us."

Lucky for him and his traveling companion, they soon saw headlights. He turned his flashlight on and off to get the attention of the driver of the vehicle, which turned out to be a police car. The police took them to a café just up ahead, where he found a long-haul trucker willing to pull his truck out of the ditch.

Disaster averted, they carried on: "It started to snow, and soon I couldn't see the highway at all." To stay on the road, he followed the tracks and distant taillights of the semitruck that had pulled them out. Once the semitruck was out of sight, he used the rows of trees on each side of the road as a guide, steering his automobile down the middle and hoping to stay on the road. Gonzalo continues, "I drove slowly and cautiously all day. Although we didn't have any food left, we didn't stop. Night fell, and I noticed that my hands were jumping involuntarily on the wheel from two days and one night without any sleep or food. Finally I saw lights and a sign: Fort Nelson, British Columbia." They pulled into the parking lot of the first motel they saw, and drank coffee and ate sandwiches before falling asleep. Gonzalo said, "I woke up at 5am, thinking of the road ahead. We got up and continued along the Alaska Highway until Vancouver, driving with more confidence now that the weather was better."[38]

In Gonzalo's retelling of his trip, the terrain that he traveled appears as a vast wilderness, uninhabitable and empty. However, this would be in direct contradiction to the experience of the land for some local residents, especially Alaska Native and First Nations people who have lived in these regions since time immemorial, and for whom the landscape has immense significance.[39] Instead, Gonzalo experiences the land and weather as obstacles.

While the length and terrain of the highway makes for a long and tiring drive, the very existence of the highway makes it possible to travel by car between Alaska and the rest of the continent. Gonzalo, in fact, drove down to Mexico several times. Once he did so just because he was missing his *rancho*. He said that once he got it into his head that he wanted to be back at his rancho, he could think of nothing else. For this reason, "like a madman," he would drive all the way from Anchorage to Los Angeles nonstop, drinking coffee and smoking cigarettes, hands jumping on the wheel. Being on the road therefore connected him powerfully to the rancho and eventually let him get there by jumping into his car and driving.

Gonzalo's rendering of his road trip repeatedly reiterated the excruciatingly long distance between Alaska and Mexico and, in particular, the roughness of the terrain one needs to drive through in wintertime. Indeed, in his telling and retelling of the story, the detail and events along the road from Anchorage to Dawson Creek take up the majority of his tale, and in comparison, they seem to have traveled quickly from Seattle to Los Angeles and, later, to Mexico, even though this stretch involved thousands of kilometers. Especially in the northern part of his trip, he experienced many stops and starts, some of which almost ended his trip completely. The cold, ice, and snow of the northern winter added another level of friction, one that almost brought his trip to an end.

Most of Gonzalo's trip took place along the Alaska Highway, which begins in British Columbia at mile 0 at Dawson Creek and continues over 2,349 kilometers of mountainous and forested terrain to the historical end of the highway at Fairbanks.[40] Prior to the construction of this highway, Alaska could only be reached by air or sea. This became a military concern after Pearl Harbor was bombed in December 1941, as the U.S. government became anxious about the vulnerabilities of Alaska to an attack by Japan. Since building the highway meant crossing through Canada, the U.S. government agreed to pay for everything, and Canada agreed to provide the right-of-way.[41] In March 1942 construction by U.S. Army troops began, starting from Dawson Creek, Whitehorse, and Big Delta simultaneously, all locations that were difficult to supply with materials.[42] The road was finished just over eight months later.

Ideas about how Alaska fit within the U.S. national narrative shaped the project in profound ways.[43] At the time, the construction of the highway had great symbolic importance, especially as Alaska was on the forefront of national defense during World War II. The road was important for protecting the nation from an impending Japanese attack, demonstrating political will and providing a wartime success story.[44] The highway can also be seen as part of the ongoing attempts by the United States to settle and develop the Alaskan landscape, conceptualized as the "Last Frontier."[45] Ultimately, according to Willis, the road served neither an economic nor a military purpose.[46] The highway failed to link Alaska meaningfully with the Pacific Northwest or with large cities elsewhere on the continent.

Heroic narratives of conquering wilderness aside, roads like the Alaska Highway have fundamentally reorganized experiences of space and perceptions of distance. According to Julie Cruikshank, for Yukon First Nations, who never had fixed boundaries between them, roads are part of an ongoing colonial process that has changed the relationship between humans, land, and animals. Fur prices fell in the early 1940s, and people were looking for other options to support their families. The highway drew Yukon First Nations away from hunting territories toward the construction of the road. The construction of the Alaska Highway was a "gravel magnet" that drew people to it in anticipation of short-term jobs.[47] New villages were established along it, and the people became "stuck" or more fixed in place, with their mobility more limited than ever before. It was not until fifty years later that the highway provided routes for visiting family, access to hunting, gathering and fishing sites, and even to document territory and mobilize for land claims.[48] The overlapping boundaries claimed by different Yukon First Nations now overlap along highway routes.[49]

This disruptive, dividing, and boundary-making aspect of the highway is one way in which social relations were reorganized in the North by the Alaska Highway. However, the highway also fundamentally reoriented Alaska as a space accessible by automobile, bringing the state into the network of roads that stretch across the continent. The Alaska Highway facilitated mobility into the region by newcomers, including those from Acuitzio who travel along the same highway all the way south. For Gonzalo, the road is much more than a connection between points.[50] It narrates his experience of the sociospatial distance between Mexico and Alaska at the same time as it links him to his hometown.

*A Farewell Song*

After our flight together from Mexico City to Los Angeles, Juana, Verónica, Sophia, and I were at our gates at LAX about to go our separate ways: me to Vancouver and they onward to Anchorage via Seattle. When we arrived at our gates, music was playing at a low volume from speakers built into the ceiling of the airport. Juana heard the music and said to me, "This song is called 'Golondrinas.' It's sad. They play it at the end of school or things like that."

"Like a farewell?" I asked. "Is it about saying goodbye to the *golondrinas* at the end of the season?"

"Yes, it's a very sad song," and she said it makes her feel sad just to hear it.

As I described earlier in the chapter, *golondrinas* are long-distance migrants too, making this moment particularly poignant. They are a lovely allegory for long-distance, annual travel.⁵¹ This is a different song from the one at the beginning of this chapter, but the lyrics of this song are also about leaving home. The song was written in 1862 by Narciso Serradell Sevilla, who was in exile in France at the time. It became the anthem of Mexicans in exile then and has since been recorded by many artists in Mexico and beyond. And as Juana said, it is played to say farewell—at graduations, at funerals, and at airports too. Consider the final two verses of the song:

> I have also left
> My beloved homeland
> That home
> That saw my birth
> My life today
> Is wandering and anguished
> And I can no longer
> Return home
>
> Dear bird
> Beloved pilgrim
> My heart
> Is close to yours
> Remember
> Kind swallow
> Remember
> My homeland and cry⁵²

Mobility between Anchorage and Acuitzio is an essential part of transnational life for Juana and for many others who travel on airplanes, across borders, and along highways all across the continent. Transnational lives and communities are constructed and sustained, along the lines, routes, trajectories, or corridors that connect them and across the distance, difference, and borderlines that divide Michoacán and Alaska. This infrastructure reconfigures social relationships across the continent, and the roads, routes, and border crossings make mobility between Mexico and Alaska possible. Such long distance and cross-continental mobility is lived by Acuitzences on regular travels back and forth: as a sense of sadness when hearing a particular song like Juana; in the need for luck when crossing the border like Claudia's aunt; as overwhelming fatigue manifested in jumping hands on the steering wheel like Gonzalo. In the next chapter I continue to analyze the mobilities of Acuitzences who move between Mexico and Alaska, but rather than focusing on the materiality of mobility through space, I explore mobility through time and across generations. Transnationality between Mexico and Alaska is lived across the continent, and also through the generations.

# 3 "My Grandfather Worked Here"

## THREE GENERATIONS OF THE BRAVO FAMILY IN ALASKA AND MICHOACÁN

Juana's children had their U.S. citizenship interview in Anchorage in 2005. Her youngest daughter Sophia was about five years old. Their father Luis had told them beforehand to say "yes" to every question, and the two older Bravo siblings—Verónica and Toño—said, "Okay *papá*, we will."

Since the children didn't speak much English yet, a *tejano* immigration officer interviewed them in Spanish.[1] He asked them: "Do you accept this country as your own? Do you feel like this is your primary country, that you'll no longer be Mexicans, you will be Estadounidenses, Americans?" Then the officer said to them, "Do you understand what I am asking you?"

Toño said, "Yes."

"Okay, sign your certificate of nationality. Verónica, do you understand?"

"Yes."

And Sophia. The officer asked her, "Do you understand what I am saying?"

"No."

Juana protested, "Sophia!"

But the officer said, "No, it's okay, let her be, she's young, and it will be more difficult for her to understand, it's okay. She can sign her certificate."

The family left the immigration office, and Luis said, "Ay, *hija*, what did I tell you?"[2]

Sophia said, "I understood the questions. But, well," she paused, "if I sign that paper, do I stop being Mexican?"

Luis said, "No *hija*, no. If you sign it means you accept this country because we live here and this place gave us the opportunity to have what we have, to work, and to study. But you will always be a *mexicana* in your heart. It's what we have inside of us, it's another country that we also love."

"Ah, good," Sophia said. "But they didn't say that! Because if I sign and I'm not going to be Mexican anymore, then I don't want to sign! But the man didn't say that."

Juana concluded the story, "Sophia was so worried, she felt that by signing the paper she wouldn't be Mexican anymore. At five years old, Sarita."

In this chapter, I continue to analyze the mobilities of Acuitzences who move between Mexico and Alaska, but rather than focusing on the materiality of mobility through space across the continent, I focus on the history of mobility *through time* between Michoacán and Alaska within multigenerational family and *compadrazgo* networks.[3] Over time, relationships are spatialized between Anchorage and Acuitzio, and people move within a social world that links these two locations.

Migrants do not act alone but as members of families and households,[4] and the history of migration from Acuitzio to Alaska is family history. Members of multigenerational family units who live in Anchorage and Acuitzio today tell it this way, and most Acuitzences who have traveled to Alaska to work and live are connected to each other through kin relationships. Kinship, constellations of relations created through alliance and descent, provides access to travel and work and creates the traction that keeps people moving between Mexico and Alaska.

I tell the history of mobility between Acuitzio and Anchorage within a multigenerational family—the Bravo family—whose members have moved between Acuitzio and Anchorage since the early 1960s and whose relations are spatialized across the continent. Individual members of the Bravo family orient themselves to take advantage of opportunities on both sides of the border, moving between Alaska and Acuitzio, reestablishing a primary residence in Acuitzio or expanding northward once again. I show how they have spatially expanded from Acuitzio to Alaska, how mobility is taken up in alignment with shifting life circumstances, and how this connection has gained traction over time.[5]

The concept of traction "seeks to convey how the efficacy of situated practices articulates with contingent constellations of geography, history, and environment."[6] The unevenness of the terrain, the specificity of the historical moment, and the characteristics and abilities of individuals have allowed these family networks to establish footholds that gain ground. Traction, in this regard, refers to the resilience of certain patterns of mobility. Mobilities between Acuitzio and Anchorage are repetitive and rhythmic not only by individuals over the course of their lives but by different generations over time.[7] The trip between Anchorage and Acuitzio is thus repeated over and over again across the generations. This repetitive aspect of *multigenerational* travel specifically is important because over time, back and forth mobility between Anchorage and Acuitzio is spatially productive and leads to the production of a social space between these locations, based on the shared experience of each location and of the mobilities between them.[8] The initial trajectories of individual Bravo family members, and other Acuitzences, gained traction over time, engaging with changing geography, economies, and citizenship regimes to eventually produce the more resilient mobility patterns that today extend between Acuitzio and Anchorage. A multigenerational focus on mobility and transnational migration also illustrates that the connections between Alaska and Michoacán are not especially "new" and that the development of such a way of life and a transnational habitus occurs over generations.

For five-year-old Sophia Bravo at her citizenship interview, this would have been a relief. Migration is not a linear or unidirectional movement between distinct, bounded nation-states, nor is it a progression from Mexican to U.S.-American over time. Instead, over time, people orient their lives to the circuit as a whole where the shared experience of mobility produces a transnational social field across the continent. By transnational social field, I mean the field of social relations that extends between points in different nation-states between nations (i.e., Alaska and Mexico),[9] but also the specific social relations that extend between localities (Acuitzio and Anchorage). Here, the transnational social field is produced through the shared experience of mobility and the mainte-

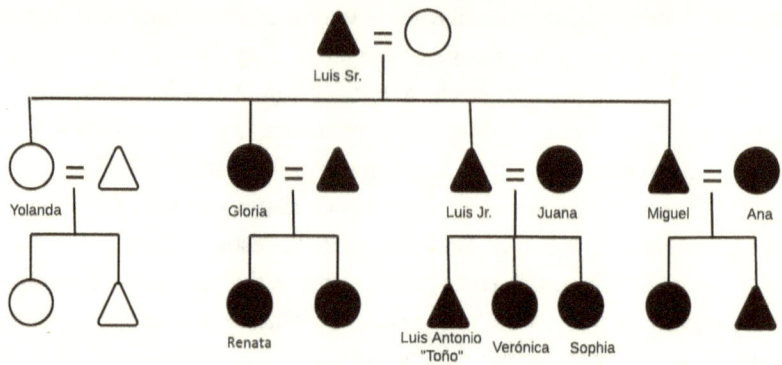

FIG. 4. The Bravo family, 2012. Black indicates that the individual has lived in Alaska. Figure by author.

nance of familial, economic, social, organizational, religious, and political relations between Anchorage, Alaska, and Acuitzio, Michoacán. This type of process offers a counterpoint to the idea that someone could "lose" their *mexicanidad* and become U.S.-American, an idea that is taken up in the language of citizenship and in studies that investigate acculturation or level of belonging in a new country. Instead, over time, generations of Acuitzences have developed a habitus that is oriented to both locations within a transnational social field and the common experience of mobility between them.

*The First Generation: Producing Corridors for Future Generations*

The initial expansive movements between Acuitzio and Anchorage began in the 1950s and have continued through the generations to the present moment. Early migrants produced a social space between Acuitzio and Alaska as they moved between these places, and they also made it possible for that spatial formation to gain traction and persist over time. Moreover, they also literally produced Alaska as it is today, contributing to projects that are currently considered iconic parts of Alaska history and identity—Alaska's highways, pipelines, fisheries, and military projects. The production of particular kinds of links to elsewhere was part of the process of state building in Alaska. At the same time, these early

Mexican migrants facilitated the movement of subsequent generations of Acuitzences, forging trajectories for new generations to move along. I met and interviewed five men of this cohort, and I asked other interlocutors in both Acuitzio and Alaska for stories they heard about *los primeros*, the ones first known to have sojourned in Alaska.[10] All of these men are similar in age and have a similarity of experiences and type of work in Alaska. As well, each of them worked in Alaska before 1980. This is significant because by 1980 the Alaska pipeline had been built, the Alaska Native Claims Settlement Act (ANCSA) had been signed,[11] and Alaska was increasingly linked to the rest of the continent by corridors that move oil, fish, people, and other goods into and around the state. Mexico was becoming more integrated into the North American economy and levels of migration to the United States remained high. As well, all of these men traveled without spouses or children, either because they had not married yet or because their wives remained in Acuitzio. Finally, in 1986 U.S. president Ronald Reagan granted amnesty to all migrants who had entered the United States "illegally" before 1982.[12] Although none of the Acuitzences I spoke to mentioned Reagan or this change to immigration law explicitly, this act provided a path to residency and citizenship for many of this generation and their families.

Luis Bravo Sr. is one of these men. I met with him for recorded interviews over two afternoons in his living room in Acuitzio, and we visited informally at family events and exchanged greetings in the plaza or while he was driving his shiny red pickup truck around town. When we met at his home, he sat in a burgundy armchair, the walls around him adorned with photographs of family members, Alaska souvenirs new and old, and tapestries, one depicting a dogsled team running across the snow. His wife sat on the couch across from him, and the three of us talked together as their pet parrot chattered in the other room. The doors to their living room opened to a patio, and sounds from the plaza and the rumblings of an afternoon thunderstorm drifted in as we talked.

"How did you end up working in Alaska?" I asked. Some friends he knew in California, one from Acuitzio, invited him to Alaska, and he went there to work there in 1960. He had been earning $2.50 per hour in California, but in Anchorage they told him he could earn $4.50 per hour for the same work—washing dishes in a restaurant. The first time he went north, he traveled to Anchorage on an airplane. He found employment washing dishes in a restaurant in the evenings and after his shift, he and a group of other *paisanos* worked as janitors, cleaning banks and offices in downtown Anchorage. Each day, they did not go to bed until four or five in the morning and then started working again at five in the afternoon. After the Good Friday earthquake in 1964 there was a lot of work in construction, to fix train tracks, rebuild the port, and rebuild the city, which had been shaken apart.[13] This work paid even better, about $8 per hour. Luis joined a union and continued to work in construction in Alaska for the next twenty-five years.

For most of his time in Alaska, Luis Sr. was employed in the construction industry in the summer and as a janitor in the winter, and he even worked on the Alaska pipeline for a time. He proudly showed me a book about the construction of the Alaska pipeline that he purchased in Anchorage and brought back to Acuitzio to have in his home.[14] The Trans-Alaska Pipeline was built to transport oil from the remote North Slope of Alaska to the ice-free port of Valdez. Construction began in 1974 and involved not only pipeline construction but also building roads and camps to the oil fields and the work camps along the pipeline route.[15] The pipeline was built to accommodate unique factors of the Alaska terrain: almost half of the nearly 1,300-kilometer-long pipeline was built above ground to avoid thawing the permafrost, and it was constructed in a zigzag pattern to absorb shock from thermal expansion or seismic activity. It was also constructed to accommodate well-established animal crossings. The terminal at Valdez, where Luis Bravo Sr. worked, was built to withstand even major earthquakes.[16]

Luis Sr. also helped construct highways and bridges around the state, living in camps and working outdoors everyday. He described a highway construction project along the Richardson Highway: "I was working where there was a steep valley, and to get the highway through they had to build a viaduct. I was a flag person there for three or four months, *fíjate*. As the flag person, I directed traffic: big trucks bringing building material and the passenger traffic heading to Valdez. *Híjole!* It was cold up there. It rained, and the wind blew, and up above us was what they call Thompson Pass." He talked about working in construction within the city of Anchorage too and described patching the pavement on city streets, building new roads, and laying water and drainage pipes for new Anchorage neighborhoods.

Ernesto Cárdenas Sr. now lives in Morelia, but he too spent many years working in Alaska in the 1970s and 1980s. He also labored on a pipeline construction crew and showed me a commemorative trophy made out of a piece of the pipeline when I interviewed him at his home. All of his children and most of his grandchildren still live in Anchorage. Another Acuitzence worked in the king crab fishery in Dutch Harbor and at Ft. Richardson Military Base just outside of Anchorage. Gonzalo Calderón was employed on Amchitka Island as a cook during the nuclear tests there.[17] He also worked to build Cold War–era Distant Early Warning radar stations and helped reconstruct parts of the Alaska railroad, built in haste during World War II and reconstructed in the 1950s. The *primeros*, then, represent an initial expansion from Acuitzio to the Last Frontier in Alaska, not only to Anchorage but also to points in rural areas of the state as well. Like Luis, these men worked on highways, on bridges, in canneries, on Amchitka Island, and constructing the pipeline. In this way, this generation of men had a role in producing Alaska as a new kind of place in the 1960s and 1970s. No longer a territory, Alaska had to be produced as a state, and connections were *built* to facilitate travel to the Lower 48 and out into the expanding global economy. Part of that meant producing corridors through which such connections could be made. Men like Luis, and many other workers who were attracted to Alaska by relatively high wages, were building corridors to move oil, fish, products, and people around the state and to points Outside: roads and bridges, pipelines, military facilities, and homes. Many of these were iconic projects that are key to the history and identity of the state. Acuitzences were part of them because they were part of the labor force that built them.

Moreover, some men from this first generation align their life course with the landscape, describing their own coming of age and adulthood alongside the development of the state of Alaska. For example, Octavio described how he grew up alongside the state: "Alaska has been somewhere where I grew because it has opened up doors to the whole world for me." Gonzalo made a similar point—"*Crecí yo con Alaska*, I grew up with Alaska"—and went on to explain what he meant: "I lived exactly when Alaska started to progress and develop, and I saw myself developing too, developing in an environment that was developing at the same time as me, right?" Like other Alaska sourdoughs, these men emphasize their experience with iconic Alaska projects, critical events in Alaska history, and time spent in the wilderness. Their stories thus fit in with established Alaska lore and legend, and yet to date the stories and experiences of Mexicans in Alaska have been totally excluded from dominant narratives about Alaska.

These iconic events are always described in terms of work. After all, these men were in Alaska to work and spent most of their time doing exactly that. Luis's experience of the 1964 earthquake is a good example. "Did you hear about the big earthquake in Alaska in 1964?" Luis asked me when I interviewed him at his home in Acuitzio. "We were there." He said that they were just about to start work at a restaurant downtown called La Cabaña when it hit. He said the earth cracked and lifted up all down Fourth Avenue from the Denali Cinema to the post office. After the earthquake a month passed before he could contact his wife to let her know that he was safe. She said that she had heard about the natural disaster on the radio in Acuitzio, and that she cried upon hearing the news. Luis was not the only one who mentioned the 1964 Good Friday Earthquake in their narratives; many men referred to it as an important historical event in their personal narratives.

Narrating key events in terms of work reminds us that these mobilities were profoundly shaped by a class experience and by the labor inequalities between Mexico and the United States, where then, as now, men faced few prospects for jobs at home but could *brincar*, or "jump" the border, to earn substantially more compared to what they could earn at home. They certainly started out with more resources relative to others in Acuitzio. For example, they had enough money to get to Alaska at the very least, as well as the social contacts to facilitate that. Going to Alaska meant good work, good pay, and adventure. These young men left Acuitzio for Alaska as they entered adulthood, and many of them aligned their life course with the remaking of the Alaskan landscape as they worked and grew up in the "Last Frontier."

These men also explained their mobility between Michoacán and Alaska in terms of contingency or serendipity. As they tell it, it is only partly by chance that they went to Alaska in the first place and ended up staying on. Luis Sr. said that when he was initially invited to go to Alaska by a friend in California, he also had an invitation to go to work in Australia. Jaime initially worked as an ice road trucker in Canada, and when the season ended, he decided to follow his friend north to work in the king crab fishery in the Aleutian Islands of Alaska. Gonzalo and Octavio both talked about making plans to leave Alaska when finding work was difficult, but unforeseen opportunities arose that led them to stay. Over and over again, Gonzalo said that he was about to give up and head back to Mexico when he reunited with a friend or met a new acquaintance who offered him work, prompting him to extend his stay. Similarly, Octavio thought his return to Mexico was imminent, at first due to lack of work but then due to problems with immigration. But his social network helped with jobs, and since he also developed a close friendship with a well-connected North American woman, he also got help with his immigration problems.

Men like Luis also produced corridors for future generations of Acuitzences to move along. I use the term "corridor" because it denotes a pathway that makes movement smoother and more direct, while also restricting mobility to that pathway, like a highway or a pipeline does. The first generation produced corridors for following generations through the traction provided by immigration status and social capital, namely contacts in Alaska, U.S. permanent residency, and raising children in a household oriented toward migration.

Luis worked in Alaska until about 1985, traveling back to Acuitzio every year or two and staying there for two or three months each time. He described his working life as *"echarle vueltas y vueltas y vueltas,* going back and forth and back and forth." This repetitive mobility was important for encouraging others to make the trip north. Those who traveled between Acuitzio and Anchorage showed people in their hometown what was possible to gain by going to Alaska. As I describe in chapter 2, Gonzalo's first trip back to Mexico was pivotal. For one, it assured him that he did not want to continue his training in medical school. As well, some Acuitzences who saw his fancy car, his new clothes, and his plentiful spending money decided to follow his path north. As he tells it, "When I arrived in Mexico with the car, after being a poor student, and after five years arriving with a new car and with a lot of money, it aroused tremendous interest in Acuitzio. And all of a sudden everyone wanted to go to Alaska! Everyone who wanted to go to the United States wanted to go to Alaska specifically." Not everyone could go to Alaska, however, since the trip to the northernmost U.S. state required significant social and economic capital. But the perception of Alaska as a place where people can do well for themselves continues among Acuitzences today.

Social capital, in terms of strengthening existing relationships and building new ones, was key for reproducing ongoing forms of mobility between Alaska and Mexico and was influential in paving the way for future generations to go north. For instance, many of the first generation of men are *compadres* with one another, and their *ahijados*, or godchildren, also worked in Alaska at a later date. It is unclear to me whether these relationships were close before going to Alaska or reinforced because all of these men worked together there, but these *compadrazgo* relationships link these men with each other through a mutual experience at a baptism, shared experiences of mobility between Acuitzio and Anchorage and time spent together in Alaska. Gonzalo told me that he helped some family members and *paisanos* go to Alaska, some of whom are still there with residency or U.S. citizenship. "I helped them in Alaska, and they started to bring their family and friends." His brother brought him, and he brought all the others, and "that's how we started to go to Alaska." Over time, "the number of people started to grow, and as you know, there's almost a *colonia* or neighborhood of Acuitzences in Alaska."[18] Ernesto and Octavio both said that they wanted to go to Alaska because they saw that others from town had done well for themselves there. For example, Ernesto, who went to Alaska in 1965, had seen that "*paisanos* who had gone to Alaska, among them my *compadre* Humberto, my *compadre* Luis, and others that went to Alaska, they did well for themselves there. And I said, well, I'm going too to see how it is too, ha! And so I went." I asked what his *paisanos* had said about Alaska, and he said, "Well, just that one day you should come, you can do well for yourself, right? I understood simply that things went well, and I said, I am going there too."

These men also built entirely new relationships in Alaska. Gonzalo met and married his first wife in Anchorage, the Anglo-American daughter of a powerful local businessman. Other men made friends who helped their children later on: to cross the border, to get settled upon arrival in Alaska, or, in one case, even to sponsor them for residency. These relationships made it easier to live and move between Acuitzio and Anchorage for the first generations and for those that followed.

Arranging immigration status was also key for the mobility of future generations. In 1980 Luis Bravo Sr.'s daughter Gloria asked him for a trip to Alaska instead of a *quinceañera* party, and to facilitate that, he applied for residency for his wife and daughter so that they could visit him. Later, he arranged residency for his two sons. Luis himself never became a U.S. citizen and explained that since he did not need to be a citizen to arrange papers for his children, he did not bother with that procedure. Today, three of his four children live and work in Anchorage, while he himself moved back to Acuitzio in 1985 to enjoy his retirement there. "Those kids are there now, they made their money and bought their house there, but always with the dream to come back here."[19] He says that his grandchildren always want to come back to Acuitzio, "They want to be here. So they come and go every so often."

Another way in which the first generation made it possible for the next to follow them to Alaska was by raising them in a household oriented toward migration. Raymond Wiest wrote a dissertation about out-migration and household economics in Acuitzio, based on fieldwork conducted in the town in 1967. In his sample of seventy households, three individuals were working in Alaska as what he classified as "temporary migrants."[20] He found that those migrating to the United States at that time were major income contributors to their household incomes, and moreover, that U.S.-migration households strongly tended to be single-contributor households. Migration to the United States was also shown to be associated with above-median household income, whether considered in terms of the total income of the household or as a per capita measure. U.S.-migration households at that time were least bound to a subsistence level of living and were more economically independent. Male household heads who migrated to the United States maintained their headship, and aside from spatial expansion of the household to the migration destination, there were no changes in residence or composition of the family unit.[21]

Wiest also noted that a large portion of the earnings of U.S.-bound migrants was spent on consumer goods such as television sets, household appliances and furnishings, or improvement of the house.[22] Many migrants to the United States at that time also invested their earnings in land or livestock. But this investment does not provide a basis for maintaining the household unit at a level similar to that based on wage-labor migration to the United States. Moreover, for those who remain, prices of land and livestock are higher because of U.S.-migrant demand for them.[23] Finally, "few technical skills are acquired in the United States that are applicable to the present state of development in Acuitzio."[24] For instance, large-scale industrial agriculture in the United States is and was different from small-scale Acuitzio agriculture. The types of crops differ greatly as well: fruit and vegetables in the United States and cereal crops in Mexico. "Semi-skilled . . . labour in the United States . . . does not prepare one for life in the small Mexican community, but instead it prepares the labourer for eventual permanent relocation."[25]

Wiest concludes as follows: "The data clearly show that wage-labour migration to the United States results in maintenance of normative domestic groups, continued economic support by the husband-father, and general economic betterment of the household."[26] He saw this pattern as unsustainable in the long term: "Migration to the United States does not represent *long term* reliable income. Provision for the migration of Mexicans to the United States may be abruptly cut off."[27] To date, however, migration has not been cut off. Rather, it *has* become a long-term and somewhat reliable income for future generations of Acuitzences. Moreover, Acuitzences in Alaska and elsewhere have not permanently located to the United States; they continue to maintain a link to their hometown.

I discuss these findings at length because in 1967 all of the first generation of Acuitzences that I met, interviewed, and write about here were already working in Alaska. This out-migration was a way for individual families to *superarse*, or get ahead. As a result of their success in producing corridors for future generations, for many of these men, most of who are now retired in Acuitzio, their connection to Alaska is ongoing. Most of Luis's children and grandchildren currently spend most of the year in Anchorage. Ernesto Cárdenas Sr. has also retired in Michoacán while most of his children and grandchildren live and work in Anchorage. Gonzalo's nephew lived in Alaska for a long period of time and is married to one of Ernesto's grandchildren. Octavio continues to live in Alaska full-time and vacations in Puerto Vallarta although he owns property and homes in Acuitzio. Many from his kin network have worked for him in his Anchorage restaurant. Moreover, Luis Bravo and Ernesto Cárdenas Sr., both retired in Mexico, continue to collect pension payments from their work with the labor union.

*The Second Generation: To Be Together*

While suffering the absences of their fathers, the sons and daughters of these first migrants to Alaska were likely to have grown up in households with a higher income. They also grew up within households oriented toward migration. No wonder, then, that some in the next generation grew up to say to me in interviews many years later: "I always knew I would go to Alaska."

By "the second generation" I refer to a cohort who were born in the 1950s and 1960s, and whose fathers also worked in Alaska. This generation first went to Alaska in the 1980s and 1990s, and most of them currently reside in Anchorage with their spouses and children and make annual trips to Acuitzio. Many of them own homes in both Anchorage and Acuitzio. Most Acuitzences of this age work in the service industry—at Costco, in restaurants, or in landscaping. Some work in the construction industry.[28] A few families own their own restaurants, landscaping, or janitorial companies in Anchorage.[29] Usually people start doing "whatever" (usually, washing dishes) and move on to more preferred kinds of occupations in Anchorage, which have good benefits, an ample salary, and the flexibility that allows for winters to be spent in Acuitzio. Others own their own businesses. As with the first generation, many who live in Alaska are linked as kin or *compadres* of one another. Many of these men and women went to school together, migrated to the United States together, and refer to each other by nickname.

This cohort expanded the Anchorage-Acuitzio network significantly. For example, replacing Luis Bravo Sr. in Alaska were two sons, a daughter, their spouses, and seven grandchildren. In this section, I introduce you to Luis's three "Alaskan" children and their spouses and to how their mobile lives interact with life events and broader social forces like the North American economy, the U.S. citizenship regime, improvements in travel and communications technologies, and changing ideas about love, marriage, and family.

The mobilities of second-generation men and women from Acuitzio show how geography and gender intersect and mutually influence each other.[30] For one, geography matters to gender: gender relations vary over space, and the construction of gender relations varies between places. Moreover, places are themselves gendered and reflect and affect how gender is constructed and understood.[31] For example, Alaska has been gendered as a masculine space due to the historical emphasis on wilderness, adventure, frontier life and resource exploration, and the domination of nature implicit in those pursuits.[32] This is also why the first generation of migration was male dominated. But this changed with the second generation. Other researchers have drawn attention to gender as a key part of the migrant experience; gender relations shape mobilities within multigenerational family networks and uneven experiences of place in Alaska and Mexico so that the social construction of gender changes with both migration and generation.[33]

Deborah Boehm writes about how, for migrant men, migration to the United States represents a coming of age, while for women it is a *quinceañera*, which celebrates a young woman's fifteenth birthday. In her book, the transition to adulthood for men is mobility, whereas for women it is stasis because young women's mobilities are controlled more closely.[34] Gloria first visited Alaska in the summer of 1980 when she asked her father to take her there for her *quinceañera* present. Gloria's coming of age was also associated with mobility, although in a significantly different way from that of her brothers. She told me about this trip during an interview at her home in Anchorage in 2011:

> I told my father that I didn't want a fiesta for my *quinceañera*, that I wanted to come to Alaska. I wanted to see snow, to see something different. So my father started to investigate how he could *arreglar*, or arrange papers for me, and he did the application for resident for my mother and for me. A letter arrived for us, saying that we had to cross the border in mid- to late July. At that time we didn't have a

telephone in the house, everything was done by mail, and we very rarely spoke by telephone with my father. We advised my dad that the papers were ready, and he said to come. So my mother, she said, "well, let's go," and so we went, ready to go to Alaska. We arrived to the border at McAllen, Texas, where my father had a friend. The friend was working in Alaska and his family lived in McAllen, Texas. So, we took the bus from Acuitzio to McAllen and in McAllen we had to pass the, the immigration. And so there they gave us the *permiso* and the paperwork, and we had to cross the border. After that, the wife of my father's friend bought us the plane tickets with my mother's money and told us that we leave for Alaska the next day. She put down for us that we didn't speak English and arranged it so that we would travel directly to Alaska.

Gloria said that she wanted to go to Alaska because her father had worked there: "My father worked here for thirty years. He always sent postcards, he sent photos, he brought us photos, and it looked so beautiful. The snow, the scenery, as if they were paintings. You've seen how it is. I really wanted to know Alaska for myself." Her father said that she could come to Alaska on the condition that she went back to Mexico to continue her studies. She agreed, and Gloria and her mother visited Anchorage in July and August, returning in September so that Gloria could go back to school. Her brothers, on the other hand, left school early to go to work in Alaska. Among this cohort, women from Acuitzio achieved higher levels of education, often completing high school and some postsecondary training. Men, as I discuss later in the chapter, often left school early to work.

In Gloria's narrative, coming of age was associated with travel to Alaska, in that instead of a *quinceañera*, she asked for a trip to Alaska.[35] She wanted to mark this point in her life with a trip instead of a party. For Gloria and, later, her daughter and nieces, their fifteenth birthdays were a time where relationships were built and connections were made between Acuitzio and Anchorage. Overall, looking at the life course of Acuitzences in Alaska across generations, it is clear that life events influence mobilities—adulthood, marriage, birth of children, baptism, the death of parents or older family members, and retirement.

For example, Gloria and her husband decided to come to Alaska after another life stage: marriage. By that time her brothers were also living and working in Anchorage. Meanwhile, Gloria had finished her degree in dentistry, married, and given birth to her oldest daughter. In 1995 there was an economic crisis in Mexico, one of two peso devaluations that rocked the nation's economy after the North American Free Trade Agreement (NAFTA) was signed in 1994. Her husband did not fare well, since he was involved with raising and selling livestock. They lost a lot of money. Gloria's father, Luis Bravo Sr., had already arranged Green Cards for his children, meaning that Gloria would be able to travel to the United States with the Green Card that her father obtained for her, and she could apply for her husband to accompany her. This led Gloria to say to her husband, "*Pues*, let's go to the United States to work."

They traveled to Tijuana and then crossed into California, where they stayed for one week to visit family before departing for Alaska. "The idea was to work here in Alaska. Since I had already been here, I had an idea of what it was like. My husband wanted to go to Texas because he had family there. But I wasn't interested in Texas. No, I was more interested in coming to Alaska since I already knew the place a little bit." Gloria, her husband, and their daughters arrived in Alaska in 1995.

Gloria's brother, Luis Jr., arrived in Anchorage in May 1983. He left high school early and first came to Alaska at age eighteen. Luis told me that his father wanted to arrange papers for all of his children, so that they would have the option to go the United States later in life. However, "[my father] didn't want us to come here—he wanted us to stay in Mexico and study." But Luis wanted to go "*al otro lado*, to the other side" because his father had traveled back and forth between Mexico and Alaska, and Luis said to himself, "when I grow up, I better go there too." Because he had the option to go to work in the United States, he said he didn't try very hard at school, and as soon as his papers arrived, he went to Alaska.

Luis Jr.'s father had obtained a Green Card for him, and he also benefited from having a relative in Alaska—Octavio.[36] When Luis Jr. first arrived in Anchorage, he worked at his uncle's Mexican restaurant and lived at his uncle's house, and then he later moved into an apartment with friends from Acuitzio. "We all chipped in for the rent, and but yes, everyone was from Acuitzio. Birds of a feather flock together.[37] And as you know, there are plenty from Acuitzio here."

Across generations, people move between Mexico and Alaska within a wider network of relationships often expressed as kin or *compadrazgo* relationships. Indeed—Gloria, Luis, and Miguel came to Alaska because their father arranged papers for them, and upon first arriving there, Luis and Miguel both lived with and worked with their uncle Octavio. It is useful to point out here how access to work and mobility is produced through maintaining or building relationships with people in different sites. Multigenerational families like the Bravo family have been especially successful at creating corridors for family members and other close relations to move through, as well as for access to work. Moreover, the families with the longest experience in Alaska intertwine with one another so that in Anchorage, people move within a network that is tightly bound up with kin and *compadre* relationships.

The network facilitates access to work as well. In the Bravo family, all of the women (Juana, Gloria, and Ana) work at the same place: a large industrial food services center that provides cafeterias in institutions across Anchorage with prepared food. They all enjoy working there for many reasons, but especially because it is run by the school board, which means they always get the summers off. Luis and Miguel work in the same restaurant, a Mexican restaurant co-owned by Miguel Bravo and Bernardo Cárdenas, both of multigenerational Acuitzio-Anchorage family networks. Octavio in particular has been instrumental in hiring Acuitzences at his restaurant. For example, both Luis and Miguel Bravo worked as dishwashers at his restaurant when they first arrived. Many other Acuitzences have worked for him too. Octavio says, "Well, most of the people who come from Acuitzio [have worked for me]. And now look, [some of them] have their own businesses. They worked with me, they started out washing dishes, and they learned the business."

Multigenerational family networks like that of the Bravo family thus structure opportunities for mobility to Alaska and to work upon arriving there. Over time, trajectories became formalized into corridors whereby close family members move between Acuitzio and Anchorage and build their lives in both locations.

In this cohort, there is a pattern of couples meeting each other in Acuitzio and, after marriage, of husbands arranging to bring their wives and children with them to Alaska after a certain period of time *para estar juntos*, to be together. Intimate practices of marriage and performances of love have emerged as key aspects of transnational mobility, enabling long-term transnational circuits and illustrating how global capitalism is redefining personal lives.[38] Indeed, research about transnationality, love, and marriage shows that migrants enmeshed in shifting structures of feeling and constrained by immigration and citizenship regimes use intimate relationships to provide for family members but also to fulfill their own needs for meaningful relationships.[39]

For example, Luis and Juana met on one of Luis's annual visits back to his hometown from Alaska. After they married and had their first child, and with the money Luis had saved from his work in Alaska, he decided to stay in Acuitzio and invest in livestock, much like Gloria's husband and many other men in Acuitzio did at that time. He had taken out loans to finance his operation, but after the currency devaluation Luis found that his livestock was not worth as much as before, feed was more expensive, and he had to find a way to pay his creditors. Juana said, "At that time many people lost property. Luis had put up his father's *rancho* as collateral. Since he didn't want to lose his father's *rancho*, and he had the option to come back to Alaska again, he decided to leave." Luis went back to Alaska to work and pay his debts, but it was only supposed to be temporary. He tried once more to *hacer la lucha*, make things work, by returning to Acuitzio to sell leather after a difficult summer in Alaska.[40] Luis said, "I knew that if things went bad, I could come back here [to Alaska]." Unfortunately, selling leather did not work out either. "I had my papers, there wasn't anything for me [in Mexico], and after that I went back to coming back [to Alaska]." But Juana had told him, "I don't want you to come and go and come and go because little Toño is upset a lot when you're there and we've stayed behind." He decided, "Okay, I'm going to go, but I'm going to try to arrange papers for my family."

To do that, he first applied for citizenship for himself, which he received in 1995. After that, he applied for residency for his wife and their young children. The family arrived in Anchorage in 1996, and ever since then they take annual vacations to their hometown, lasting one or two months. As Luis put it, "I almost always come and go, you know."[41]

I spent a lot of time with Juana during fieldwork in both Acuitzio and Anchorage, and we sat down for a formal interview at their home in Anchorage during the spring of 2011. We talked about many of the same things that I discussed with Luis, but Juana had a different perspective. When I asked Juana how it is that she came to Alaska, she said, "Well, I married Luis," and then laughed. I asked for more details, and she explained that ever since he was eighteen years old, "Luis came here [to Alaska] and since then he has made his life here." She told me about how they met in Mexico, began dating, and then married. After that, "supposedly he wasn't going to keep coming here [to Alaska]." She talked about the currency devaluation that had caused him to lose money on livestock in which he had invested, and since he had always worked in Alaska, he went back there "supposedly" only to save money and pay the debt he had with the bank before coming back. Juana thinks that he was also accustomed to the relatively high salaries in Anchorage and was uncomfortable with the comparatively small amount he earned in Mexico. Juana's statement—"*supposedly* he wasn't going to keep coming here"—was echoed by other women who married Alaska-migrating men and intended to live together as a conjugal couple in Mexico after the wedding.[42]

Living together as a family was really important to both Juana and Luis. One day in Acuitzio, Luis told me how hard it was to grow up without a father, since Luis Sr. was always away, working in Alaska. Tears in his eyes, he described acting out as a young man before meeting Juana, who helped straighten him out. Juana said that one time she asked Luis about how he felt about being away since his own father was always away in the United States, and he only saw his father for a few months a year. Juana told him that she was lucky to grow up with both her parents, and because of this she knows what it is like to have the support of both parents, and she wants that for her children. She asked Luis how he felt when he was a child and his father wasn't there, and she encouraged him think about what he wants for his children.

Luis and Juana decided to move the whole family to Anchorage, but this was very difficult for Juana, who was—and is—very close to her siblings and parents. She said,

For me, it was really difficult to come here. My whole family is there [in Mexico], and I've never been apart from them. I knew it would be difficult to separate me from my family, but I wanted my children to be with their father. That they lived what I had lived with father, mother, and children together. And not to live only seeing their father every two months, or every few months, no. In fact, my mother said, "*Hija*, my soul aches to see you go, but I prefer it even though I will only see you when you visit, than see you here with your children alone." *Ay, mamá*. And it's true, because when I would go to my mother's house I went with my three children, and sometimes I felt so alone. Alone.

In the second generation, Bravo family mobility shifted to focus on keeping the family together, the most important concern for Luis and Juana. Once the applications for permanent residency for Juana and the children were submitted, and interviews and appointments were scheduled in Ciudad Juarez, the family made arrangements to move.[43] At the time, Luis was working at a supermarket in Anchorage, and he asked for time off so he could travel to Acuitzio, then to Ciudad Juarez, and finally to Anchorage, where Luis had already rented an apartment for the family. Juana explains: "What happened is they only gave my husband a few days off of work. He left Anchorage on Friday after work, and arrived on Saturday afternoon to Guadalajara. On Sunday we baptized our youngest daughter, we had a *comida* and spent time with our family, and it was also a way to say goodbye. My brothers took us to the bus station on Monday morning and we left, in order to make it to Ciudad Juarez in time for the appointments." Again, life events and mobilities across vast distances are intertwined. In this case, they felt they could not leave Acuitzio until the baby was baptized, and as part of the intense mobilities demanded by the U.S. bureaucracy as part of their applications for permanent residency.

After their appointment in Ciudad Juarez, Luis, Juana, and their children had to go to El Paso, across the border in Texas, to drop off an envelope filled with all of the necessary paperwork to complete their application for residency. They took a taxi to El Paso to drop it off and then traveled directly to the airport, where they flew to Los

Angeles, then Seattle, and finally to Anchorage. Juana said, "Finally we arrived in Anchorage at six in the morning on the sixth of December. And I remember it was a Friday because Luis left to go to work at the grocery store." This was December 1996, and they did not return to Acuitzio until 1998.

The youngest brother in the Bravo family, Miguel, came to Alaska two years after Luis did. I asked him how he came to Alaska in the first place, and he said, "Well, to improve my life and to work. My father worked here, he was the one who arranged papers for us, and he brought us. Or like, it was to find work, right? A better way of life." But when he finally arrived "on January 15, 1985," he felt disappointed.[44] "When I arrived here, I said, this is *el norte*? I didn't see anyone. There was no one at all in the street, it looked so lonely. No, I wanted to go back after eight days!" He paused to laugh and then continued, *"Primero soñaba con venir y después soñaba con regresar*, first my dream was to come here and then my dream was to go back. First my dream was ay, *when* am I going to go to the United States! But as soon as I arrived here, I dreamed of going back. But now I have more than half of my life here, twenty-seven years. It's a long time, already."

Miguel's statement about how first he dreamed of coming here and then of going back is also essential for understanding the experience of this generation. As I have described, members of this second generation have attempted to contract the network and return to Acuitzio. Diverse life circumstances and contingencies interacted with larger social forces that led to people becoming migrants in the first place and also led to continued migration.

There are also important reasons to continue mobility between Mexico and Alaska. Women emphasized the importance of mobility to visit extended family. For example, Juana said, "When I am in Acuitzio I spend pretty much all my time with my mother." Ana also visits her mother every day when she is in Acuitzio. And many of the women I interviewed told me that being with family was one of the things they miss the most about their hometown. Some women also described visits back to Mexico as necessary to endure life in Anchorage. For example, Serefina, who moved to Anchorage with her husband, said, "When you go back to Mexico you recharge your batteries so that you can make it through the year in Anchorage." Men, on the other hand, talk about enjoying life in town, visiting the plaza, and spending time with friends.

Nevertheless, some still plan to go back to Acuitzio. Even though many consider it ideal to move between the two places, some are in the midst of planning a more permanent move to Mexico. Luis said that nowadays he feels comfortable, "*me siento a gusto*," in both Alaska and Acuitzio. In the future, however, he says he wants to move back to Acuitzio: "I want to do like my dad and go. Take myself over there [to Acuitzio] when I'm older, to live peacefully and relax. Here [in Anchorage] it's good, a person can work and everything is good. We don't have a big house like in Mexico, but we don't need much space since we spend most of the time working, and you just come home to sleep." His wife Juana is less sure—she does not want to be apart from their children, who she expects will continue to live in Alaska.[45]

This generation is defined by a tension between desires to keep the family together as important relationships have been spatially expanded across the continent. Moreover, alongside structural changes in U.S. immigration policy and the North American political economy, ideas about love, marriage, and family changed between the generation represented by Luis Sr. and that of Luis Jr. These changes had impacts on mobility patterns and the experience of both Anchorage and Acuitzio. Specifically, this generation of U.S.-Mexican dual citizens, with important relationships in both locations, travel regularly across the continent. Their generation developed a transnational habitus and way of life, orienting themselves to both locations within a transnational social field and the common experience of mobility between them. As I discuss further in chapter 4, this is not a smooth process but one fraught with tensions and difficulties. Like Miguel, many Acuitzences dreamed of going to Alaska, only to dream of going back upon arrival. Luis wishes to retire in Acuitzio, but Juana knows her children may not join them there.

### The Third Generation: Transnational Futures

The third generation of Acuitzences who move between Anchorage and Acuitzio were born between 1980 and 2000. In some cases, like Toño, Vero, and Sophia Bravo, these youth were born in Mexico and spent the early years of their life there, before moving to Alaska with their families as young children. They currently spend most of the year in Anchorage, making annual trips back to Acuitzio to visit family and friends there. Others were born in Alaska but move between Anchorage and Acuitzio in a similar way. Some have more complicated mobilities and have relocated their primary residence multiple times throughout their lives.[46] Others have stopped moving between Anchorage and Acuitzio, but instead move between Alaska and other locations in the Lower 48 where they have built their lives.

This group in general experiences the tension between "here" and "there" most strongly. This generation has to work to build relationships, find out where they belong, and imagine where their future might be. Some dream of "going back" to Mexico, and others slowly lose ties to the hometown of their parents and grandparents. In terms of mobility, younger Acuitzences in Anchorage often have lived their entire lives moving back and forth between Mexico and Alaska. As a result many of them orient themselves to a transnational way of life that depends on mobility even more than past generations. It is now well understood that children play an important role in guiding transnational migration decisions, so that "children's perceived needs, interests, and desires influence the decisions families make within the constraints of particular circumstances."[47] When adults make decisions about leaving children behind, bringing them along to Alaska, or sending them back to Mexico, they "are actively engaged in the process of 'developing' their children towards the goals and values they hold for them."[48] Indeed, these young people have grown up traveling between Mexico and Alaska, orienting themselves to the transnational social field as a whole. Many have been socialized to live in both locations, acquiring the necessary language and social skills to move between social contexts and nation-states. Many of them, like Sophia, see their potential futures in both locations, with ongoing mobilities between them.

Sophia was really nervous about her *quinceañera* in the days leading up to it. For one thing, her uncle was sick, and I knew she had been worried about getting everything done and learning the dances that she and her *chambelanes*, or escorts, would perform at the reception.[49] Today, however, she looked beautiful and confident in her strapless red gown with a full skirt and sequins stitched across the bodice. Her escorts were dressed in black tuxedoes with matching red cummerbunds and bow ties. Over the past weeks, I had helped Sophia, her sister, and her mother glue red and white flowers onto salt shakers, baskets, and napkin holders to place on the tables at the fiesta, as well as on plastic wine glasses to toast Sophia at the party. I had also watched Sophia and her escorts practice their dances, and I talked to her family about who would be invited to the party.

Sophia Bravo was born in Morelia and lived in Acuitzio for the first months of her life. Her father worked in Alaska and moved back and forth between Acuitzio and Anchorage until 1996, when the whole family moved to Anchorage. At that time Sophia was a small baby and does not remember living in Acuitzio full-time. However, the family visits Acuitzio every year, and Sophia said that she always knew her *quinceañera* would take place in Acuitzio. After all, she said, "most of my family is in Mexico, and if I had it in Alaska, not very many people would be able to come."

Her party was a transnational affair. After the mass, as is customary at *quinceañeras* and weddings that I have attended in Acuitzio, guests posed for photographs with Sophia at the front of the church. Many of those guests also live in Anchorage and had come to Acuitzio for the summer, timed so that they would be able to attend Sophia's *quinceañera*. In fact, many people say that they intentionally schedule fiestas like *quinceañeras*, weddings, baptisms, or anniversary parties during the summer months or in December when most migrant family members come back to town.[50] But, as Sophia said, it was also very important to her to celebrate this special day with her mother's family, most of whom live in Mexico. Thus, her celebration was in part about reaffirming social ties within a kin network that has expanded to include both Acuitzio and Anchorage. Indeed, for the third generation, reaffirming social ties and developing new relationships in Acuitzio is key to maintaining a connection there.

Although vital conjunctures like *quinceañeras* and other milestones such as baptisms, weddings, or funerals reaffirm social relationships and trace the boundaries of kin groups,[51] these events can also produce new relationships. For example, Verónica, Sophia's older sister, celebrated her own *quinceañera* two years earlier. In an interview on a snowy winter day in Anchorage, Verónica told me that her *quinceañera* was when she made friends her age in town. Since she did not go to school in Acuitzio, establishing nonfamilial relationships in Mexico was more challenging. As she explains it, she started meeting different people because of her escorts. A young woman who is being celebrated with a *quinceañera* is expected to learn and perform dances with her escorts, and they meet to practice on a regular basis leading up to the *quince*. In this case Verónica said that her close friend and cousin initially suggested possible escorts to her. After practice she would hang out with her escorts, who then introduced her to their friends, and "that's how I started meeting people over there." Although I realized that a fiesta like a *quinceañera* reaffirmed and solidified existing bonds of family and friendship, I had underestimated the role of a *quinceañera* as an opportunity to build *new* social relationships in the hometown. But for some young women, it seems, choosing escorts, getting to know them while practicing the dances for the *quince*, and meeting their friends becomes the basis for a whole new social network in Acuitzio.

Verónica's brother, Toño, has made friends his own age through the weekly *cabalgatas*, or horse parades, in Acuitzio. These are Tuesday evening man-only rides into the mountains, followed by food, drinking, and socializing.[52] Toño told me he met his oldest friend in Acuitzio there and soon got introduced to other young people in town. "That's how I started making friends," he said, and he met even more people when his younger sisters had their *quinceañeras*. Toño and his sisters have dated people from Acuitzio over the summer, and sometimes their relationships continue long-distance. Sometimes these relationships become even more serious, and third-generation migrant-immigrants visiting Acuitzio meet and marry their spouses there. As explained earlier, many couples in their parents' generation also met in Acuitzio, when men were in town on a break from work in Alaska. However, other young people with a connection to Acuitzio have met and married people they met in Alaska, some from Acuitzio, some from different parts of Mexico, and some of other backgrounds entirely.

Across all generations, spatializing relationships between Acuitzio and Anchorage is essential for maintaining mobility between these points. For young people in this network especially, who have lived most of their lives in Anchorage with annual trips back to Mexico, developing these kinds of new relationships is critical for maintaining a connection to their hometown.

Verónica Bravo is Luis and Juana's oldest daughter. She was born in Mexico in the early 1990s but was raised in Alaska after her family moved there when she was age two. We met for a recorded interview on a cold winter afternoon in Anchorage. The sun that time of year is permanently low in the sky, as though it is always dusk or dawn. Vero was dressed for the weather in typical Anchorage style—a puffy North Face jacket, jeans, and brown leather boots. We ordered coffee, and I sat the digital recorder on the lacquered wooden table between us. After we read through the consent form, I pushed "record" and asked: "What is the first thing that you can remember?"

She said, "The first thing I actually remember is the first time we went back to Mexico." This was in December 1998, when Verónica was around five years old. She remembers being in the airport a lot, waiting, traveling. She remembers actually leaving Anchorage on an airplane and then attending parades and holiday festivities in Acuitzio. Verónica's brother is named Luis after his father and grandfather, but his family calls him Toño, a short form of his middle name, Antonio. In an interview, he recalled the family's initial move to Alaska:

> I don't remember the plane, but I remember stopping somewhere, maybe California. And we waited in a long line, I'm pretty sure it was something about paperwork for like visas and all that stuff. But, we were just in a big line. Waiting, waiting, I remember I was getting frustrated. I was a little kid and I hated standing still. The next thing I remember is waking up, getting out of the cab, and going to the apartment where we used to live. And seeing this white stuff and water all over the ground. My dad was carrying me cause I had these little shoes that were gonna get wet so he was carrying me. And I was just like, "What is that?" He's like, "That's snow." I'm just like, "Snow? What is, what's snow?" And that's my first memory of Alaska.

Toño describes how, over time, as he and his sisters grew up, the family traveled to Mexico more often:

At first we started going like maybe once every few years, then once every two years, then maybe once every year. And when I hit high school, that's when we stopped going for Christmas and for New Year's 'cause I had finals. So then we started going every summer. At first since most of our cousins used to live in the same town. They'd show us around and introduce us to their friends. But then they started moving away too. They got older, we got older, some moved to the U.S., some moved to Morelia. So then we just started actually having to meet people in Acuitzio.

Considering Verónica's and Toño's individual life histories and their family's multigenerational mobility, the fact that their earliest memories are of *travel* is not all that surprising. For over fifty years, their family members have moved between Anchorage and Acuitzio, tracing long lines across the continent. Vero explains her family's history in Alaska:

My dad told me stories about working in Alaska, and I've seen a lot of pictures too, like my grandpa when he was on the pipeline or like in the middle of snow. They would send a lot of pictures back to Acuitzio. A lot of the pictures would be outside of a store or next to a huge pile of snow. And that's what they would send over there to Mexico. My dad mostly talks about how much snow there was and how his dad had always been in Alaska on and off, and I guess that's basically why he brought us here too because he didn't want to be like on and off coming and visiting. He just wanted to have everybody be here, in the same place.

Vero's sister, Sophia, also described her family's long-term connection to Alaska: "I say we're here because my grandpa came to work on the pipeline or something like that? From California he came here and then, yeah. People kind of ask me why, and I say I have no idea, you should ask my parents. But I think it was just 'cause of work. Like they needed work and they had jobs here, so."

Sophia is right; past generations do talk about going to Alaska for work, for better paying jobs and more opportunity. As I have shown, keeping family together was important for her parents, the second generation. So how does this third generation explain why they are in Alaska? And where do they imagine their future?

It is Verónica who wants to go back to Acuitzio most often, her mother says: "If she could go every vacation she would, spring break, in December, in the summer. I said, no *hija*, you can't. Plus, it's so far and aside from that, like Luis says, *hija*, it's another country. Right now you can't, but you can go when you are older."

Her parents attempt to restrict her mobility because the distance and difference is too great, but they tell her that "you can go when you're older."[53] Here age intersects with sociospatial distance, a key aspect of transnational life between Acuitzio and Anchorage. Verónica and her siblings express an ambivalence: although they want to go to Acuitzio whenever possible, they also echo the concerns of their parents—it is too far, and too different for them to go on their own.

There is an irony here: although youth are discouraged from traveling to Acuitzio alone, they experience much more freedom in terms of mobility once they are there. Striffler described how young women experienced more freedom in the United States, and young men in their hometown in Mexico.[54] But I found that young people in general experience more freedom in Acuitzio than in Anchorage. For example, Alina Cárdenas's nine-year-old daughter would play with her cousins all day in Acuitzio, not returning home until dusk. Alina would tell her not to get used to it, "*acá es pura calle pero allá es pura casa*, here it's all street, but there it's all house." In Anchorage every day after school Alina's daughter came straight home and was not allowed out alone. Similarly, the Bravo children were afforded a lot of liberty to go out and stay out late while in Acuitzio, as long as they checked in with Juana regularly by text message.

Verónica talked about the possibility of living in Mexico one day when I asked her what kind of life she imagines for her future, if she will stay in Alaska or not. She responded, "I've never really thought if I'm going to stay here or not because a big thing was that I wanted to go to college in Mexico. I feel like the easier thing to do is just stay here [in Anchorage] because I know how everything works here. Over there, everything is just so different. Getting used to being over there. Because like a lot of people tell me that the only reason why I like it is because we're just there for vacation. Actually living there is, like, way harder."

I often heard this sentiment from young Acuitzences in Alaska, and I asked Verónica, "Do you think it's true? Would it be harder to live there?" before taking a sip of my coffee.

"I think so. But I also don't think that you need that much. Over here [in Anchorage] you have to have a car to get around and stuff, and then over there [in Acuitzio] it's not really that necessary." Vero pauses, then continues, "I would think about moving back, but then what's the point of my parents bringing me over here? They wanted me to have a better lifestyle, so I feel like it would be pointless to go back if they're the ones that brought me over here. But I know they want to go back; my parents want to move to Acuitzio someday. After they're retired and stuff. I think I could do that, like, many years from now."

"Yeah totally, but then what if you have kids?"

"They can come visit," Vero says, laughing.

Vero aims to continue to travel between Alaska and Michoacán, and if she does retire in Mexico, her children "can come visit," as she said.

In an interview with Sophia at the Bravo family home in Spenard, Anchorage, I asked, "Where do you feel most at home, do you think?" Sophia immediately replied, "Acuitzio," but then went on to explain: "It's weird. I've had that question asked before, like, where do you feel at home and I don't know. I guess you could say Acuitzio is my home, but my life's here. If you kinda get it."

She said she hopes she always goes back: "I hope when I'm older and when I have kids of my own I'd want them to go visit Acuitzio. I'm not saying I'd take them every single year, but I'd definitely want them to visit Mexico and tell them stories about it, have them know where they came from, just as much as I know where I'm from."

Like his sisters, Toño is ambivalent about the future:

> I really don't know. That's the thing, like I, I love it over there and everything, but I know that over here I have a great opportunity and I shouldn't just waste it. 'Cause a lot of friends that I have over there *really* wish they could be up here. I have a couple of friends that have come up here, that have come up illegally, and it is just like a really terrible journey for them. When I was younger I couldn't appreciate that, you know. I have all this paperwork handed to me when I was

little, but now I really can't, I know that I can't just move back to Acuitzio. Not when there's all these people trying to come over here.

This ambivalence indicates that Vero, Sophia, and Toño have built a social network that stretches between Anchorage and Acuitzio, a way of life that depends on mobility between these places. They know that their position in terms of dual citizenship and class is a privileged one, built over many years of work in the United States by their parents and grandparents. They imagine a future whereby they are able to keep moving between both Anchorage and Acuitzio. For them, home is found in both places, and in the shared experience of moving between them.

*Mobile Generations*

In this chapter, I have analyzed the ongoing expansion of Acuitzences to Alaska through the narratives of people in an extended family network. Using the example of the Bravo family, I have traced the family's mobility over the generations to show that there is no linear movement, nor straightforward progression over time from Mexico to Alaska or from Mexican to U.S.-American identities. Instead, mobilities are ongoing, and people increasingly orient themselves to the social field as a whole, to a transnational setting that spans the continent. Grandparents, children, and grandchildren have all experienced life in both Anchorage and Acuitzio. Or to put it another way, the habitus of transnational life between Anchorage and Acuitzio is the "product of a chronologically ordered series of structuring determinations" that integrates similar experiences together.[55] The development of such a habitus happens as generations are socialized into life between Acuitzio and Alaska. Indeed, places like Acuitzio and Anchorage remain important sites of personal belonging only as long as migrants maintain close relations with people there.[56] Within one multigenerational family I show how, over time, Acuitzio and Anchorage both become key sites of personal belonging, along with the common experience of travel between them. People draw from and work within their positionality within family networks as well as other resources, systems, and structures in Alaska and Michoacán to keep moving between "here" and "there."

Even so, not all members of the Bravo family have moved to Alaska. Don Luis also arranged papers for his eldest daughter, Yolanda, but her husband would not let her go. She is the only one of Don Luis Sr.'s children who has never gone to live and work in Alaska. As well, other families have not been as successful at working the sociospatial distance between Anchorage and Acuitzio. For example, I visited Sr. Jaime at his home many times when I was in Acuitzio. From the outside, his home it is a low, nondescript building. However, inside the windows along one wall open onto an expansive view of the town going down the hill, *ranchos* and fields in the valley, and avocado farms at higher elevations. Jaime himself is an imposing but soft-spoken man, tall, with white hair and a full moustache. He worked in Alaska beginning in 1960, but he returned to Acuitzio after receiving a deportation order in 1968 and never went to work in the United States again. Neither did any of his children. "The vagabond's wings were clipped," he said.

Processes like citizenship, land ownership, and life events that give people roots also provide traction and paradoxically facilitate mobility between both points. Larger structural forces in North America and globally shape and condition abilities or necessities to expand northward.[57] This is what it means to live transnationally: moving between Alaska and Acuitzio, reestablishing a primary residence in Acuitzio, or expanding northward once again are all possibilities that are taken up in alignment with life circumstances within a transnational social field. Mobility between Anchorage and Acuitzio has continued over time and will likely continue as the youngest generations are socialized into a transnational social world oriented around mobility.

But, across generations, getting used to life in Anchorage and Acuitzio is a process. In the next chapter I discuss spatial practices that people use to *acostumbrarse*, or "get used to" life in Alaska. I analyze *acostumbrarse* as the everyday practices indicative of the development of a transnational habitus. For Acuitzences in Alaska creating a sense of home is a *process*, and developing a transnational way of life takes time and work. As well, this kind of work is done in both Mexico and Alaska. Acuitzences say they have to get used to life at either end of the continent as they move across borders and boundaries to secure not only a livelihood but also a way of life.

# 4 "You Have to Get Used to It"

LIVING THE NORTH AMERICAN DREAM

On the day of Sophia's *quinceañera* in Acuitzio, I got dressed, did my hair and makeup, and then went to the store to buy some potato chips to eat as a snack before mass at the Parroquia de San Nicolás Tolentino. The store next door was closed, so I went to the next closest *abarrotes* on Melchor Ocampo. I chose a bag of lime-flavored potato chips, and as I was counting out pesos, the man working there asked me where I am from. I told him that I am from Canada, and that I am in Acuitzio working on a project about Acuitzences who live and work in Alaska.

He said, "I worked in Alaska, in Barrow on the *North Slope* or however you say it," and he took an Alaska ID card out of his wallet to prove it.[1] "I'm Diego. I was in Barrow when some Alaska Native people had a whale hunt there. I even have photos. Let me go and get them."

He came back with a photo album with a map of Alaska on the front, the kind I have seen for sale all over Anchorage in tourist shops and grocery stores. He pointed out the locations where he worked: Barrow, Anchorage, Kotzebue. Then he flipped through to a photo of himself in front of a giant whale on the shores of the Bering Sea, in Utqiaġvik (formerly called Barrow). This whale was likely hunted by local Iñupiat whalers who have been harvesting bowhead whale for thousands of years and continue subsistence hunting activities today. Diego told me that he worked in Alaska for twelve years in total: at a Mexican restaurant in Barrow, building a school in Kotzebue, and working on construction sites all over Anchorage.

I met Diego at his store again the following week for an interview. He talked about how when he was in Anchorage, "I remembered Acuitzio like it was a dream." When he came back to Acuitzio and thought about Anchorage, it was the reverse: "everywhere that I went and all that I saw, everything seemed just like a dream." He explained that when he leaves Mexico, he feels like his life there is cut off, but when he comes back, "it's like starting over again from when I left."

"I understand," I said, "you carry on where you left off."

"Yes, I carry on from there. And when I went back to Anchorage, I went back to the same house, my same things. I left my clothes, my bed, my blanket, my room, everything. I went back to it. But," he continued, "it takes a few days *to get used to* those same things again, to feel normal again, and then the memories of Acuitzio become just a memory, like something that happens in a dream."

Unfortunately for Diego, when I met him he was unable to go back to Alaska, even though he has a young son in the United States. Without papers and fearing deportation, he left for his hometown and resumed life in Michoacán. Like Diego, however, many Acuitzences talked about having to *adaptarse, acostumbrarse*, or *get used to* living life between these different worlds. The verb *acostumbrarse*, used again and again by Acuitzences in interviews and conversations, shows that creating a sense of home is a *process*, and developing a transnational way of life takes time and work. This is a way of life based on mobility, as in chapter 2, and it takes place over generations, as in the previous chapter. "Getting used to" this way of life is also about working to secure a livelihood across the continent. This is a profoundly bureaucratic process that depends on applying for and receiving statuses and certifications: ID cards, passports, citizenship, driver's licenses, and certifications. It is also a paradoxical process of territorialization: purchasing land and property in both locations in order to facilitate mobility and access to a livelihood between them. It is also an embodied process, described in terms of "getting used to" the weather, or feeling *encerrado* or closed in at home in Anchorage. And it is also a social process, as people talk about things like difficulties with language and norms about appropriate clothing. This everyday and multifaceted process of getting used to it happens in both Mexico and Alaska, so that people talk about getting used to life in Acuitzio and use the same language to talk about getting used to life in Anchorage.

I have described this way of life, with the ability to move and build a life across the continent, as the North American Dream—a goal for many but only achievable by a few. Indeed, the fact that people argued that they "have to get used to" transnational life indicates that it is not a smooth process but one fraught with tensions and difficulties, in which this way of life has to be gradually *created* over time through repetitive practices and experiences and shaped by the immigration and class status of these people and the political economy of North America. For dual-citizen transnational migrant-immigrants in Alaska, "getting used to it," is a process of building a livelihood and a way of life by working across sociospatial distance and sociocultural difference and the unequal political and economic space of the continent.

*The Money: "You Get Used to the Salaries"*

I wrote in chapter 3 about how Luis Bravo Jr. tried to return to Mexico to live and work. Recall that Luis's attempts to secure a livelihood in Michoacán after he and Juana married were unsuccessful, and the whole family ended up moving to Anchorage together. Juana suspected that Luis had become accustomed to the salaries in Alaska. During the time he moved back to Acuitzio, he earned less money and was paid in pesos, not U.S. dollars. This was a big change for him. Ernesto Cárdenas talked about this in more detail when I interviewed him at his home on a winter day in Anchorage. Ernesto's father had worked in Alaska for many years in the 1960s and 1970s, including work to build the Trans-Alaska Pipeline, but Ernesto himself didn't come to Alaska until 1987. This was supposed to be temporary. But, as Ernesto said, he got used to both the salaries and the way of life in the United States: "You get used to the salaries, and it's difficult because you have another way of life, another way of living. The customs, the education system, the laws, whatever. In Mexico right now there's a lot of organized crime, there's more corruption, and it's hard to adapt to all of that."

He went on to explain that his mother was born in the United States, but his father is from Acuitzio. His mother and her family moved back to Mexico when she was very young, and later on she met Ernesto's father and they married. When they had children, "there weren't any good economic opportunities, and my mother decided to go back to the

United States and help my father emigrate." Meanwhile, Ernesto and his siblings lived with their paternal grandmother in Acuitzio. "Later, they emigrated all of us." When he finished school and had to make his own life and find work, he was not interested in going to any other state but Alaska. His sister and brothers all lived in Alaska by then, and he knew about the place from what his father told him about it. Importantly, he was also already a U.S. permanent resident.

"I have adapted, I think it's good," he continued, "because Alaska has been a great option for me, and for many people from my town. A lot of money that people have earned here in Alaska has been invested in [Acuitzio], in houses, in a better standard of living for the people, for everyone, no? So, it's good. Alaska has helped Acuitzio del Canje a lot."[2]

"In Alaska," Ernesto continued, "*nos hemos adaptado bastante bien. We have adapted pretty well and we have managed to get ahead. We have had to work really hard, but all in all, we live pretty well."

He went on to explain that he believes that if he had spent his life working in Michoacán instead of Alaska, he would not have been able to get ahead. "Life in Mexico isn't very cheap. To live more or less like we have been living in Alaska is not cheap. If I go to Costco in Morelia, for example, I spend about the same, it costs about the same there as it does here for many things. *Igual.* So I need to earn almost the same . . ."

I interrupted, ". . . and in pesos."

Ernesto responded, "In pesos, yes, and it's more difficult because the salaries are so low, right? *Entonces tiene uno que tener un ritmo de vida mas bajo también para poder adaptarse.*" Ernesto implied that moving back to Mexico would also mean adapting to a lower standard of living. He points to the fact that consumer goods and food in Mexico are not very cheap, nor is cellphone credit, or property, or many other things that are necessary to live "more or less like in Alaska." In this chapter and the next one, Acuitzences compare relative salaries and prices between Mexico and Alaska. Relative, because what matters for transnational life are the differences between these *specific* places. This kind of North American economics is challenging to do formally, as in table 2. I found it difficult to find local-level, comparable information for Acuitzio and Anchorage. Yet this is something Acuitzences in Alaska do all the time.

Table 2: North American economics, 2012

| LOCATION | EXCHANGE RATE (USD/MXN) | COST OF LIVING INDEX | AVERAGE WAGE | MINIMUM WAGE | AVERAGE HOUSE COST |
|---|---|---|---|---|---|
| | 13.154[a] | | | | |
| Anchorage (USD) | | 129.6[b] | $203.44/day[c] | $62.00/day[d] | $337,018.76[e] |
| Acuitzio (USD) | | 58.65[f] | $16.15/day[g] | $4.49/day[h] | $171,050.63[i] |

a. Based on Federal Reserve Bank of St. Louis, FRED Economic Data, fred.stlouisfed.org.

b. This value is an *index* and measures the relative price of consumer goods and services in Anchorage as compared to a national average. A value of 129.6 means that the cost of living in 2012 was 29.6 percent higher in Anchorage than in the average U.S. city (Anchorage Economic Development Corporation, "Cost of Living Index," http://aedcweb.com/wp-content/uploads/2014/10/2013-Anchorage-Cost-of-Living-Report.pdf, accessed March 24, 2017).

c. Daily average wage based on an eight-hour day, $25.43/hour average wage (U.S. Department of Labor, "Occupational Employment Statistics," https://www.bls.gov/oes/2012/may/oes_11260.htm #35-0000, accessed March 24, 2017). Note that the average wage for food preparation and serving (in which many Acuitzenses are or have been employed) was $11.34/hour.

d. Alaska Department of Labor and Workforce Development, Division of Labor Standards and Safety, "Minimum Wage Standard and Overtime Hours," http://labor.alaska.gov/lss/whact.htm, accessed March 24, 2017.

e. Anchorage Economic Development Corporation, "Cost of Living Index," http://aedcweb.com/wp-content/uploads/2014/10/2013-Anchorage-Cost-of-Living-Report.pdf, accessed March 24, 2017.

f. I was not able to find a Cost of Living Index (COLI) for Michoacán, so this number is based on an average COLI for three Mexican cities in 2012: Mexico City, Guadalajara, and Monterrey (Numbeo, "America: Cost of Living Index 2012," https://www.numbeo.com/cost-of-living/region_rankings.jsp?title=2012&region=019, accessed March 24, 2017). The average cost of living in these three cities is 41.35 percent lower than in New York City. Since this COLI value is relative to New York City, not a U.S. national average, it is not perfectly comparable with the Anchorage COLI.

g. Average salary for Michoacán, January–June 2011 (Comisión Nacional de los Salarios Mínimos, "Salario promedio diario de cotización por entidad federativa según mes," http://www.conasami.gob.mx/pdf/entidad%20federativa/salprofentfed_2011.pdf, accessed March 24, 2017). Mexican federal law states that a work day is eight hours, but this does not necessarily apply to the work day or earnings for the "informal" economy.

h. Minimum wage November 2012 (Servicio de Administración Tributaria, http://www.sat.gob.mx/informacion_fiscal/tablas_indicadores/Paginas/salarios_minimos.aspx, accessed March 24, 2017). Area geográfica B includes Michoacán.

i. Average house cost is approximately $2,250,000 MXN in Acuitzio according to information provided by Tony Calvillo (personal communication, 2017). Tony is a real estate agent in California, and his parents live in Acuitzio. He said homes in Acuitzio in 2017 range from $1.5–3 million MXN. An average- to large-size home would cost approximately $2–2.5 million MXN, with smaller homes available for about 1 million pesos. Information was not available for 2012.

For a long time now, one way for Acuitzences to get ahead has been to go to the United States and exploit the inequality between the economies and the disparity between the peso and the dollar. As Gloria Bravo said, "There isn't money [in Mexico]. Here in Alaska there's work and so we've adapted [to that]." According to Ernesto, Gloria, and Luis's logic, the way to get ahead, secure a livelihood, and live well is to cross the border to work in the United States but continue to return to Acuitzio. To do this, Acuitzences have drawn on a variety of strategies to live transnationally. This includes seeking U.S. citizenship and other official statuses, developing skills and certifications to work in a chosen field both here and there, traveling with things to feel at home in transnational space, and purchasing homes and property in Acuitzio and Anchorage.

*The Paperwork: Bureaucratic Processes and State Regulations*

Crucial to a way of life that depends on regular travel between Alaska and Mexico is access to the official statuses that facilitate mobility and the ability to work and live in both nation-states. Gaining U.S. citizenship and other official statuses makes it much easier to travel across the U.S.-Mexican border and work in the United States. Individuals are limited in what they can do when they come up against state regulations and the bureaucracies that enforce them.

The most obvious obstacle is the difficult process of obtaining legal immigration status in the United States such as a Green Card or U.S. citizenship. In other chapters I analyzed the process of getting U.S. citizenship in relation to mobility, how citizenship makes it possible to move more easily, and how the very business and bureaucracy of citizenship *requires* mobility as a matter of procedure. For Acuitzences, it is not citizenship per se that is important; it is the ability to come and go.[3]

When I was in Acuitzio in 2011, Alina Cárdenas studied for her U.S. citizenship test all summer. One rainy evening in her house, she showed me her study materials and explained the tricks she was using to remember the answers. Although she is critical of U.S. policy ("Can you believe they ask kids to show their immigration status in schools in Arizona, Sarita?") and the food system ("The fruit tastes like cardboard in Alaska, and it's so expensive!"), becoming a U.S. citizen is important to her. For one thing, she's "tired of going in the other lineup." After all, her husband Ernesto and most of her children are U.S. citizens, while she holds a Green Card as a permanent resident. At the airport when passing through immigration review, Alina must go in the line for visitors or "aliens," while her family can go in the line for citizens.

After studying for her citizenship exam for about two years, Alina took the written test. A few weeks later, she received a letter notifying her that she passed and asking her to visit U.S. Citizenship and Immigration Services (USCIS) for her interview. Alina went to the interview, answered the questions, and waited to hear back. However, unlike other Acuitzences that she knew who had become U.S. citizens, Alina was invited back for a second interview, and this worried her. The reason why she was worried was that she had come to the United States before, "illegally" and without papers.[4] While they were there, Alina got a traffic ticket, and she believed that because of it, the authorities knew she had been to Alaska before and could possibly deny her citizenship as a result.

She invited me to come with her to the second interview, and she and her husband Ernesto picked me up at my apartment in their white minivan. She was neatly dressed, wearing makeup, and carried a folder with her paperwork in it. I could tell she was nervous. She showed me the letter that she received, which instructed her that her appointment would consist of an interview that could take up to two hours, and advised her not to arrive too early because there is limited space in the waiting room. Finally, it asked her to bring her paperwork (U.S. Green Card and Mexican passport) for review.

We sat in the waiting room, Alina, Ernesto and I, watching other people exit from interviews or ask questions at the windows. Ernesto and I talked, while Alina sat quietly, fidgeting and turning a ring around on her finger repeatedly, until she got called in for her interview. We wished her good luck. While she was being interviewed, Ernesto reminisced about getting his own citizenship in the late 1990s. Ernesto received U.S. permanent residency when he was younger, because his parents applied for it for him and his siblings. He described the process of getting citizenship as easy, and the whole process took about a year.[5]

Many men from Acuitzio told me that they sought permanent residency or citizenship in order to facilitate mobility for themselves and their families. Ernesto received his own citizenship, and then he applied for his family to come to Alaska, which took another year. He said that this was expensive because they had to make multiple trips to Ciudad Juárez, he had to find a sponsor in Alaska, and a lawyer, and so on.[6] All five of his kids are now dual U.S.-Mexican citizens except for one: she is a permanent resident but married to an American, so she could naturalize if she wanted to. His youngest daughter often jokes that she is different from her Mexican brothers and sisters because she was born in Alaska. But really, she is a dual citizen too because they arranged for her to have Mexican nationality as well.

Alina returned to the waiting room after her interview and told us that she was asked a series of questions: Did you come here illegally? Have you ever sold drugs? She then had to read some sentences in English. We left the office and went for lunch together.

Three weeks later she called me on my cell phone. She had received a letter from USCIS, and unfortunately her application for citizenship was declined. She said, "It's their decision, there's nothing I can do. But I passed the test, Sarita! I did everything I needed to do to be a citizen, but they said no." I could hear her holding back tears at the other end of the line. "At least I can go back and forth easily, I don't have to cross through the desert, in dangerous conditions, and all of that."

Alina was clearly upset and disappointed, but as a permanent resident with a Green Card, she reiterated that she can still move back and forth, differentiating herself from those who "have to cross through the desert." And at this writing, even though she was unsuccessful at her application for citizenship, Alina continues to move between Mexico and Alaska.

Many Acuitzences have applied for citizenship and received it, and like Alina, they see it as important for facilitating mobility between Alaska and Mexico. Juana Bravo told me that when she filled all the requirements for U.S. citizenship, "I felt like if I could do anything." Octavio talked about feeling "free" after getting a U.S. Green Card and eventually becoming a U.S. citizen. More specifically, he talked about how he felt free to *travel*, to move. He says that he "feels the same" in Alaska as in Mexico, now that he has his papers. He said when you do not have papers, "you have to be someone really quiet," he laughed. "But since I got my papers I feel the same here as I do in Mexico. And in whatever place." Traveling with a U.S. passport reduces the friction of the U.S.-Mexican border and makes it possible to move back and forth, without limits to the length of time a person is permitted outside of the country (as for U.S. Green Card holders) or the possibility that they will not be able to cross back in either direction. It is not only a piece of paper; obtaining it can make a place *feel* different.

Bureaucratic processes are part of building a way of life at both ends of the continent, and people seek official state statuses in Mexico too. Many Acuitzences who had children in Alaska obtain Mexican citizenship for them. Some Acuitzences told me that they faced difficulties getting ID cards or similar documents in Mexico, since they are not technically residents there. For example, midway through my fieldwork in Anchorage, I told Ana Bravo that my Canadian insurance company would no longer insure our vehicle and that I would have to somehow get an Alaska driver's license and insurance. She said, "The same kind of things happen to us in Mexico, Sarita, because we don't live there all the time." She told me about how her husband, Miguel, was trying to get a Mexican voter registration card, used as identification in Mexico, to facilitate business now that he owns an avocado orchard and is involved with selling avocados in Mexico. When he tried to get his ID, they said he could not have one because it was municipal election time, and there was a blackout period before elections. It was also challenging for him to get an ID in Mexico because they do not live there all the time, Ana said. In the end Miguel could not get an ID card, so he could not cash a check, and as a result they had no cash when they went on vacation to Ixtapa that year. Miguel gave the check to his father, who cashed it and deposited the funds into his account in Mexico.

Bureaucracies work to fix people in place by making it difficult to live in places temporarily or seasonally, for example, the difficulties faced by a Mexican citizen like Miguel who while visiting Mexico temporarily needed to get the proper ID card and open a bank account. State definitions of residency do not allow for mobility, and there are minimum requirements for the amount of time one must spend in a nation-state to be considered a resident. For Miguel, not having the ID he needs obviously makes it difficult to run a business in Acuitzio from Alaska. In order to be successful he relies on family members in Mexico, so again, maintaining relationships in Acuitzio is important.

To live within a transnational social space, then, people work to get not only official statuses, such as ID cards in Mexico or U.S. citizenship and passports, but they also develop skills and certifications that serve them both "here" and "there." Men of the first two generations of Acuitzences often arrived in Anchorage with the equivalent of a high school education, or sometimes less. They began by working as dishwashers or laborers and worked their way up to more preferable jobs. Women that I interviewed were more likely to be better educated and sought skills and statuses that would serve them in both Anchorage and Acuitzio. I talked to Serefina at her home as she prepared breakfast for her children, and she explained how things were very difficult for her when she first arrived. Serefina was in her early thirties when I interviewed her in 2012, and she told me about how she met her husband in Acuitzio, when he was there on vacation from work in Anchorage. He had already worked in Anchorage for many years before they met, and most of his brothers did too. At the time, they planned to live in Morelia together after they married, but that didn't work out, and they moved to Anchorage together in 2002. Serefina had been a hairdresser in Mexico, but to work as a stylist in Alaska means recertifying to meet the requirements set by the state Board of Barbers and Hairdressers. Being a hairdresser is important to her,[7] and she worked hard to study and get the credentials she needed to work in her field in Alaska. "Since I started studying hairdressing in Mexico, I really identified with it because part of me loved it; I loved doing what I did as a hair stylist. That was why I was focused on studying it here in Alaska." But it was not easy for Serefina to become a hair stylist in Alaska. She explains all of the difficulties she faced: "At first the doors were closed to me in every way. First of all because I didn't speak English. Second, I didn't have a Social Security number. And the third reason was because I didn't have the money to pay for additional training."

With time, her husband filled out her papers, and she got a Social Security number and started working, cleaning houses and offices. She was making money, and she could speak some English by then, so she told her husband that she still wanted to study hairdressing in Alaska.

Serefina continued, "He didn't want me to. He said, how will you do it while working? Also, it's all in English, how will you do it? But I said to him, look, it's something that I've already invested in. It's something that I carry with me, that I already know how to do."

"Well, you had your own salon," I said.

Serefina replied, "I had my own salon in Mexico for three years. So I already knew the techniques, I knew what I was doing. The only thing was that I had to demonstrate to the state of Alaska that I knew how with a license, with a piece of paper." Serefina described the frustrations of this bureaucratic process:

> I applied for a license, and they asked me to send in the documentation and transcripts, so I sent the hours that I had already worked in Mexico. It was so much work, plus all the money I spent to get the papers sent to me and translated into English because they didn't understand Spanish. All of that took five months or so, like five months fighting with this. And finally they told me no, they couldn't count those hours because it had been more than two years since I studied there, and that here they just count the past two years of your studies.

Since the state Board of Barbers and Hairdressers would not count her training and hours in Mexico, Serefina had to complete a training program in Anchorage, a very expensive and time-consuming endeavor. However, she did complete it and is now certified to work as a hair stylist in the state of Alaska. It is not only immigration status that makes it possible to get used to life in a transnational social field. There are other kinds of certifications and regulations that also make it possible to build a life and a livelihood in Anchorage and Acuitzio. Serefina also had to change the expectations of her husband, who did not want her to study to become a hairdresser in Alaska. However, for Serefina, being a hairdresser is a key part of who she is, whether in Acuitzio or in Anchorage.

But not everyone is able to get the certifications that they need in Alaska. For Serefina, to become certified as a hairdresser took a lot of time, money, and additional education. Getting used to life in Alaska thus means either investing in the requirements and certifications that you need to continue in your career or switching to something else altogether.

Recall that Gloria first visited Alaska as a *quinceañera* present. She studied dentistry in Morelia, but in Alaska she works in an industrial food preparation facility. As she said, "I know people who come from Morelia to Anchorage who have a career in Mexico already, like a dentist or a doctor, but their training doesn't count for anything here. You don't start to work in your career here, you start here in whatever. In a restaurant, as a waiter, whatever. I know that when you study, you always have that and it's training that you always have. But to develop a career here in Alaska, it doesn't do anything for you. And eventually you forget."

Training in Mexico may not be recognized by U.S. employers, but on the other hand, moving to Mexico with a U.S. education also presents challenges. I spoke to Araceli about the possibility of attending school in Mexico. When we met for an interview in Anchorage, Araceli was just about to graduate from high school in Anchorage. She was born in Alaska, but like her cousins Vero, Sophia, and Toño, she travels back to Acuitzio every year with her parents. We met for coffee, and she told me that going back to school in Anchorage in September is always hard:

"I'm not into anything, I don't want to do anything because I just came back from Mexico. It's so depressing. Finally when the new year hits it's like, I'm kind of, I don't know, *adapting* again I guess."

"So you think you feel more at home in Mexico than here in Anchorage, or it depends?"

Araceli immediately replied, "No, I kinda like it more over there [in Mexico]. But school wise, I think I wouldn't be able to stay over there. I mean I've already gone to school here my whole life so it'd be a hard transition. Even though I took AP Spanish, I don't know if it would be enough to go to school there."

In her narrative, Araceli oscillates between feeling at home in Acuitzio and Anchorage, and the difficulties of getting used to life at each point in the transnational social field. Although she says she feels more at home in Acuitzio, she realizes that in other ways, like at school, she is more accustomed to Alaska. The educational and certification structures in Alaska and Michoacán do not match up, and moving between them and navigating their ambiguities is challenging from either side of the border, as Serefina, Gloria, and Araceli all show.

Obtaining skills and statuses that make it possible to work in a specific field in both Mexico and Alaska is a challenge, requiring time, social capital, and financial resources. Even people who have dual citizenship may not have other skills or training that allow them to live seamlessly between places. This difference is enacted by laws and regulations of the federal and state governments and enforced by bureaucracies that require demonstration of citizenship, of credenciales electorales in Mexico, or certifications to work as a hairdresser, dentist, or in other occupations. As shown in this section, Acuitzences try to get used to transnational life and manage the friction of bureaucratically enforced difference by seeking skills and statuses that allow them to move between and work within regulatory frameworks in both Mexico and Alaska.

*The Property: Territorialization and Mobility*

Another spatial strategy to facilitate transnational life is the acquisition of homes and property in both Acuitzio and Alaska. Many Acuitzences who work in the United States have purchased property in the town or surrounding areas. The acquisition of homes and property in both Acuitzio and Alaska facilitates transnational life, and owning property can make it possible to build a livelihood on both sides of the border. Miguel, for instance, has an avocado orchard in Acuitzio and a restaurant in Anchorage. Lola and her husband owned restaurants in Acuitzio and Anchorage at the time of my research. Many migrants have houses on their properties in Mexico, and this also facilitates transnational life since there is somewhere to live and call home on visits to Acuitzio. Owning property as a process of territorialization that fixes people to specific places paradoxically makes it possible to be more *mobile* within the transnational social field by having somewhere to live in each location. By decorating their Mexican homes with items from Alaska, and their Anchorage homes with items from Mexico, they demonstrate their multiple attachments to each place, as I analyze further in the next chapter. And finally, by relying on local relatives to care for their homes while they are away, they strengthen social relationships that extend between Anchorage and Acuitzio. Much like the *casas vacias* in Textitlán, Guanajuato, about which Debra Lattanzi-Shutika wrote, maintaining houses in both locations indicates a desire to maintain connection to hometowns in Mexico while building a life in the United States.[8]

I was told that the price of property in Acuitzio is artificially high because of the amount of out-migration and the resulting interest in property.[9] Many Acuitzences say that they decided to go to the United States to invest in land and build or improve their house, and this has been the case for a long time now.[10] Those who are more established in the United States will purchase property as an investment or for future generations to live in. The fact that U.S. migrants and immigrants primarily want to purchase property in their Mexican hometowns has resulted in inflated prices for land and property in the area. This means that for the poorest Acuitzences, owning land and a house is out of reach without migrating to the United States.[11] Through migration people become wage-laborers and landowners and therefore change their class positioning.[12] Indeed, as people work outside of Mexico for longer periods of time, they become more able to afford land in their hometown. Thus increased mobility means people are more able to afford to put down roots, in terms of land ownership and house construction. Indeed, Luis Sr. purchased several houses in his hometown with money earned over decades of work in Alaska: the house that he lives in, one house for each of his sons, and their family rancho at Parapio. Having a home in Acuitzio means that his children have a place there and something to come back to. Processes that lead people to develop roots in a place, such as citizenship or land ownership, again simultaneously facilitate a mobile and transnational way of life between Mexico and Alaska.

As mentioned, some Acuitzences who live and work in Anchorage own properties for income in Acuitzio, such as restaurants or avocado orchards.[13] For example, Miguel Bravo co-owns a restaurant in Anchorage, but he also co-owns an avocado orchard with his father, Luis Sr., along the Acuitzio-Villa Madero highway. The highway twists and turns up into the mountains, offering spectacular views of the valley below. Miguel bought the orchard in 1988, only three years after arriving in Anchorage. The *rancho* was his maternal grandfather's and was inherited by his aunt. When she decided to sell, "I bought it to keep it in the family, *que no pasaba a otros manos, verdad?*" Miguel saw it as "something to remember my grandfather by. Since I was a little boy I remember going to that *rancho*." Around the year 2000 they planted the avocadoes. Avocadoes take up to five years to begin producing fruit, and in recent years Miguel's plants have begun producing "*más o menos bien*," as he put it. When Miguel returns to Acuitzio, much of his time is spent arranging contracts for harvest and sale of the fruit. While he is away, he depends on family members to manage the orchard and the contracts: his father manages it, and a cousin works for them. When they need more help, they contract people and pay them by the day.

In our interview in Anchorage Miguel also talked about the reasons why he decided to invest in an avocado orchard and about the uncertainty that now surrounds the future he had planned: "Well, my idea was when I couldn't work anymore and once I was retired, I wanted to go back to Acuitzio. For that reason we invested in the avocado orchard. To have money in Acuitzio when we live there, and so that we would be earning money from there. But now with the violence in Mexico it's become more difficult. I wanted to live there in the future but . . . it depends. Every day it seems worse and worse. I wouldn't be comfortable, *pues*."

I said that it could also be difficult to decide where to live since his children live in Alaska and may not want to return to Mexico or move away. Miguel continued, "That too. They're going to want to work here [in Alaska], and they won't want to work there [in Mexico]. So I don't know. I think about the future, and sometimes I say to Ana, maybe we should buy a house in another state."

But then Miguel points out that places like California are not ideal either. He continues, "*No hay para donde irte!* Here the main thing is the snow, right? But we are good. We just have to be able to stand the cold, right? But we will wait and see, *a ver que pasa*."

Miguel and others like him are able to "wait and see" and leverage statuses, skills, property, and expertise across the continent to build their lives transnationally. Owning property, homes, and income-generating businesses in both places is one way that this class of migrants can be differentiated from others in Acuitzio and other migrants in the United States. This kind of flexibility is only possible due to Miguel's structural position as a second-generation migrant and dual citizen with a class status that facilitates the kinds of practices and strategies to *acostumbrarse* to transnational life that he can engage in, in both Acuitzio and Alaska.

*The Everyday: Practices of "Getting Used to It"*

So far in this chapter, Acuitzences have talked about navigating economic, legal, and regulatory systems in terms of salaries, citizenship, and certifications. Acuitzences also put down roots and at the same time facilitate their mobility between Acuitzio and Anchorage by purchasing houses and establishing businesses at either end of the continent. But these dual-citizen migrants also engage in a variety of everyday spatial practices to *acostumbrarse* or "get used to" life between Mexico and Alaska.

Weather figures prominently in people's spatial perceptions of this transnational field. In interviews and informal conversations, I asked Acuitzences what it was like when they first came to Alaska, and they emphasized how hard it was getting used to the cold weather and darkness at a high northern latitude. As Oscar said, "Alaska has helped us a lot because we have always had work, but *it is not the weather for us. When I arrive in Acuitzio I feel totally different, I feel ready to do things, I have more energy. Here, everything is different.*"

Getting used to the weather happens at the level of the body, and people not only talk about getting used to the cold and dressing appropriately for it but also the long, dark winter nights and adjusting to effects on the body like dry skin from the winter air and a lighter complexion from less time spent in the sun. So when people talk about getting used to the weather, it is with reference to its effect on the body.

I met Esteban and Laura at their cozy home in Anchorage in the middle of winter, with snow piled high along the street and either side of the driveway. They are both from Michoacán: Esteban is from Acuitzio, and Laura is from Morelia. They met and married in Anchorage and have since had two children. The whole family lives together in Anchorage and travels to Acuitzio and Morelia every year or so. In an interview, Esteban and Laura told me about how, after living in Alaska for many years, their bodies got used to cooler temperatures, and they were no longer accustomed to hot weather when they visited Mexico. Laura talked about a recent trip to Morelia when they decided to take the tourist bus around town. Her sons were dressed up in suits for a fiesta, and she took advantage of the nice clothes the boys were wearing to take photos around town before their suits had to be returned. But it was May, and it gets very hot in Morelia at that time of the year. "*Y ya no estamos acostumbrados a la calor de allá.* We're not used to the heat there anymore. We felt like we were drowning."

Her husband continued, "Now we don't feel the cold as much, either. One December we went to Mexicali to visit my mother's brother. It was in December, right?"

Laura said, "Yes, it was in December."

Esteban continued, "We said, let's go out to eat somewhere. My uncle said, let me go and get a sweater; it's starting to get cold. And us, nothing! We went around in shorts and a T-shirt!"

I said, "So, you get used to a place, like that."

Esteban nodded, "The body does."

Getting used to the weather takes place at an embodied level, but women I interviewed in Anchorage also talked about getting used to a different way of life in Anchorage, captured in the phrase "feeling *encerrado*": closed in and at home all of the time. This is partly related to weather and geography, especially considering the cold temperatures and short hours of daylight during the winter. It also has to do with a different rhythm of everyday life, and a different way of living in and moving through a city or town. For example, in Acuitzio, many people, and especially women, do not drive. It is possible to walk or take transit such as a bus or collective taxis to travel within and from Acuitzio to Morelia and to destinations around Michoacán or even Mexico. Anchorage is spread out over a very large area. Walking or taking the bus is less convenient, and most people in Anchorage consider it necessary to drive to work, to school, and for shopping and leisure activities. In Anchorage, and many other places in the United States, automobiles are considered essential for everyday life and an important symbol of individual freedom.[14] Women who arrived in Anchorage unable to drive or speak English could not work, and thus felt closed in, or *encerrado*, in their homes. This adds an important gender difference to the experience of "getting used" to living in Alaska upon arriving from Mexico.

To illustrate this gendered process for women from Acuitzio, consider what Serefina told me about what it was like when she first arrived in Anchorage. When she first came to Alaska, she said life was very difficult for her because she has always been very independent. "But," she continued, "when I arrived in Anchorage, it was difficult because I depended on my husband for everything." She only spoke Spanish then and described how she could not go to the store alone or ask any questions. If she wanted something, she could not ask for it. "It was really hard for me because I had to depend on my husband for everything, and that made me really frustrated. I wanted to go back to my country because I felt like I wasn't anyone here, and I couldn't do anything."

"How long was it until you felt more independent again?" I asked. Serefina replied, "When I started to drive. I came to Anchorage with a visa, and so I couldn't have a driver's license until my husband arranged papers for me."

Feeling *encerrado* has to do with feeling closed in because of being unable to drive and a different rhythm of social life, but it also has to do with one's ability to work in Anchorage. For example, Lola told me that she doesn't feel completely at home in Anchorage. She described life in Anchorage like living on an island. We met in Acuitzio after she finished work, and we talked on a bench in front of the municipal buildings on one side of the plaza as cars, buses, and trucks drove by on their way into town. Lola explained that she married someone who worked in Alaska and spent the first ten years of her marriage there. She since moved back to Acuitzio with her two children because she believes that educational opportunities are better in Mexico than in the United States. Meanwhile, her husband continued to travel back and forth between Anchorage and Acuitzio, working as a server at a restaurant in Anchorage and running his own restaurant near the highway at the entrance to Acuitzio.

She said that living in Alaska frustrated her, and described herself as the kind of person who's "always doing things." In Anchorage, however, she felt like she couldn't go out, especially in the winter, and more importantly that she didn't have anything to do: "At first I wasn't very happy with such a big change. I studied accounting and I'm trained as an executive secretary. I worked here in Acuitzio, and when I arrived in Anchorage, well, I didn't know the language and I couldn't work because of that but also because my husband was arranging the documents for me. So I had to stay home, and it was so boring. It was a very unpleasant experience for me because I was *used to* being productive."

With time, she got used to life in Anchorage: "*Después se acostumbra uno*, one gets used to it, and I felt more productive when I started to work, take my children to soccer, and get involved with the dance group at the church. I kept busy, and this gave me stability and peace. I was content. But I always planned to go back to Mexico to live."

In fact, she did go back to Acuitzio to live and became involved with municipal politics while her sons went to school and her husband continued to work in Alaska. However, in 2012, she moved back to Anchorage to open a restaurant with her husband. Lola shows how getting used to life in Anchorage means that for her and her family, Anchorage is always an important spatial point of reference, and it is possible to relocate her permanent residence to either Acuitzio or Anchorage to pursue professional or educational opportunities, like sending her children to university in Mexico, relocating there to become involved in politics, and moving back to Anchorage to open a restaurant.

Both women and men told me they feel *encerrado* because of the different ways in which people use public spaces in Acuitzio and Anchorage. In Acuitzio, town residents and returned migrants are accustomed to going to the plaza to visit with townspeople.[15] There are regular fiestas in town, celebrated with food, music, and socializing. In Anchorage, there is no plaza, and social activities have a different dynamic and rhythm. This takes some getting used to. For example, Iván and I met for an interview at his kitchen table on his birthday. When I came over that day, the house was unusually quiet with Claudia at work and the kids at school. Iván's uncle is one of the very first Acuitzences to go to Alaska, and Claudia's father and grandfather have both worked in Alaska too. However, Iván did not come to Anchorage until after he and Claudia were married. Iván and Claudia often told me about how much they both appreciated the relaxed attitude of people in Anchorage. For example, he said, you do not have to dress fancy or drive a nice car to fit in. In the interview Iván reiterated how much he likes Anchorage: "There are many things to do in Anchorage. *You have to know how to live in the place where you are.* Even the winter is nice if you know how to enjoy it. But being from the south, we don't enjoy it the same way. Because it is sometimes too cold for the activities you were once used to doing."

"Like what?" I asked.

"Well, you're used to going out more, to the *calle*.[16] More than anything you're used to going out, a *pasear por afuera*." Iván continued: "You feel a little, not depressed, but sometimes your energy level changes. And it's difficult sometimes, and that's why I said, *me estoy yendo desde que llegué!*" Iván laughed and explained, "I've been leaving since I got here! And I haven't been able to go back yet!" He stopped to laugh again, and this time I joined in.

Iván went on: "But we are here now, and I think it's really nice in Anchorage. It's really nice to raise a family here because there isn't much violence, and it's far from the big cities where there is more corruption and violence." I know as he spoke he was thinking of Los Angeles, where he lived and worked as a young man, but also of Michoacán and other parts of Mexico and the violence there attributed to state corruption and drug cartels. He continued: "It's so different here, on this side of the border. It's difficult because you wish for things that aren't here. But you get used to it. *Se acostumbra uno a hacer otras cosas.* You get used to doing other things."

In Iván's narrative, even though he is used to life in Alaska, he admits he still does not feel completely at home there. Instead, he maintains his hometown in Mexico, or even Mexico in general as an important spatial and affective point of reference. Lola, Serefina, Iván, Oscar, and others have had to get used to the differences in weather and ways of life, or as Acuitzences say, *acostumbrarse*. This takes time and the development of a transnational habitus at the level of the body and the rhythm of everyday life. This is a profoundly gendered process, as Serefina and Lola attest. Over time, both men and women orient themselves to the wage-labor economy in Alaska, and some, like Lola and her husband, have been able to own their own businesses in Anchorage and Acuitzio. People start to feel less *encerrado* once they are able to move around within Anchorage, get used to a different rhythm of life, and are able to secure a livelihood through wage labor or entrepreneurship.

Another major difference between Anchorage and Acuitzio that people say they have to get used to is language. People used the same verb, *acostumbrar* or "to get used to," to refer to speaking English or Spanish. More so than in states further south with larger Spanish-speaking populations, everyday life outside the home in Anchorage is conducted in English. Especially among those who moved to the United States as adults, many do not feel comfortable speaking English. Speaking both Spanish and English is the ideal for people oriented to transnational life. However, it is not easy or possible for everyone to become perfectly bilingual.

Indeed, most of those in the second generation, as described in chapter 3, told me that they know enough English to *defenderse*, defend themselves, or get by. For example, Soledad and Efrén, both in their forties, were very active in the dance group Xochiquetzal-Tiqun, and I met them for an interview at their home in south Anchorage to talk about their experiences with the dance group and about life in Anchorage and Acuitzio. Efrén had started out working at a salmon cannery in Alaska, but he now works as a manager of a janitorial services company with contracts throughout the state. Most of Efrén's brothers also live in Alaska, while his mother and father move back and forth, spending the summer months in Anchorage and the winter in Acuitzio. Soledad is from Mexico City, but her grandparents live in Acuitzio. She and Efrén met through mutual acquaintances at a *comida* in Acuitzio when she was there visiting family, and he was temporarily back from Alaska.[17] I asked Efrén about speaking English at work. "Do you have to speak English at work?"

He said, "Yes."

Soledad said, "He speaks English really well."

"I had to learn," Efrén clarified. "*A martillazos*, it was drilled into me, as we say."

Everyone laughed, and Soledad continued, "No, but he speaks it. Me, I can just defend myself. I talk a little crooked, I can understand and everything, but it's still a little more difficult to speak."

"It's more difficult to speak, yes," I agreed. "You have to practice, I think."

Soledad said, "Yes, *ya te vas acostumbrando*. You get used to it as you go. Now all that's missing for me is to speak it. I've become used to English, but my mouth doesn't listen! *Falta la boca!*" She laughs, "But I carry on studying, I carry on."

As Soledad works to learn English in Anchorage, like other Acuitzences in Alaska, she also works to ensure that their children can speak Spanish. Young people in the third generation were more likely to say they felt comfortable in both languages. However, their parents are concerned their children do not speak Spanish well enough, and they work to ensure their children are able to speak Spanish, because they want their children to be able to go back to Mexico and communicate easily with family members there. In Alaska I met parents of school-aged children who were considering moving temporarily to Mexico so that their children could attend school there for a year or two and thereby become more fluent in Spanish. Alina moved back to Mexico in 2013, partly because she wanted her daughter to go to school in Mexico for at least part of her education. Going to school in Spanish is important not only for spoken fluency but especially for reading and writing Spanish correctly. Anchorage also has a Spanish Immersion program at Government Hill School, and some parents from Acuitzio have enrolled their children there. Many high schools in Anchorage offer Spanish language classes for fluent speakers, which are different from classes that teach Spanish as a new language. However, in these programs, children may learn Spanish, but they will not learn the way of life, social rules and norms, and history and culture that they would learn while at school in Mexico.[18] A final concern for parents is that their children learn to speak Spanish without an accent. Parents are proud when their children can speak Spanish in Michoacán with the right accent, and people comment negatively when young people come to Acuitzio speaking Spanish with a U.S. accent.

It is not easy to move between nation-states, school systems, and languages as a child, however. Claudia, who is Alina and Ernesto's daughter, talked to me about this. As explained in chapter 3, Claudia has experienced a lot of mobility in her life, and when I interviewed her at my Anchorage apartment, she talked about moving back and forth between Anchorage and Acuitzio and the difficulties she experienced adjusting to the shifts in language and to everyday life in both places. Her family arrived in Anchorage together in 1985, when Claudia was four years old, and her father already had an apartment set up for them. "But everything looked so weird to me," she said.

"How come?" I asked.

Claudia said, "I don't know, it was a shock, probably like a culture shock. When I first came to Anchorage, the houses were different, the streets, like everything was different. And when I go back to Mexico, it's like," she paused and took a sharp breath in, "it's completely different than Anchorage because I got used to this type of lifestyle or whatever, where the roads are more clean and the houses are more well taken care of and stuff like that."

Claudia's family lived in an apartment on Northern Lights Boulevard in Anchorage for four years until 1989, when Claudia's maternal grandmother got sick and her mother decided to move back to Acuitzio to be closer to the grandmother, taking all four children along. They lived in Mexico until Claudia finished high school. Meanwhile, her father continued to work in Alaska and travel back and forth between Anchorage and Acuitzio.

Claudia talked at length about moving back to Acuitzio at age eleven after living in Alaska for four years. She talked about all of the difficulties that she faced moving across social and geographic distance and between places: adjusting to family members she didn't know, to a different school system, to the way people interact with each other, to the way buildings look. In sum, different ways of life. When I asked her if she remembers being excited to go back to Mexico at all, she talked about this in terms of language:

"No, we were not excited," and she went on to explain why. "First of all, we knew how to speak Spanish, but we did not know how to write it." She explained that she felt anxious about how she would be able to go to school in Spanish, and that people would laugh at her. "It did happen, they did laugh because for Mexico we said Mexico, not *México*. We used the wrong accent so they laughed at us. It was hard, but we had a teacher who taught us every morning and evening so we had double schooling every day.[19] We stayed in Acuitzio, and we had to adjust so that's what we did. We didn't have a lot of friends though."

In 2012 Claudia, her husband, Iván, and their young children moved back to Mexico after living in Anchorage for many years. Based on the difficulties she faced moving back to Mexico as a child, she was worried about her own children adjusting to life in Spanish, since they were not fluent speakers and could not read or write in Spanish at all. They enrolled the children in an English school, at least for the first year so that they could get used to everyday life in Spanish before having to go to school in Spanish too.

Being able to speak both English and Spanish is one way that people manage the difference between Anchorage and Acuitzio and ensure that future generations are also able to move between English- and Spanish-speaking social spaces in both the United States and Mexico. Although language is one way that people get used to the difference between places, they also create spaces that produce sociospatially distant locations as linguistically connected. For example, Luis and Juana Bravo only speak Spanish at home and with their children. Alina only speaks Spanish with her children. Parties and events in Anchorage may be Spanish only, Spanish mass is available twice every Sunday at Our Lady of Guadalupe Church and the Holy Family Cathedral, and Spanish-speaking businesses and services are available throughout Anchorage.

Language work therefore takes place in both Acuitzio and Anchorage. So does the related work of learning local social rules and norms, including informal norms about what is appropriate to wear in Mexico and how that is different from what is socially appropriate in Anchorage. When I interviewed Sophia Bravo, she talked about dressing appropriately at different points in the transnational social field. I had asked her about the differences that she noticed in Anchorage and Acuitzio. Sophia talked about clothing, and how people dress in both places: "Here in Anchorage, people care if you repeat your outfit. Like if you wear something once and you wear it again the next day people are going to be like, 'Oh my God she wore that yesterday' or something like that. You could wear two different pairs of sweat pants and look like a bum, but people wouldn't judge you cause they're different outfits. But in Mexico, if you wear sweat pants, people would pay more attention to you for that than if you wore the same thing twice. Do you get it?"

I clarified, "So in Anchorage it doesn't really matter how nice you look as long as you wear something different. And in Acuitzio if you're dressed in sloppy clothes, like sweat pants, people are going to notice that more than whether or not you're wearing something new, right?"

Sophia said, "Yeah."

I continued, "So in Mexico it's more important, even if you wear the same thing every day, that it's clean and you're not wrinkly and everything like that and you look nice."

"Yeah."

"Whereas here it doesn't even matter if you're wrinkly or whatever, just as long as you're wearing different stuff. Is that what you mean?" I said.

Sophia said, "Yeah that's exactly what I mean."

"That makes sense," I said. "I always feel bad when I'm wearing wrinkly clothes in Acuitzio."

Sophia laughed and said that she once wore what she later realized were socially inappropriate shoes in Acuitzio. "I remember one time in Acuitzio I wore flip flops. Here in Anchorage I'd wear them all the time in the summer, but in Mexico my cousin asked me, 'Why are you wearing your bath slippers out in the street?' And I was just like . . ." Sophia laughed out loud, and I did too.

Sophia identifies a distinction between how someone of her gender and class position would dress depending on their location. She identifies the need to dress *differently* in Alaska, as opposed to in Acuitzio. In Alaska, new clothing is valued above all else, whereas in Acuitzio, clean, pressed, and more formal clothing is valued. On the other hand, men like Luis Bravo, Sophia's father, use clothing to identify their rural roots in Mexico or Alaska. At special events in Anchorage with mostly Acuitzences, men swap the T-shirts and running shoes they wear every day for cowboy shirts, decorative belts, and cowboy boots. Acuitzio is a rural town, and men dress to express their identification with rural *ranchero* culture when they are in Acuitzio and at events in Anchorage such as a Jenny Rivera concert or a New Year's party, for example.

Along similar lines, Jaime told me that he brought a *charro* suit with him to Anchorage in the 1960s: "I only brought clothes with me when I went to Alaska, and what I liked to bring were my *charro* suits because I always liked to dress like that, in the clothes I wore for *charrería*.[20] That was the sport that I liked the most in Mexico, and that's what I brought with me. *Charro* shoes, the whole suit of clothing. A *traje de gala*, formal wear for fiestas and parades."

He showed me a photo of a friend of his in a *charro* suit, and he pointed at it as he talked, "You see how it has a button design made of silver? Mine was the same style."

"Like the mariachis wear?" I asked.

Jaime continued, "Yes, like the ones the mariachis wear, but the *charro* suit is something else, more beautiful, more formal. And you only wear it to formal events, nothing else." He also brought chaps with him to Alaska, which is a good thing because he was invited to participate in the state fair in Palmer. "They invited me to ride a bucking bronco, coarse and wild."

Clothing signifies a point of connection to a rural Mexican hometown, as for Jaime and other men from Acuitzio, and social norms around clothing and what is appropriate to wear are another set of differences that Sophia says she has to navigate to live between Michoacán and Alaska. To live transnationally, people have to know how to dress appropriately, depending on their location in the transnational social field.

*"Like, I Have to Get Used to Being Over There Again"*

Back at the café in Anchorage, I asked Verónica Bravo where she feels most at home. She answered that she feels at home in both places, but she has to get used to life in Acuitzio when she goes there to visit: "Like I told you, the first couple days are kinda weird, I have to *get used to* being over there again. You know how it is to live over there, too! I don't even know how to turn on the boiler at our house in Mexico!" She laughed.

"Do you feel like when you come back here to Anchorage that you have to adjust too?" I asked.

"Yeah. I definitely miss it over there when I come back. I mean, I still do right now."

Verónica is talking about adjusting to the everyday life in Acuitzio when she goes there every summer, and again getting used to everyday life in Anchorage upon her return. Doing this required the development of a habitus that allows Vero to adjust to everyday life within a transnational social field that includes both Anchorage and Acuitzio. This process of adjustment is not smooth, for as described here, it requires "getting used to" different types of weather, social life, bureaucratic rules and regulations governing immigration and work, and language, among other things. People *se acostumbra* by learning what to do and how to be in both Anchorage and Acuitzio, a process that can be challenging.

Acuitzences like Verónica and her family have been very successful at working the border, developing a way of life that depends on access to dual citizenship and ongoing mobility and allows people to take up a number of strategies that facilitate life between Alaska and Acuitzio. These range from seeking official statuses to understanding how to dress appropriately depending on one's location within the transnational social field. But people also get used to life in both places by traveling between Acuitzio and Anchorage with a wide variety of things: food, souvenir goods, photographs, and even animals. In the following chapter I extend the discussion to the stuff of transnational life: material culture and the things people travel with as they move across the continent.

# 5  The Stuff of Transnational Life

SUITCASES FULL OF *MOLE*, T-SHIRTS,
ROOSTERS, AND OTHER THINGS THAT MOVE

I visited Oscar a few times in Anchorage during the winter of 2011, before he went back to Mexico. He and his brother have a system worked out. They are both taxi drivers and they alternate: Oscar spends four months working the taxi in Anchorage, while his brother spends four months in Acuitzio. Then they switch. Their boss is happy because the cab runs all year, with alternating brothers at the wheel. In Anchorage Oscar lives in a yellow single-wide trailer in a mobile home park across from a mall. In the mobile home park the streets loop around each other, and I found it difficult to find his place, especially with tall drifts of snow on either side of the narrow road. When I arrived, I parked my Jeep at an angle behind the two vehicles already parked in the driveway. I walked through the little gate, down the sidewalk, and to the front door, which was located to one side of the trailer in a little open-air porch.

I did not immediately notice the pet carrier to one side of the porch and instead walked straight up to the front door to knock. As I waited for Oscar to answer the door, I heard some clucking sounds. I turned around and peeked into the pet carrier. "A chicken!" I thought. "How odd." Oscar answered the door and invited me inside. I sat down on a leather sofa across from the one on which he sat, and after a few moments of conversation, with the TV on in the background, he asked if I would mind if his rooster came inside.

"No," I said. "Actually, I thought it was a chicken!"

Oscar explained, "No, in fact, it's a rooster bred for fighting, a *gallo de pelea*, of a line that I created myself."

FIG. 5. "Oscar" and his rooster, 2012. Photo by author.

As we spoke his rooster walked around the living room, and I asked Oscar if I could take a picture of them together.

In Acuitzio he has a farm where he breeds, raises, and sells his roosters. However, he also brought some eggs with him to Alaska to hatch and keep. He said that the roosters that live in Anchorage can handle the weather, but bringing a live bird from Mexico to live in this cold would be difficult. The one walking around the living room was brought to Alaska as an egg, was incubated, and then hatched in Anchorage.

This story provides some insight into what is necessary, important, and valued enough to be packed in a suitcase and brought along on travels between Acuitzio and Anchorage. For Oscar, taxi driving pays the bills, but roosters are his passion. He advertises his champion fighting roosters and keeps in contact with clients on both sides of the border and all over the world through specialty magazines and the Internet, specifically on Facebook and YouTube. As he said, "I don't need to travel the world, the roosters have brought the world to me." Oscar told me that he doesn't feel like himself without these roosters, and that is why he brought them with him all the way to Alaska. He keeps most of them in a trailer in a storage yard elsewhere in Anchorage, but sometimes he brings a younger one home, to keep him company. When it gets old enough to crow, and for the neighbors to notice, he takes it to live with the rest.

Oscar explains, "I have very few here because the climate doesn't help us at all. But I raise them anyway just because when I'm here in Anchorage, and I start to miss Acuitzio, and I start to miss my animals, and the people, I go and see the roosters, and this helps me a lot. The roosters have helped me a lot psychologically because when I'm with them, I forget my problems, I forget the bills."

"So that's why you have one here with you?" I asked him.

He explained that since his brother is in Acuitzio, and his parents also left to spend the winter in their hometown, he is in Anchorage by himself. The rooster keeps him company. "When I get home from work, I spend time with him. He makes good company. He's like a pet. It makes me happy because he comes in and sings and like I said, psychologically it's helped me a lot. I give him his food, and some water, I clean the cage, and it helps me a lot."

Throughout this book I show how Acuitzences in Alaska build a way of life in *both* locations and across the continent. This chapter focuses on things that travel transnationally: roosters, material culture, and food. Because the particular class of transnational dual citizens—like Oscar—work to build a life in more than one place, the movement of material culture is not only in one direction, that is, from Mexico to

Alaska. Instead, material culture travels with people between both locations since "feeling at home" may require things from each place. People travel with things to feel at home, connect distant places in their everyday lives, and build social relationships in Acuitzio and Anchorage. They also sometimes travel with things to buy, sell, or give away in another location in the transnational social field. They often flirt with the legality of it all, something that others who move across the U.S.-Mexican border with a more precarious legal status could not afford to do because it could mean putting their ability to continue moving between places at great risk. Traveling with things therefore reinforces the socioeconomic status of the transnational class. Things that move are both a marker and a material reality of transnationality: a symbol of a way of life based on mobility as well as an object that has literally traveled between Mexico and Alaska.[1]

*Transnational Material Culture*

Although there has been much academic and policy research on remittances, or money sent by migrants in the United States to family members in Mexico, there has been less interest in the *things* that move between these two nation states.[2] But the movement of people is always also a movement of objects, and the movement of material goods is always embedded in social relations. In the pages that follow, I show that the movement of material goods is embedded in social relations at multiple levels: from particular local networks of kinship and material culture to the level of the North American economy and immigration rules and regulations that shape mobility of people and things across the continent.[3] People travel with things to "feel like themselves" and make a life for themselves at different points in the transnational social field, but they also travel with objects to create a livelihood. Material culture is the stuff of transnational life—an important part of building a way of life between locations, of building transnational livelihoods, and of forming a specific class status based on access to dual U.S.-Mexican citizenship and transnational mobility. And finally, the way in which these people travel with things distinguishes this class of dual citizen migrant-immigrants from other Mexican migrants in the United States.

There is a growing body of research about the material culture of migration and of the movement of things across the U.S.-Mexican border specifically. For example, Emma Ferry has studied the mobility of minerals between the two nations as scientific specimens, religious offerings, works of art, and valuable collectibles. The movement of minerals across the U.S.-Mexican border through mineral exploration and trade has defined the transnational space between these nations in terms of value.[4] Shaylih Muehlmann's study of narco-culture in the U.S.-Mexican borderlands includes those who travel with drugs or money across the international border in a broader framework of illegal, illicit, or black market activities taken up by the rural poor who have lost other ways of making a living.[5] Jason De León has researched the material objects left in the desert by clandestine border crossers in remote and treacherous parts of the borderland. Such border-crossing artifacts both reflect and shape a way of being that is specific to the desert migration process. The camouflage and dark-colored clothing, specialized water bottles, first-aid equipment, high-salt-content foods, hydration beverages, and religious objects provide evidence of techniques and modifications that are connected to the widespread suffering experienced by those who cross the desert.[6] All of these authors theorize how the political economy of the U.S.-Mexican border can be understood in terms of the mobility of things—minerals, drugs, money, and the artifacts of illegal crossing—in the borderlands.

Here I focus on the things that travel with dual-citizens between Mexico and Alaska. As I describe, the value of objects varies across the U.S.-Mexican border, especially in terms of *flavor* and *price*. This is important as mobile objects become tied to place, even as they move. As well, dual-citizen migrants are able to capitalize on the value differentials along the border in the kinds of everyday economics in which they engage. Material culture is sometimes crossed surreptitiously, in terms of foods that are not allowed to cross or items that will be sold on the other side of the border. As well, related to De León's findings, the material culture of migration also reflects and shapes a way of being specific to this particular form of U.S.-Mexican transnationality.[7] Since these are dual-citizen migrant-immigrants, rather than evidence of bodily suffering discussed in De León's work, the material culture of this kind

Table 3: Things that travel, 2011–12

| FROM ALASKA TO ACUITZIO | FROM MEXICO TO ALASKA |
|---|---|
| Alaska pipeline commemoration trophy | Animals (puppy, rooster eggs) |
| Alaska license plates | *Artesanías* (handicrafts) and other souvenirs |
| Automobiles | Calendars |
| Books (including one about the Trans-Alaska Pipeline) | Clothing and accessories (bags, *charro* suit, dance costumes, dress for first communion, *huaraches* (sandals), jewelry, *rebozo* (shawl), serape, team Mexico jerseys) |
| Baseball caps that say "Alaska" | Cooking equipment (*molcajetes* [a stone tool made of basalt used for grinding food, similar to a mortar and pestle], *molinillo* for making hot chocolate, *ollas/cazuelas* [pots, some handmade of clay]) |
| Camping trailer | Custom bumper stickers |
| Clothes (new and used, winter jackets) | Electronics (cellphone, tape recorder to record music) |
| Decorations for the home (coasters; figurines of husky dogs, bears, etc.; paintings; posters; wall hanging/tapestry) | Food (*barbacoa de borrego* [lamb barbecue], bread, candy, *carnitas*, cheese, chiles, cheese, chorizo, dried meat, chamoy chile sauce, chocolate gum, churros, *gorditas* filled with meat or cheese, *gorditas de nata* [biscuits], mezcal, *mole* paste, pinole [toasted ground corn that can be made into a drink, similar to *atole*], *rompope* [an alcoholic drink similar to eggnog], tequila, wheat seeds) |
| Dream catcher | Guitar |
| Electronics (MP3 player, video game system and games) | Makeup (e.g., mascara) |

| | |
|---|---|
| Food (salmon, smoked and fresh) | Photographs and videos |
| Hair products | *Recuerdos de fiestas* (party favors, usually from a *quinceañera*, wedding, or baptism) |
| Home appliances/fixtures (bathroom fixtures, cutlery set, enameled cast iron pots, toaster) | |
| Maps of Alaska and Anchorage | |
| Newspaper clippings | |
| Party invitations | |
| Photographs | |
| Rooster cages | |
| Souvenirs (coffee mugs, key chains, magnets, photo albums, postcards) | |
| Stickers and bumper stickers | |
| Toys | |
| Ulu knife[a] | |
| Vitamins | |

a. A ulu is a knife with a rounded blade that was traditionally used by Yup'ik, Inuit, and Aleut women. Many people continue to use ulus, and they are also sold as tourist souvenirs throughout Alaska.

of migration indexes nostalgia for and links produced between homes and homelands for those who live across the continent.[8] This difference also indexes the inequality between different classes of migrants: illegal migrants who take treacherous routes through a hot desert, and dual-citizen migrant immigrants who travel through air-conditioned airports and on comfortable buses.

I have been interested in things that travel since I first started fieldwork in Anchorage and Acuitzio in 2005. I went to the field with an interest in everyday dimensions of transnational life, and specifically food. Once in Anchorage, and through conversations with Acuitzences there, I realized that food was one of the things that traveled in people's suitcases on trips from Mexico to Alaska. People said then, and continue to say now, that food doesn't taste the same in Anchorage—especially *mole*, bread, and cheese.

A focus on things that travel thus comes out of the ethnographic context and provides insight into the material culture of transnational life and the mobility of things.[9] As I followed the people, I also followed the things. For example, at a meal at her home, Ana pointed out to me that the *mole* she had used was from Acuitzio and that was why it was so delicious. Gloria invited me over for enchiladas, promising to use the cheese she brought from Acuitzio and keeps frozen for use throughout the year.

Upon returning to fieldwork in 2011 and 2012, I expanded the focus on food to ask more broadly about the things with which people travel, and in formal and informal interviews in both Acuitzio and Anchorage I asked what kinds of things people bring with them when they travel. Oscar's roosters are certainly one of the most exceptional nonhumans that travel. A traveling rooster, even in the form of an unhatched egg, also emphasizes the lengths that people will go to make a place for themselves, to feel they belong, to feel like themselves, as Oscar put it. For him, getting used to transnational life means having roosters around in Anchorage, the same stock that lives at his home in Acuitzio.

Roosters and other things that move trace the connections between locations. Through mobility, particular things, and especially food, become increasingly associated with particular places within the transnational social field. At the same time that material culture links locations within the transnational field, objects are wrapped up with the everyday economics of the transnational class. Traveling with things is therefore a strategic spatial practice and an important part of living across the continent.

*Eating Transnationally*

When my friend Rosa in Acuitzio makes *mole*, she carefully toasts each ingredient and mixes them together to make a thick brown sweetly spicy-bitter paste. Each time I travel to Acuitzio I purchase a bag to take home, frozen and packed in double plastic bags so that it will not leak in my suitcase. As soon as I get home from the airport, I put it into the freezer. Many of the Acuitzences I have met over the last decade also purchase *mole* in Acuitzio to take with them to Anchorage.

People travel from Acuitzio to Alaska carrying not only *mole* and bread but also such things as cheese, candy, and dried and crushed chiles. For the most part, these are foods that travel well and are permitted to travel across international borders. They are also foods that have the right flavor since they are prepared and purchased in Mexico, or they may be foods that are not available in Anchorage, or they may be much cheaper, fresher, and of higher quality in Mexico. The very first time I was invited over to Juana and Luis Bravo's home in Anchorage in 2005, it was for a dinner party that was attended by others from Acuitzio, Ana and Miguel, Ivonne and Fernando, all of their children, and my thesis supervisor and his wife. I wrote in my field notes:

> We had *mole* from Acuitzio—Maria and Ivonne each had a bit left and they mixed it together. We had chicken with *mole*, rice, beans, salsa, cheese (cheese also from Acuitzio) and tortillas. For dessert we had flan from Costco that Fernando himself actually made at work. Ana talked about how she and her family just got back from Acuitzio and they brought the cheese we had, and I guess they brought back bread and some other things—eight suitcases worth! She says she loves the bread from a woman named Mercedes—it's homemade and she said she especially loves the *conchas*. Her parents live on the last street in town and I understand the bakery is near there.

As I continued my fieldwork, I learned that many Acuitzences travel with food. I accompanied Juana to a small stand in the plaza in Acuitzio to purchase *pinole* to take home, and I helped Alina package *carnitas* and *uchepos* at her house in Acuitzio for travel to the United States. I went to the market with Vero and Sophia to purchase candy. I went shopping for my own favorite foods to take home and was given other foodstuffs as gifts. All of it was packed into suitcases and carried north. Ivonne, who is originally from southern California, and Fernando, who was born and raised in Acuitzio before leaving to work in the United States as a young man, talked about the foods they bring with them when I interviewed them in 2005. "What foods do you usually bring with you?" I asked them, as we sat together at their kitchen table.

Ivonne started out, "We always bring bread, cheese . . ."

Fernando piped up, "*Mole*."

And Ivonne continued the list, ". . . cheese, powdered *mole*. Uh, we bring *chile perón*. It's a yellow chile, small; they also call it *chile manzano*. Sometimes you can find them in Alaska, but you can't find them regularly. Anyway, we bring those, we bring foods that the family [in Acuitzio] makes for us, and my mother-in-law always makes tamales before we go. We bring a lot of tamales."

"How do you bring all of that food," I asked. "In suitcases?"

"We put them in a Rubbermaid container. Because if we don't, they [the airline baggage handlers] throw them and break some of the things," Ivonne said.

Women are much more likely to say that they travel with food, but men bring food with them too. Consider Eduardo, for instance, whom I interviewed in Acuitzio. He talked about bringing bread from Acuitzio to share with his friends in Alaska:

"My friends in Alaska really like the bread, the bread from here [Acuitzio]. I brought them each a piece or two or three. I took something like, seventy pieces of bread. I also took *corundas*, *uchepos*, cheese, and *mole*. And I brought sweets."

Eduardo pauses and describes the logistics of traveling with that much food, "I brought two suitcases full of . . . of bread and that." Laughing, he continues, "They [the airline] didn't charge me, I didn't pay anything extra. But yeah, the suitcases were really heavy. I had the *corundas* in my backpack. But it was so heavy, right?" He laughs again.

Eduardo shared the food he brought back with friends in Alaska. It is typical to invite friends and family over for a *comida* in Acuitzio, and in Alaska too. As Claudia explains: "The food does bring us comfort somehow . . . like if we're gonna make a party we always cook Mexican food, and it does bring family together. For me if I'm gonna make *menudo*, I call my dad and my mom, just come and eat it. And that is the way that we get together 'cause food brings us together."

Food therefore plays a role in building social relationships across the continent, building links to cooks in Acuitzio who prepare the food, to those who travel, and to those friends and family in Alaska who eat and share the food.

Ana, Ivonne, Antonio, and many dual-citizen Acuitzences like them travel with food even though the basic ingredients and foods necessary for Mexican cooking are available in Anchorage. *Lo básico*, the basics, can be purchased at specialty shops such as Mexico Lindo, Red Apple, and New Sagaya Market, as well as at large, mainstream grocery stores like Carrs-Safeway, Fred Meyer, and Costco. Taco Loco is a *tortillería* in town that makes both flour and corn tortillas. While things like tortillas, dried chiles, and Maseca brand flour now are available in Anchorage, they were not always. Even five years ago it was much more difficult to find the necessary ingredients, and I was told that people used to bring even more food than they do now. Anchorage is changing, and more products are available as different stores open. More of nearly everything, and not only Mexican ingredients, is available now, whereas it was not in the recent past. Specialized or unusual ingredients are still unavailable or are available only sporadically and often at a high price. And even when specific ingredients are available for a similar price, people still bring them from Mexico.

When I first analyzed foods that travel, I wrote about food and especially *flavor* in terms of a nostalgic link to a home community.[10] In other words, people travel with food to create a sense of home. I cited Lisa Law, who writes, "the absence of familiar material culture and its subtle evocations of home is surely one of the most profound dislocations of transnational migration."[11] I wrote that it was important for Acuitzences that I knew to travel with a piece of home to alleviate this dislocation, so much so that, as Alina's husband said, "when she came here her suitcase was all food, hardly any clothes!" I traced the contours of a material and an imaginative *foodscape* that linked Acuitzio and Anchorage. I quoted Gilberto, who works at a Mexican restaurant in Anchorage, who said that people bring food with them because "we want to bring a little piece of Mexico with us . . . even though a person has their U.S. citizenship, your heart is always in Mexico." I defined eating transnationally as "meals that connect places and the people in them or foods that depend on interconnectedness and mobility across space."[12] *Mole* is one instance of traveling food, one example of how food connects places (how *mole* literally moves, is packed in suitcases, and is taken from one place to another), and how food is connected to place (how it just is not the same if you buy it in Anchorage). *Mole* from Acuitzio has the "right" flavor. For example, Rosa's sister, Ana Bravo, said, "I bring my *mole* with me to Anchorage, *mole* prepared the way they prepare it in Mexico. And if I bought it here in Alaska? It's very different, the flavor."

So food, and especially the *flavor* of particular foods, is linked to place. To put it another way, attachment to place becomes legible through taste. This includes not only ingredients that give the right flavor to foods but recipes and cooking equipment also. Flavor, then, is shorthand for the relationship between local practices of cooking and individual expertise, as well as the place itself in terms of terrain and terroir. If it is not from there, it does not taste right.

Through mobility, material culture can become more evocative of place, more tied to place, more firmly *territorialized* in a location even as it moves. As I explain in chapter 4, as people become more tied to place as citizens or homeowners, they are able to be more mobile. In this case, as material culture travels, as it is deterritorialized from one location to move across the continent in a suitcase, it also becomes more firmly territorialized there. It becomes symbolic of that place, a signifier and material link to a location, a home, or a homeland. In a global and interconnected world, things that travel remain firmly emplaced even, or perhaps especially, as they move. This is the case for people who are fixed to place as citizens and homeowners in Acuitzio and Anchorage, and it is true for the food that they pack in their suitcase as well.

Because of my interest in food, I was often invited to cook and eat with friends and research contacts. Cooking and eating with dual-citizen migrants means a constant back-and-forth comparison of places, prices, and flavors. In Acuitzio, someone might say, "Oh, you can't get guavas that taste like this in Anchorage! And they would be much more expensive!" or, "I wanted to make a particular dish that I make in Alaska, but the ingredients weren't available in Morelia." In Anchorage, Juana and I got together with a friend to make tamales, but a Oaxacan style of tamale wrapped in banana leaves instead of corn husks. We had purchased some at the market on our last day in Mexico City, and months later we met at a friend's house to make them together in Anchorage. As we cooked, we reminisced about our time in Mexico and purchasing the tamales that day. Juana told me what was different and what was the same. For example, we used mozzarella cheese and only a small amount of cotija for flavor, since mozzarella is much cheaper in Anchorage. This is typical of my experience cooking with Acuitzences in Alaska, a constant back and forth discussion of how it would be done "there" (i.e., in Acuitzio or in Mexico in general) and how we are preparing the food that day a little differently because of what is available or affordable in Anchorage. Selective use of ingredients brought from Mexico with those available in Alaska brings back memories of another time and place, as well as always a commentary on either the flavor or the price.[13]

Food and ideas about food and eating travel regularly between Mexico and Alaska, connecting those places and the people in them. This traveling food becomes both a marker and a material reality of the transnational connection between places and the transnational lives that people live. Food is deeply symbolic of place, in this case of Acuitzio, and it is a place that travels alongside people in their suitcases and Rubbermaid containers on their way back to Anchorage. In this way people are sometimes "eating transnationally" in Anchorage in that they are eating food that is a "condition of cultural interconnectedness and mobility across space," anchored in particular places and homes, in this case Acuitzio and Anchorage.[14] While people are away from Acuitzio, food becomes even more important, and food from Mexico in general, and from Acuitzio specifically, becomes an important marker of identity, of home. As this food travels, it becomes even more fixed to particular places. *Mole* becomes *mole from Acuitzio*, cheese is cheese *from Acuitzio* and these items are traveled with, packaged in plastic and foil, frozen and saved to eat at family dinners or special occasions, and shared with social networks in Alaska.

The movement of food across the Mexican-U.S. border involves dealing with the regulations, bureaucracy, and legal force of the U.S. government, which uses policy to restrict the type of food items one is allow to bring to the country from abroad. People who travel without papers and who are considered "undocumented" in the United States are likely to say that they travel with nothing at all, only the clothes and personal items in their suitcase. Those who migrated to Anchorage from Acuitzio in the 1950s and 1960s said they brought nothing but their clothes and personal items with them. But dual-citizen or permanent resident Acuitzences often travel to Alaska with foods that are not permitted, fully realizing that these foods may still be taken away and disposed of by customs agents if their suitcase is inspected and the food item is deemed inadmissible. Serefina complained about this when I interviewed her in 2012: "Right now they're not letting you bring much. They add more requirements all the time."

"Do you think they are stricter at the border now?" I asked.

Serefina replied, "Yes, if you bring a cheese, they search you thoroughly. Because they think that you might have something hidden inside the cheese. You can't get mad about it because it's their rules, and it's for the best for everyone, or whatever."

Two arms of legislation and policy are responsible for the rules and regulations about the travel of food into the United States: the U.S. Department of Agriculture and U.S. Customs and Border Protection. Travel of food into the United States is thus seen in terms of protecting domestic agriculture, and especially the massive agro-industrial fruit, vegetable, and animal operations, from "foreign" pests, plagues, or fungi, to "protect community health, preserve the environment and prevent the introduction of devastating diseases to domestic plants and animals."[15] Even so, food products are permitted to travel into the United States in personal baggage. Which food products are permitted depends on where an individual is traveling from. Travelers are supposed to declare food products, or face fines and penalties up to $10,000. Regulations about which foods can be brought into the United States change over time, and determining exactly what is allowed means consulting an online database.[16] But people from Acuitzio are well versed in what is allowed and what is not. When traveling with foods that they know are not allowed, they perceive the biggest risk to be losing the food item, assuming that the border guards will throw it away if they find out about it.

For example, Alina shared, "I always bring food, even food that I shouldn't bring, Sarita!"

I laughed, "Like what?"

She lists off the kinds of items she has surreptitiously traveled with: "I brought some chiles, *chiles perones*. It's a chile, like smaller than an orange but yellow in color and really hot!" Pausing to explain, she continues, "And you know that we can't bring fresh things here [to the United States]. But I've brought some, Sarita! I've brought chiles, all the food, I've brought *carnitas*, meat, you can't bring pork. But they [U.S. Customs] didn't look through my bag! They didn't look through it! I also brought bread . . ."

"*Pan dulce?*" I ask.

Nodding her head, Alina says, "Yes, *pan dulce*. What else have I brought? The *cazo* [saucepan]. Well, but it isn't an ingredient. But the saucepan I use to make *atole*, I brought." Gesturing around the kitchen, she continues, "The saucepan, these dried chiles, the ones I have here for making *mole*." In addition to food, copper *cazuelas*, tamale steaming pots, *comales*, and clay pots are some of the food-related things that people bring. Clay pots, used for cooking beans in Mexico, are said to give a special and delicious flavor to them. It is not just about where the beans are grown but how they are prepared, and even what cookware is used to prepare them, that gives them the right flavor.

Antonio, who brought food to Alaska to share with friends, described regulations and the ways to get around them: "Chorizo, they won't let you pass with. Nor chiles that have seeds. We've brought chiles with us but in vinegar. We make it with those yellow ones, the *manzanos*. We put them in just a little bit of vinegar so that it won't spill. If it spilled in the airport opening the bags, there would be vinegar everywhere! And all the way to Alaska!" He laughs and shakes his head.

Fresh or dried chile peppers are not allowed to travel across the border into the United States, so people often find a way to bring them that is permitted by the rules and regulations of the state. With chiles, for example, people might put them in vinegar, like Antonio did, so that they are permitted through customs even though this changes the flavor. Or they pack them in their suitcases and take their chances. Food may also be purchased or sent from elsewhere in the United States. California, for example, is "just like Mexico," according to Alina. Ingredients are available at a similar price in California as in Michoacán. Alina's daughter, Claudia, told me that her aunt from California often sends her guavas or other things in the mail. She laughed as she told me about it, "I wonder what the mail man must have thought delivering such a fragrant package to the house!"

On the other hand, I have never heard anyone talk about foods that are not allowed to enter Mexico. That said, people are much less likely to travel with food on trips from Alaska to Mexico. The one exception is smoked salmon: caught, smoked, and purchased in Alaska and brought to Mexico to share with friends and family there. I think people travel with salmon because it is profoundly linked to the Pacific Northwest and Alaska: salmon is a fish that lives only in a certain area, has been a traditional source of food for local Indigenous peoples for millennia, and has been one of the major drivers of the Alaska economy, along with resource extraction and tourism.[17] Salmon is often marketed as "Alaska salmon" specifically, or as hyperlocal "Copper River salmon" in restaurants or grocery stores. Some Acuitzences in Alaska enthusiastically participate in salmon fishing, dip netting on the Kenai River to stock their freezers with fish.

Dual-citizen migrant-immigrants from Acuitzio are able to travel regularly across the border, and many bring food with them. This food has the right *flavor;* it is linked to their home communities and is carefully packaged in plastic and foil, in suitcases and plastic containers, portioned out for meals in Anchorage. On trips back to Acuitzio, Acuitzences replenish their supply of bread, cheese, *mole,* candy, and other goods, or they ask friends or family members who travel there to bring things for them.[18]

*What's in Your Suitcase?*

Food, then, typically travels one way: from Mexico to Alaska. However, people travel with other things in both directions. These objects are similarly everyday items: makeup, home decorations, photographs, souvenirs, or clothing for family members. Through mobility, such objects, like food, become representative of place. Much like souvenirs, these things link people and places, marking and reproducing relationships between people in Anchorage and Acuitzio. In Anchorage, many Acuitzences decorate their homes with arts and crafts brought from Mexico or images of Acuitzio. For example, one woman commissioned a painter in Acuitzio to paint a scene of the street just outside of her mother-in-law's house in Acuitzio, where he grew up. They hung it on a stairwell so that when he was leaving the house, it was exactly same view and perspective that he has when leaving his childhood home in Acuitzio.[19] Another family also owns paintings of street scenes in Acuitzio by the same painter, displayed prominently in their home in Anchorage. Others have photographs or calendars hanging up that feature Acuitzio.

In Acuitzio, on the other hand, people have decorated their homes with posters and images of Alaska: Denali mountain, the Anchorage city skyline and its spectacular mountain backdrop, the northern lights, dog sleds, moose, bears, and so on. An ice cream shop owned by Juana Bravo's brother and sister-in-law had Alaska postcards framed and on display, icy scenes appropriate for a shop selling frozen treats. Other people had ulus, posters, and magnets on display in their homes. One day I said to Luis Bravo, "In your house in Mexico you have a lot of things from Alaska, like posters of Denali and Anchorage."

He replied, "We don't have those pictures on our walls here in Anchorage, because those things are located here. We have them in Mexico so people can see what [Alaska] is like. And have you noticed that here [in Anchorage] we have stuff from Mexico? *Y allá de aquí*, and there from here."

Another time, I asked his sister Gloria about the Alaska theme that she has used in decorating her home in Mexico: "Why do you take these things with moose and mountains and all of that to decorate your house with?"

She replied, "Well, because you plan to one day return to your country to live and remember all that was part of your life here in Alaska, right? And I like to bring things from Mexico to Anchorage, to decorate my house here. Like all these hearts that I have here, look, almost all of the decorations I have are from Mexico." She gestured to some ceramic decorations painted in a Mexican style, perhaps from Jalisco. "I have all of these little things from Mexico to remember with."

Claudia's home in Anchorage was also decorated with items from Mexico, especially the kitchen. As I wrote in my field notes: "In Claudia's kitchen there is a clock and some pots and other things hanging on the wall from Santa Clara del Cobre. She says that her kitchen is too small [in Anchorage], that in Mexico her grandpa ground corn so there were always lots of people in the kitchen there. She also has shelves with little miniature pots on them. She said that in Mexico her grandma has shelves all around her kitchen with little pots on them. Claudia said she wants to do that too." For Claudia, the idea of what a kitchen should look like is one that comes from her grandmother's kitchen in Mexico, and so do the pots and other decorations with which she adorns it.

Oscar, who brought his roosters with him to Alaska, also has some decorations from Mexico in his mobile home. When I asked him about them, he said, "To live this life you have to be in both places, so that when you're there, you try to remember here, so these things help you to remember. Or even just when friends or family come to your house, you can show them and explain: look, this is where I live. As you say, here I have only things from Mexico. And in Acuitzio, I have many things from Alaska."

Oscar and his rooster are also exceptional because it is usually women who emphasize the importance of traveling with things. Men often downplay their role in this, and many say that they don't bring anything. For example, when I interviewed Esteban and Laura, I asked them "What do you bring with you when you travel from Mexico to Alaska?"

Esteban said, "Nah, nothing."

Laura protested, "Yes, we bring things!"

He said, "Well she does, I don't." And they both cracked up laughing.

Esteban continued, "When we go to Mexico we just bring our clothes, and we leave some things there because we forget them. I got a hat that

I took to Mexico, and I left it there, and no one knows what happened to it! But from Mexico . . ."

Laura finished his sentence: "We always bring, we always bring things from there. *Always*. Food . . ."

Esteban cut in, "*Huaraches*."

Their son said, "This guitar."

Esteban said, as he gestured around the room in their brightly decorated home, "All of this. The painting, many things. The little house decoration above the kitchen door, the painting of Morelia."

"This photo is from Morelia too!" Laura said.

Gilberto and Mónica are another example. Gil says that he doesn't bring anything, and Mónica explains how the practice of traveling with things is gendered:

Gilberto said, "Sometimes people say, 'I bring things.' Well, I don't. No, no, no, I don't like it.

Mónica continued, "Well, that's a man. But a woman always brings a lot of things," she laughed, "lots of food, decorations."

Gilberto says, "It's going through Los Angeles and having to carry those damn suitcases, no, no, no, no!"

Mónica says, "But it's because you're a man."

Gil continues, "I never liked it. And for that reason I never bother my fellow Mexicans to bring me something when they travel. I just bring my bag."

Mónica concedes, "It's much easier [not to carry things]."

Gil agrees, "It's much easier [not to carry things]. Before, people came loaded with stuff because . . ."

Mónica finishes his sentence: "Because there weren't a lot of things here [in Anchorage]. But now there are lots of things here."

However, even though men said they did not bring anything, it often turns out that they did. For example, when I asked Jaime what he brought with him to Alaska, he said: "Nothing, only my clothing. That's all that I took, I didn't take anything else." Granted, it had been decades since he had gone to work in Alaska, but later in the interview he told me that he brought a *charro* suit with him to Anchorage in the 1960s.

People also travel back to Mexico with photographs that they took in Alaska. This is true across generations. Diego kept his photos in a souvenir photo album with an outline of the state of Alaska on the front, and other people I met in Acuitzio had similar photo albums containing collections of images taken in Alaska. These photographs say "I was there" and show friends and family what Alaska is like. Don Luis Bravo, for example, has a whole album of photographs of himself at work. Of course, most people go to Alaska for work, so it makes sense to take photos of their labor experience. The other kinds of photographs that people commonly have are photos of themselves with ice and snow in order to highlight the extreme weather conditions in Alaska. Don Luis and his son both have photos of themselves in the snow, Don Luis in front of a large snowdrift in the 1960s, and Luis Jr. pretending to take a bite out of a piece of ice from a frozen waterfall in the 1980s. Diego showed me a photo of himself in Barrow, Alaska, posing on the sea ice with his shirt off. Wearing only a tank top and smiling in spite of the cold. "Weren't you cold, Diego?" I asked.

He smiled and said, "Sure, but I look tough, don't I?"

These photographs and the kinds of souvenir items that people travel with are often stereotypical images that reinforce perception of Alaska as a frozen, wilderness land. For Acuitzences who have not been to Anchorage, Alaska is an exotic and distant place, and the image of the "Last Frontier" as an icy wilderness where people live in igloos persists even as the mobility of Acuitzences to Alaska disrupts these stereotypes.

Many of these items are brought as gifts for friends and family members in Acuitzio or Anchorage instead of sent by mail or courier, which is considered unreliable and expensive. People from Acuitzio bring items themselves when they travel, or ask friends and family to carry things for them.[20] These practices build and maintain social relationships within the transnational social field. At the same time, they also tie people to place. For example, souvenir items that say "Alaska" on them are given as gifts from a particular place. In Acuitzio I saw Juana Bravo give an acquaintance a fridge magnet that said "Alaska" across an image of polar bears frolicking in an icy landscape. When she gave it to the acquaintance, she said, "Here you go, *un recuerdo de mi*, something to remember me by!" The Alaska magnet is something to remember *Juana* by: she identifies herself with the place the magnet indexes, so that Alaska comes to represent her, her identity, what makes her "her."[21]

However, even though Juana and Luis identify themselves as Alaskan in some contexts, such as in the decorations in their home, or in a souvenir gift to a friend, the links between places, people, and things are uneven. One evening I went with Juana and Luis to Morelia. We took Luis's mother to an appointment and then spent the rest of the evening walking in the *centro histórico*, the historic downtown of Morelia. As we walked along the *portales* to one side of the plaza, I saw a teenager wearing a T-shirt that said "Alaska" with the outline of a bear. Juana pointed it out to us, "Look at that, Alaska!"

Luis said, "I don't like wearing a shirt that says Alaska here, so that everyone knows."

I said, "I know what you mean. I wouldn't like to wear one that says Canada either!"

Juana talked about her nephew who wears a sweater that they brought him from Alaska all the time: "it's *original de allí*, he always says."

I said, "Your nephew Adán is always wearing his hat too." Adán's hat has an eagle and the word "Alaska" emblazoned across it. I know they bought the hat and gave it to him as a gift on this trip. Adán is very interested in going to Alaska himself and often asks me about what it is like there and if it is easy to find work.

Juana said, "When we're here and people ask where we are from, I always say Michoacán, never Alaska." Of course, those who know her well know that she lives in Anchorage most of the year. But this complex dynamic of back-and-forth travel and transnational life is not emphasized as Juana moves around in the city, or goes to the beach, or meets people elsewhere in Mexico. Luis and Juana don't want to be branded as being from Alaska when they see themselves at home, in Mexico. But giving Alaska souvenir gifts to family and friends in Mexico creates and reinforces relationships between people who travel to and live in Alaska and those who live in Acuitzio. They link the people through representations of the places on fridge magnets and hats and photo albums and other souvenir items like that. And for Adán and others like him, it could represent some social capital to have a link to successful dual-citizen migrant-immigrant families in Alaska. He could potentially draw on those links to go to Alaska himself someday.

So people unevenly identify themselves with places, and they often do this through the things they choose to travel with, such as decorating their home in Acuitzio with pictures of Alaska or putting a bumper sticker on the back of their vehicle in Alaska that says "Acuitzio del Canje, Mich."[22]

Luis Bravo has not driven his vehicles between Acuitzio and Anchorage, but as discussed in chapter 2, some Acuitzences have. This is as true today as it was in the 1960s when Jaime was working in Alaska. Jaime told me that he still has a car and small camper from Alaska:

> I wanted to sell them [before I left Alaska], but I couldn't get much for it. So one of my bosses said, don't sell it for cheap, leave it with me and I'll sell it for a good price and send you the money. So I left it and came back to Mexico. Two years later, he told me there was a problem, the pipes froze and he couldn't sell it. It needed work. But he told me he's coming to Mexico. He said he'll use it along the way and leave it here with me. And he brought it and left it here.

"And you still have it?" I asked.

Jaime continued, "I still have it yes. It's old now, and I never take it out because I never registered it here. It used to be very difficult to legalize a car. Better to keep it hidden. *Tiene placas de Alaska*, it has Alaska plates."

In Acuitzio you can see license plates from all over the United States, but many other owners of vehicles with Alaska plates that I met in Mexico are particularly proud of their navy-blue-on-yellow plates, with the Alaska flag depicting the Big Dipper and North Star. For example, one young man I interviewed in Acuitzio had a shiny black SUV that he purchased in Alaska, and his cousin later drove it to Acuitzio for him. He kept the Alaska plates on it. I asked if people say anything to him about them when he drives it around, and he said, "People ask 'why those plates?'" He laughs. "*Desde allá, verdad?* They're all the way from there, right?"

In previous decades there was contentious opposition to out-migration in Mexico, reflected in bumper stickers on vehicles in Acuitzio in the

1980s that said *"Y no fui al Norte,"* I didn't go north, implying that the individual driving the truck did not have to migrate to the United States to earn the money to buy it.[23] Then, with the onset of the Mexican debt crisis in 1983 and the negative impact of NAFTA, many Acuitzences were back to a warm and uncritical embrace of migration as a strategy that continues unabated today.[24] Cars evoke attachment to place, social capital, and links to larger economic formations and regulatory regimes, and they also give insight into the kinds of everyday economics in which Acuitzences engage, as I describe further in the following section.

### North American Economics

So far in this chapter I have discussed material culture as tied to and evocative of particular places in the transnational social field. *Mole*, the way it is made in Acuitzio, is *of that place* in terms of ingredients, preparation, and, importantly, flavor. Souvenir magnets, home décor, and license plates evoke locations and represent a link between people and place. These objects remain territorialized and attached to place, even as they move. Or, as I argue, *especially* when they move. In this section, I want to introduce the idea of an "everyday economics" in which people engage as they move across the continent. This is a strategic spatial practice, and one way in which the transnational class uses the border to make a living and make a life. Transnational Acuitzences frequently compare prices in Alaska and Michoacán. Indeed, conversations about food in the transnational social field focus on not only flavor but also *price*, two dimensions that vary across the continent.

For example, when I arrived in Acuitzio in 2011, I was unaware that my good friend Alina and her youngest daughter were in Acuitzio too. I walked to her house in the *colonía*, and she invited me to stay with her and go on day trips in the region with them. One of these was a day at a nearby *balneario*, or water park. I packed my swimsuit and met Alina at the house of her mother, who was preparing a meal for us to eat before leaving. Alina and I also walked down the street to the *tianguis*, the open-air market held on weekends. Alina gestured at the price of different fruits and vegetables, such as avocadoes and guavas, and said, "These would cost so much more over there, right, Sarita? And they wouldn't taste as good either!" I agreed and told her of the time I bought guavas in Vancouver but ended up throwing them away. Although they smelled nice, they were inedible. She followed up with a similar story from Alaska. Another time, driving along the highway with her, we saw boxes of avocadoes for sale. "Sarita, *mira*! For that price you would only be able to buy one avocado in Alaska. And here you can buy a whole box!"

Such comparisons extend beyond food and flavor. For instance, in the days leading up to Sophia's quinceañera, Sophia and Vero had their nails manicured. I had complemented them on their long sequined gel-filled nails, and this began a conversation about price. Sophia said, "One thing that's good about Acuitzio is that everything is cheaper." As another example she mentioned the false eyelashes she had applied that morning. They were free because the esthetician wanted to practice the technique, but in the United States they would cost about $100. Moreover, getting your nails done in Anchorage costs about $50, whereas in Acuitzio it costs about 200 pesos (approximately $15 at the time).

I said, "Yes, it's especially good if you have U.S. dollars, or Canadian." I continued, "Maybe not Canadian because when I went to the *casa de cambio*, they were giving me a lower rate, even though the Canadian dollar is higher than the U.S. one right now." I said I thought it was because it is less common, and maybe they do not want to have Canadian dollars around that no one will buy, so they give a lower rate.

She said, "I never thought of that!" and continued, "It's more expensive in Canada, isn't it?" She had seen prices on books and other products, and the Canadian prices were higher. Comparing prices and exchange rates across the continent is not usually a topic of conversation for teenagers. However, young people like Sophia, well acquainted with travel across the border and socialized into a world where exchange rates matter to the lives and livelihoods of themselves and their close family members, compare and contrast prices too. On a trip to Morelia with Sophia's parents, Juana and Luis, we purchased gazpachos. Gazpacho in Morelia is made of chopped mango, pineapple, jícama, and onion topped with cheese, ground chile, salt, and lemon juice. All of this is served in a plastic cup, with a fork to eat it with. It is delicious.

As we wandered the streets enjoying our gazpachos, Luis said, "They don't have these in Canada, right?"

I replied, "No, unfortunately. Maybe I could make one, but it wouldn't be as good."

"Is there jícama there?" Luis asked. When I replied yes, he said, "But it's very expensive, right?" Again, our conversation brings together price and flavor as key terms of comparison across the continent.

More than talk, people also travel with specific objects based on this continental accounting. For example, Acuitzences who work in Alaska often said that they give family members clothing as gifts and explain that this is because clothing is expensive in Mexico, relative to the cost in Alaska. Juana and Claudia both pay attention to when clothing is on sale in Anchorage so that they can purchase items in Alaska stores at very discounted prices to take to Mexico. Serefina does too: "What I bring for people is clothing because clothes are much cheaper here in Anchorage than there. Brand name and everything. You go to the stores, and when they have a sale, you can get a huge bag for $50 to bring clothes as gifts for seven or eight people. In Mexico, if you're going to buy one blouse, it costs the equivalent of $50, or maybe $25."

I said, "Yes, if you earn dollars it doesn't seem so expensive. But if you earn pesos, *pues ay*. It's a lot!"

"*Es mucho!*" she agreed and continued, "When I go to Mexico, I'm surprised. Really, I'm surprised by how people are able to live there. The salaries are so low, but food is so expensive, and clothing is too."

"Yes and here it's a rich country, with lots of money, but everything is cheaper." I offered.

Serefina said, "In Mexico you almost never encounter cheap clothing. The prices in Mexico, at the same stores, are the same. It costs the same as here. If you go to Wal-Mart, Costco, go and compare prices. Sometimes things are more expensive in Mexico than here."

Such conversations about prices of consumer goods in Mexico as compared to the United States were common throughout my fieldwork. The price of things and the currency used to purchase them are considerations that drive understandings of Acuitzio and Anchorage as places, Mexico and the United States as nations, and the kinds of material goods that people travel with.[25]

Sometimes it seemed obvious that an item had traveled between Mexico and Alaska, but the route of travel and the social form that led to its travel were less clear. For example, as I explained earlier in this chapter, my friend Adán in Acuitzio has extended family in Alaska. He really wanted to go to Alaska to work himself and took interest in my research as a result. One day he was wearing a T-shirt that had a picture of a moose with "Alaska" screen-printed underneath. I knew he had relatives who worked in Anchorage, and that they had previously brought him a hat with an eagle flying over a mountain and the word "Alaska" stitched on it. He wore the hat often, and I assumed they had brought him the T-shirt as well. However, when I asked him about it, he said that he had actually gotten the shirt from the secondhand clothing store that he and his wife own in Acuitzio. Indeed, that shirt followed a much different path to Mexico, likely first donated as secondhand clothing somewhere in the United States, then sold as part of a large pallet of used clothing, brought to Mexico for resale, and finally ending up at Adán's store.

This, then, relates to the third aspect of the everyday economics in which people engage between Anchorage and Acuitzio: building a livelihood. Beyond talking about prices and traveling with things, some people also make a living across the U.S.-Mexican border. A business like Adán's depends on the inequality of the border and different but related consumer societies for a pallet of used clothing to be worth money in Mexico. I began to describe this process in the previous chapter, but here I draw attention to the fact that sometimes building a livelihood across the border can mean traveling with things.

Iván and Claudia moved back to Mexico from Anchorage in 2012. They met in Acuitzio, after Claudia had spent many years living in Anchorage with her family, and Iván had moved back to Acuitzio after living and working in California. As they prepared for their move south, Claudia went to stores all over Anchorage purchasing clothing and consumer goods on sale. She told me that these things sold for a very good price in Mexico, especially because they are name brand. For example, an Abercrombie and Fitch sweater that she purchased on sale in Anchorage will fetch a higher price in Mexico. She said, "At least this way we will have something to sell when we first get there." So when they moved to Mexico, not only did they travel with their automobiles, personal possessions, and pets, but they also traveled with goods *to sell* upon arrival. Over the years I have heard many different ideas about how it might be possible to make a bit of extra money taking things from Anchorage to Acuitzio to sell.

Oscar, on the other hand, talked about a plan that he had to manufacture and sell a specific design of rooster cages. He has the equipment to make them in Acuitzio, and he was thinking of establishing a factory to make them in the United States as well, since "that kind of cage isn't available here." I had asked him what kinds of things he brings with him when he travels between Alaska and Acuitzio. His response illustrates that traveling with things is not only about building a way of life but potentially a livelihood too.

*Fijate*, always when I go to Acuitzio, I have to bring clothing for the family, right? And I bring many things also that I need for my work, for my hatchery. . . . I buy tools and medicine to help my animals and take them to Mexico. *Muchas cosas que me han servido muchisissimo.* But at the same time, even though there are many things here in the United States that have helped me with my hatchery, there are many things that the United States doesn't have. That's what I wanted to do. I was thinking if the economy continues to be poor in Mexico, I would do that. I have a workshop, I manufacture cages for the *gallos*. I had a business doing that in Mexico, but because of the economy my business didn't succeed. I had to close it and continue coming here to work.

"But you still have everything to make the cages, right?" I asked. Oscar continued:

I have all of the machines, so what I was thinking if things continue to go really poorly in Mexico, I was thinking about opening my shop and moving to another state, California, maybe. Oregon, or Washington. Move and *echar andarme*, make my cages because they don't make this kind of animal cage here in the United States. And right now since there are loans for small businesses, and like I said this kind of cage isn't available and like I said, if I see the economy in Acuitzio continuing to go downhill, I want to put my company here, in the U.S.

This is the kind of cross-border entrepreneurial strategy that allows people like Oscar to build a livelihood across the continent. It depends on dual citizenship or similar status that allows people to travel across borders. And in the cases of Claudia and Oscar, it explicitly includes traveling with things—clothes for resale and machines to make cages—from one nation-state to another.

### All the Way to Alaska

One evening in the plaza in Acuitzio on my first research trip there in 2005 I met a woman selling bread. She stood behind a table with colorful bread stacked up on a flowered tablecloth. I asked her about her bakery, about the bread that she makes, and whether or not she knows anyone in Alaska. As I wrote in my field notes that day, "She said that the bread with the *atole* in the middle is the most popular. A customer can call her and she'll make the bread and pack it up so it'll be ready when people leave to go back to wherever they work in the U.S. She said that her bread has been all the way to Alaska."

Acuitzences who move between Anchorage and Acuitzio often travel with things. These things connect Acuitzences with their home community while away and are important for building a transnational way of life that extends across the continent. Mobile objects are a marker and material reality of transnational life in that they trace the connections between locations and facilitate a way of life across the continent. At the same time that material culture links locations within the transnational field and is an important part of the everyday life of those who live it, I also show how objects are wrapped up with the everyday economics of the transnational class. Traveling with things is a strategic spatial practice, not only part of creating a way of life that extends across the continent but potentially building a livelihood too.

As a spatial practice that indicates a transnational class formation, traveling with things is one way that people can use the border to get ahead. People can purchase consumer goods for a lower relative price in the United States and bring them to Mexico. However, this reinforces socioeconomic inequalities within Acuitzio, since only those with dual citizenship or U.S. residency would be able to travel so freely and feel confident enough to travel with a lot of stuff. Finally, things that move can also contribute to building a livelihood, whether selling bread in Acuitzio to those who travel to the United States or traveling with consumer goods from Alaska to sell in Mexico. Rather than understanding Alaska and Mexico as bounded and separate from one another, spatial strategies such as traveling with things emphasize the contingent, entangled, and interconnected nature of northern spaces and extend the U.S.-Mexican borderlands to the "Last Frontier."

In the next chapter I move on to discuss territorialization at the level of the Mexican community in Anchorage and how people create a collective sense of belonging there. The Mexican consulate in Alaska, the dance group Xochiquetzal-Tiqun, restaurants such as Mexico in Alaska, and the Club de Migrantes de Acuitzio del Canje en Alaska are some of the organizations that produce a Mexican Alaska through images and collective action.

# 6 "It Freezes the People Together"

PRODUCING A MEXICAN ALASKA

My friend Edgar was working for the *ayuntamiento*, or municipal council, in Acuitzio when I was there for fieldwork in the summer of 2011. He suggested that I meet with Lola, who was the councilor of migrant issues for the municipality. Edgar gave me her cell phone number, and by text message we arranged a time to meet at the Palacio Municipal. Located at the south end of the plaza, the building features a clock tower. Not only is it visible from many locations in town due to its height, but it can also be heard ringing on the hour and half hour and playing songs at certain times of day. When I arrived, I asked for Lola and went upstairs where the *regidores* have their offices. Lola stood up to greet me, and we shook hands before sitting down to talk.

Lola was professionally dressed in crisp pants and a blazer with a nice blouse underneath, her dark hair curled and left down. She asked me about my project, and I told her that I was interested in migration between Acuitzio and Alaska, and how people are often surprised to hear there are Mexicans in Alaska at all. "To counteract that idea," I said, "I want to write a history of mobility between Acuitzio and Anchorage."

"*Casi todo Acuitzio vive allá!*" she said. "Almost all of Acuitzio lives there!"

Lola herself lives and works across the continent and is active in local politics and cultural activities in both Anchorage and Acuitzio. We met for a recorded interview on another day, this time on a bench outside the Palacio Municipal. Lola told me that she lived in Anchorage with her husband for ten years, but she moved back in 2001 while he continued to go back and forth between Anchorage, where he worked at a restaurant, and Acuitzio, where the couple operates another small restaurant. Lola moved back to Anchorage to open a restaurant with her husband in 2013 and then returned to Mexico the following year. As I write, she is working in Alaska again, this time in the health care field. Each time she moved to Anchorage, her sons stayed in Mexico to continue their studies.[1] In both Anchorage and Acuitzio she has been very involved with the Club de Migrantes de Acuitzio del Canje en Alaska (the Acuitzio del Canje Migrant Club in Alaska). In Anchorage she also helped to start a dance group at Our Lady of Guadalupe Church.

Lola said that groups such as the Migrant Club and the dance group help to "bring the community together in Alaska." She paused and then said, "Maybe for Alaska you could say *se congela la gente*, it freezes the people together." She laughed and clarified, "Yes, *se congela la gente*, because it's so cold there and life can be difficult, so we need to freeze the people together."

In this chapter I analyze the organizations and groups that "freeze the people together" in Anchorage, such as the Mexican consulate, the dance and culture group Xochiquetzal-Tiqun, restaurants such as Mexico in Alaska, and the Migrant Club. Lola's phrase is funny and evokes a sense of bonding in a very cold place. It also evokes the sense of a frozen or fixed cultural identity, a process that Lila Abu-Lughod argued against in her article "Writing against Culture."[2] Although "freezing the people together" could imply a process that creates something rigid and static, the examples I discuss in this chapter show a community in action. In particular, I explore how each of these groups produce representations of a "Mexican Alaska." Mexican Alaska is a "transnational conjectural space" where Alaska is practically and materially implicated in Mexico and could be said to belong meaningfully to Latin America.[3] It is a spatial formation produced through everyday social relations and meaningful practices of racialized labor migration, capitalist enterprises, and the U.S. nation-state.[4] Local and translocal connections made by individuals between the hometowns of Acuitzio and Anchorage are wrapped up with national and transnational narratives of Mexico and the United States. For example, when Alaska is conceptualized as exceptionally separate and a geographically distant wilderness frontier, people from Mexico appear out of place. People of Mexican background in

Anchorage, including but not only people from Acuitzio, produce their own spatial categories and claims in order to make Alaska into a place of their own. These groups work to stabilize, visualize, and mark a particular kind of place in an attempt to root collective identity in transnational space. By raising money among Acuitzences in Alaska for community projects in Acuitzio, dancing Mexican *baile folklórico*, or folk dancing, in traditional regional dress in Anchorage, visually placing "Mexico in Alaska" at a restaurant, and extending the influence of the Mexican state to Anchorage, these groups intervene in the usual representations of both Alaska and Mexico to produce transnational representations of space.

The dance group Xochiquetzal-Tiqun and the Mexico in Alaska restaurant bring Mexico and Alaska into the same frame, while the Migrant Club, the Mexican consulate in Alaska, and Xochiquetzal-Tiqun all create new connections between Mexico and Alaska. Other examples that are not discussed here include the television program *Latinos en Alaska*, Our Lady of Guadalupe Parish in Anchorage, and the (now defunct) Pan-American Club. All of these groups "freeze the people together" and produce representations of a Mexican Alaska through image and collective action. They bring Mexico and Alaska together into new representations of space, re-categorizing the spatial organization of North America and expanding the boundaries of Latin America northward.[5]

*Club de Migrantes de Acuitzio del Canje en Alaska*

I interviewed Leonardo, the soft-spoken president of the Club de Migrantes de Acuitzio del Canje en Alaska (Migrant Club), in Anchorage in 2011. He told me that he had wanted to go to Alaska since he was a child and finally went there in 1989 to work in a fish-processing camp after working in California, Oregon, and Washington State for many years. After a difficult summer working in Chignik at a fish plant, he decided to stay in Anchorage, where he started out washing dishes in a restaurant before getting a job in the construction industry. When I interviewed him, he had been working in construction in Alaska for nineteen years, where his children had been born and raised.

Leonardo and Lola, as friends and colleagues who have both lived in Anchorage and Acuitzio, work together to administer the club: Leonardo in Anchorage, and Lola in Acuitzio. Leonardo said that Lola usually decides what they should do, based on who needs the most assistance.

I asked Lola how the club started when I interviewed her in Acuitzio in 2011. Lola replied, "The club? I was invited to participate in politics in 2007, for el PAN, the Partido Acción Nacional [the conservative party then ruling Mexico under President Calderón]. Our party didn't win the municipal presidency, but we ended up in second place, and two councilors from PAN got in. I was the second one, and they assigned me to be the councilor of migrant issues for the municipality. There had never been a councilor of migrant issues for Acuitzio. I am the first one, and a woman." Lola went one, as automobiles continued to rumble around the plaza and onto Riva Palacio, "So I started to see what I could do."

In 2008, the year she was elected, Lola went to Alaska and, while there, met with Leonardo and another member of the club. Lola continued, "I contacted them, and we decided to form a Migrant Club of Acuitzences in Alaska. With a few members we started to work together. I proposed that we organize a migrant fair in Acuitzio and, as part of that, donate something for the community of Acuitzio." Lola believes that migrants and their families going to the United States to earn money and build a better life for themselves should also use the benefits of migration (financial and otherwise) to improve their hometowns, and the Migrant Club is one way to do this. She said, "That is the function of the migrant, and of the Migrant Clubs, to improve your municipality in Mexico." Lola explains further, "Part of the reason for doing that is because when people come back to Acuitzio from U.S. cities, we don't have all of the things they have become accustomed to there. So, they should improve the town." Along those lines, the Migrant Club has raised funds in Anchorage for a variety of projects intended to improve some aspect of life in Acuitzio. This creates social bonding among Acuitzences in Anchorage, but it also links people back to their town and helps to make it a desirable place to which Acuitzences will want to return.

In 2008, which was also the first year of Lola's term as councilor of migrant issues in Acuitzio, Lola said that she proposed that the Migrant Club donate jackets to the poorest communities in the municipality of Acuitzio. "The others in the club thought that was a good idea, and we got together, or as they say, *de coperacha*."[6] Lola laughed. The club chose a poor community in the mountains called El Tzintzun, and they chose jackets as an appropriate item to donate because, Lola said, "Alaska is cold, and therefore has a lot of jackets, and in El Tzintzun it gets really cold as well." Restaurants in Anchorage owned by Acuitzences collaborated to make *carnitas*, "which is a typical food for special events in Acuitzio," Lola pointed out, "and they sold them at the church in Anchorage after mass."[7] All of the profits from the fund-raiser went to the purchase of one hundred jackets to send to people in El Tzintzun. Although sending jackets from one cold place to another made sense, the logistics proved difficult: because Alaska is so far away it would be expensive to send the jackets. Another problem, according to Lola, was that people do not trust authority because of state corruption throughout Mexico. She said this mistrust is found not only among Acuitzences in Alaska but among Acuitzences everywhere in the United States. So they made the donation of jackets in December when many migrants came back to town for the season so that they could see for themselves that the money was used as intended. She said, "It's really important that the people see what they give and how much they give so that people can have faith in our organization." In fact, Leonardo went to Acuitzio himself to hand out the jackets, and he invited other people along to observe how it went. Leonardo said, "They saw that all the money went where it was supposed to, so people began to trust me." Lola explained, "At the first migrant fair they gave out one hundred jackets to the community of El Tzintzun and to neighboring communities of El Varal y La Peñita, which experience the coldest temperatures in the region. When people who live in Alaska who are from Acuitzio saw that we are working to do what we promised to do, they were encouraged by it. After that, more people registered in the club."

In 2008 the group also registered in the 3x1 Program for a project to improve the Chapel of the Señor de la Expiración in Páramo and build a fence and washrooms at the site.[8] The Señor de la Expiración is celebrated each year in Páramo in May and is considered one of the oldest ceremonial rituals of the community. The following year, 2009, the Migrant Club in Anchorage decided to donate blankets to people in the village of Páramo, also located at higher elevation than the town of Acuitzio del Canje. They again fund-raised by soliciting donations and selling *carnitas* in Anchorage and donated one hundred blankets to people in Páramo and another twenty-five blankets to elderly people in Acuitzio. Again, Leonardo went to Acuitzio and encouraged observers to join him to make the presentation of the blankets. In 2009 they also raised money to purchase wireless microphones to use in the town's annual Holy Week procession. The club has sent equipment to the dance group Ballet Folklórico Tzintzuni Uarhari. They also donated funds to another dance group, Danzantes Tradicionales de Acuitzio, and to a band called Acuitzence to help them attend a dance competition in Veracruz.[9]

For Lola, the activities of the Migrant Club help young people in both Acuitzio and Alaska maintain their culture. She said, "It helps the young people who are growing up here in Acuitzio, so that they don't lose their culture. And that was also one of the intentions I had when I organized the dance group in Alaska at the church." Lola pauses. "But it's very difficult. Especially when no one has time. *Viven trabajando*, everyone lives to work in Alaska. And young people are interested in other things."

Indeed, the Migrant Club chooses activities that either help those less fortunate in the hometown, or that help ensure that traditional events and fiestas in Acuitzio continue, such as the Fiesta del Señor de la Expiración, the Semana Santa or Holy Week procession, and the dance groups. Lola's concerns are similar in both Acuitzio and Anchorage: she worries about young people "losing their culture, their roots" and works to keep tradition alive both in the municipality and thousands of miles away in Anchorage.

Leonardo also organizes fund-raisers in Anchorage to help Mexican people in need in Alaska. I attended a fund-raiser organized for an Anchorage family who had lost everything in a house fire. The fund-raiser was held after Spanish mass in a small community hall attached to Our Lady of Guadalupe Church. Many Acuitzences attend Catholic services and special events at Our Lady of Guadalupe Church or at the cathedral downtown, and it is one of the few places in Anchorage where people from Acuitzio meet informally. Community events are usually announced after mass, and that day the announcer said, "Leonardo Aldama and some *compañeros* are raising funds for a family who lost everything in a fire. There will be a meal after mass, and it costs $8.00."

When I arrived in Anchorage after interviewing Lola in Acuitzio earlier in the summer, I hoped to attend Migrant Club meetings and events. I assumed they would meet regularly and have an organized structure. However, I soon learned that the club is organized informally, and this is something that is essential for its legitimacy, given the context of mistrust of organized authority described earlier.

César, a member of the Migrant Club, told me that everything the group does is informal, and almost nothing is written down. The club has a registered membership of about ten Acuitzences who participate regularly, but it draws on a larger group of approximately thirty members who participate in fund-raising events. An even larger group participates only occasionally. They do not have any formal affiliation with the town administration or state or federal governments. The organization is small, something that helps alleviate concerns about the money being spent inappropriately. They meet at their unofficial headquarters, a Mexican restaurant in Anchorage, "have a beer and talk, and that's it." Or as another club member put it, "we just get together when we need to." César said they could go to the consulate to formalize the organization, but they have not done so. They could take further advantage of the 3x1 Program and receive financial contributions from the Mexican federal government and the state of Michoacán, but they haven't bothered. This works for now. Keeping the club informal also means that undocumented Acuitzences in Alaska such as César feel more comfortable participating. Lola pointed out that Acuitzences living in Alaska without papers are afraid to formally register because they don't want to give out their information. However, Lola says, "they still participate. Or like, they contribute, but their names and information don't appear on the list."

The emphasis on keeping the club informal also illustrates how a mistrust of authorities is mirrored on both sides of the border. I have heard many people in both Acuitzio and Alaska complain about those in positions of political power or even in organized groups. For example, one man told me that he would rather give money to a group hosting a *jaripeo* or a *baile*, "something for the people to have fun," instead of contributing to the Migrant Club, where he feels there is more uncertainty about where the money goes. Indeed, many Acuitzences in Alaska choose not to participate in the Migrant Club due to the mistrust that extends throughout the transnational social field. Leonardo said, "I tell people that we can fix things, but many people don't believe in us even though we have tried to provide proof that the money has gone where it was promised. But the people that help us, they believe in us. Many people like what we're doing, and they understand that we are doing a good job."

But it is not only about mistrust. There is also disagreement among Acuitzences about what a migrant's hard-earned money should be used for. Leonardo especially seemed resentful about those who never contribute to the Migrant Club and to the collective benefit of the community in Acuitzio and Anchorage but instead flaunt their individual or family wealth. There is a disconnect between the function of the Migrant Club, which seeks to improve the community as a whole, and more individualistic migrant-immigrants who seek to improve life for themselves and close family members only. For Lola, Leonardo, and others in the Migrant Club, successful migrants in Anchorage should work to improve their hometowns and help those less fortunate. However, not everyone believes they have the responsibility to contribute their hard-earned money to the well-being of their hometown, and instead they use it for their own projects.

Lola said that she is also involved in coordinating activities with Migrant Clubs in Texas, California, and Chicago. She explained that Acuitzences are in charge of the clubs in all of the places with which she liaises. "But," Lola concluded, "*la fuente es de Alaska*, the main source is Alaska." These clubs not only "freeze the people together" within Anchorage and between Anchorage and Acuitzio; they also provide a map of the geography of Acuitzences in the United States and insight into what kinds of projects are considered important by some of those who live transnationally, namely making donations to those less fortunate in Acuitzio and in Alaska and ensuring that future generations know their culture and their roots in Mexico.

### *Performing Mexico: Xochiquetzal-Tiqun*

The Anchorage museum celebrates Hispanic Heritage Month with a day of special events in October,[10] and Xochiquetzal-Tiqun Mexican Folkloric Ballet of Alaska is always invited to perform. When I attended in 2011,

Xochiquetzal-Tiqun danced in the large atrium in the middle of the museum. On the stage young children, teenage girls, and adult women danced regional dances of Mexico, decked out in ribbons and lace. Their performance culminated in a dance to a song called "Cascabel," with everyone on stage.

After the performance the whole group moved to one of the galleries to take a photo underneath a large painting of Denali mountain by Alaskan painter Sydney Laurence. The effect was great—the large purple-blue mountain rises up behind the smiling dancers, dressed in ribbons and braids and brightly colored clothing. Parents and interested museum patrons snapped photos. I was one of them.

They have repeated this scene after other performances at the museum, and so this is only one of a series of similar photographs, marking the years of the group and their changes in front of the steady, solid, eternally snowy Denali. I think the group likes to play on the juxtaposition of their costumes in front of this huge painting. In fact, I think their consistency of photographing themselves in front of this particular painting at the museum visually represents the story they tell about themselves as a group—bringing Mexico and Alaska together.[11] This is how the group introduces itself on the Xochiquetzal-Tiqun website: "Our name comes from two cultures: Mexican and Athabascan. *Xochiquetzal* means 'Flower Feather' in the Nahuatl language spoken by the Aztecs and other native Mexican groups. *Tiqun* means 'Wolf' in the Athabascan Dena'ina language spoken by original inhabitants of this region in Alaska. We are based in Anchorage, Alaska. We got together in 2002 in an effort to honor and preserve our Mexican roots as well as to honor Alaska the place that opened its arms to us and where most of our children were born or raised."[12]

In interviews the codirectors of the group talked about how they chose the name. Ana Gutiérrez-Scholl said that they thought carefully about what they wanted the name of the group to reflect. "We chose to reflect something cultural, with the Aztec goddess Xochiquetzal, who is the Aztec goddess of women, flowers, feathers, and the arts." She continued, explaining what the other half of their name, Tiqun, represents: "The way that we saw it was that the wolf is a source of great strength in this climate, right? So we thought that the wolf was

FIG. 6. Xochiquetzal-Tiqun at the Anchorage Museum, 2011. Photo by author.

something really strong that could stand the weather here. Without offending the Athabascan people either, because they also have an important and grand culture." Together, "Xochiquetzal could represent the culture of the people, and Tiqun, the wolf, *la fortaleza humana*, the strength of humanity." The other director, Ana Del Real also talked about why it was important to them to choose a name for the group that draws on both places. For one, "our children are going to have the strength both from Mexico and from Alaska." As well, being far away from Mexico makes it important that she teaches her children where they are from. "Sometimes my children ask me where they are from, and I tell them, you are American because you were born in the United States, but your parents are Mexicans and your roots are Mexican. You are *Mexico-americano*."

In the photographs they take at the museum, in their name and the description of how they chose it, and at other times, such as the dance in the parking lot described in the introduction, Xochiquetzal-Tiqun puts stereotypical representations of both Mexico and Alaska within the same frame. These representations draw on wilderness and indigeneity, themes common to nation-building efforts in both Mexico and the United States.[13] Indigeneity has long been appropriated for nation-building in states across the Americas, relegating Indigenous peoples themselves to the past and justifying ongoing colonial schemes of modernization and assimilation.[14] By drawing their name from Mexican and Alaskan Indigenous cultures, Xochiquetzal-Tiqun explicitly builds on the association of the state and indigeneity for transnational nation-building. Mobilizing Aztec indigeneity as representing "Mexico" excludes or erases other forms of dance and culture, such as Afro-Mexicano dance, the unique dance and culture of local places like Acuitzio, or of contemporary Indigenous groups in Michoacán like the P'urhépecha.

Xochiquetzal-Tiqun thus continues a tradition of "mestizo nationalism" where "linguistic hybridization, aesthetic mixing, and cultural boundary crossing in Mexico and the Americas have coexisted with ethnoracial inequality and are bound up with it."[15] Even though the process of transnational nation building by groups such as Xochiquetzal-Tiqun produce a sense of nation across the boundaries of states, they draw on the same logics of nationalism used by the state. At the same time, their juxtaposition of Aztec with Athabascan also unsettles nation-state representations and re-categorizes space to diminish the sociospatial distance between Alaska and Mexico. They also produce new connections between these places and work to produce a sense of belonging for younger generations in both locations and to the transnational social formation as a whole.

Xochiquetzal-Tiqun has been active since 2002 when two dance teachers, Ana Del Real and Ana Gutiérrez-Scholl, and a small group of parents—all from Mexico—decided to form a group together. I met with Ana Gutiérrez-Scholl for an interview at a coffee shop one afternoon, and we talked about how the group began. She taught a bilingual computing for small businesses class at the YMCA: "It was the first time that I got to know a few Hispanic people, Mexican people, here in Alaska. And on our breaks, when we weren't studying, we talked about Mexico, and how we missed the folk customs and all of those things, no?" Along with two other women, one from Morelia, Michoacán, who still lives in Alaska, and another woman who has since moved back to Mexico, Ana and Ana started the group.[16]

From the beginning, and for more than a decade now, Xochiquetzal-Tiqun has worked to bring Mexican cultural practices, specifically regional dance, to Alaska both to help the adult members of the group deal with a sense of nostalgia for and distance from Mexico and to teach their children about Mexico. Soledad, who dances in the group herself and who has enrolled all of her children in it, told me that Xochiquetzal-Tiqun is important to her "so that my children never forget the culture, and more than anything that they like it, and see how there are such beautiful things in our country."

All of the parents involved with the group said that they primarily participated to ensure that their children would not lose their culture or their roots in Mexico. Women enjoy dancing with the group to socialize with each other in Spanish and set an example for the kids. By providing a space for participants to interact in Spanish and share knowledge and memories about hometowns in Mexico, the group actively recategorizes space, attempting to diminish the felt distance between where they are and where they are from. They also work to create roots for their children in Mexico, but they do this from Alaska.

Children may begin dancing with Xochiquetzal-Tiqun when they are as young as four years old, and they start by learning the regional dances of Jalisco. As teenagers, they take more advanced lessons, learning and performing dances from other regions. This parallels the activities of schoolchildren in Mexico, who learn regional dances at school. In Acuitzio, at the *clausura,* or end of school ceremonies, each year, schoolchildren dance for parents and others in attendance. Children participating in Xochiquetzal-Tiqun and children dancing in schools in Mexico are learning the same dances and the same affiliations between region and traditional dance. However, as Lola described earlier in the chapter, the need to preserve traditional culture is felt in Acuitzio as well as in other points in the transnational social field, including Alaska.

Although Xochiquetzal-Tiqun works to teach children about their "roots" in Mexico, the group also fits into a longer tradition of Mexican dance in the United States. Mexican communities have danced *folklórico* dances since at least the early 1900s when people raised in Mexico brought the knowledge and practice of regional dance to the United States. As in Alaska, these presentations were featured as part of Fiestas Patrias (Mexican national holiday celebrations) or other ethnic celebrations throughout Greater Mexico.[17] In the 1960s, *folklórico* dance flourished in the United States as part of the Chicano movement and its search for ways to reaffirm, promote, and preserve Mexican identity and express opposition to cultural assimilation and discriminatory practices. Xochiquetzal-Tiqun continues this tradition in Alaska, where it provides a "means through which Mexican culture could be recuperated and promoted."[18] Indeed, in other contexts as well, dance takes a key role in the formation of national identity, albeit from points outside of Mexico and within the United States.[19]

Xochiquetzal-Tiqun first began performing dances from Jalisco, the most well-known regional dances outside of Mexico. I asked Ana Gutiérrez how they decided what dances to perform, and she responded, "In general the most well-known Mexican dance in the whole world are the dances from Jalisco. So, Jalisco."

"You have to do it!" I said.

"Yes, Sarita, we have to do it," she laughed. "And right away, right? And after Jalisco, we started to think, okay, which are the states or regions that are well known that we should emphasize? So Veracruz followed, which is also well known and has Caribbean and African roots and all of that. Ana and I always think a lot about it, and I investigate what is happening culturally and everything folklore."

She explained that they have also worked directly with the Secretariat of Public Education in Mexico, and they have brought three teachers from Mexico to Alaska to teach dance, one from Puebla, one from Zacatecas, and one from Durango. The first teacher they brought was focused on teaching Mexican arts and crafts and Mexican readings to the children and the parents. One of the teachers from Mexico also taught the group a *cuadro de Zacatecas* that they still perform. After that, they brought another dance teacher, who has more than twenty years of experience teaching dance in Mexico, to develop a *cuadro Veracruzano* for the group to dance. They also invited a teacher from Mexico to teach dances from Tierra Caliente, Durango, and Baja California Norte y Sur. I was fortunate to learn some of these dances from Ana and the group. They continue to fund-raise to invite teachers from Mexico to teach dances to the group.

By inviting dance teachers to visit Anchorage from very different parts of Mexico, the group has been able to spatially expand their repertoire to cover other regions from Mexico in their performances in Anchorage. As well, bringing teachers from Mexico and working with the Mexican government also produces a connection between dance schools on both sides of the border and between Xochiquetzal-Tiqun and the Mexican state. Xochiquetzal-Tiqun has never invited a dance teacher to Alaska from elsewhere in the United States. To audiences in Anchorage, the group presents Mexican culture writ large through regional dance.

Ana Gutiérrez also talked at length about finding a balance between tradition and change within the dances that the group performs. For Ana, Mexico and its cultural forms are best understood in terms of their connections. Rather than emphasizing the timelessness of tradition, Ana Gutiérrez would point out the multiple influences from Europe and Indigenous America on "traditional" Mexican dance forms. How fitting, then, that Xochiquetzal-Tiqun's performances in Alaska continue to re-categorize space, and produce Alaska through connection as well. In our interview in Anchorage, Ana explained her ideas about how culture changes and the accommodations that have to be made in Alaska by Xochiquetzal-Tiqun specifically. She said they would really like to perform Las Tejuanas, which is a dance from the state of Oaxaca, in southern Mexico. That style of dance can be danced to a number of songs that, Ana says, "are not very well known, but are very beautiful." The clothing that should be worn to perform Las Tejuanas is an embroidered *huipil* and skirt. But the group does not have the correct clothing, and as Ana says, "we shouldn't learn and dance something with a different dress." The issue of authenticity is one of the principal distinctive features of this dance genre and has yielded a variety of creative possibilities in terms of "what counts" as a valid and authentic connection to the folk practices of *mexicanos*.[20] Ana's point about how culture changes by making do shapes the activities of Xochiquetzal-Tiqun and their re-categorization of space in Alaska.

When Soledad said that Xochiquetzal-Tiqun was important so that her children would never forget Mexican culture, she also talked about the importance of sharing that culture with others. "Because if we don't help to do that, well, other people won't know about the beautiful culture that Mexico has. *La cultura tan bonita que tiene Mexico, no?*" As Ana de Real said, "Before our group started, there was nothing that represented Mexico culturally in Alaska." Now the group actively builds connections within Anchorage and performs at many public events throughout the year. Juana Bravo emphasized that performances by the group are particularly well received by Anglo-Americans who attend performances: "More than anything, it's about sharing a little bit of our culture. You saw how when Xochiquetzal-Tiqun came on stage, people whistled and shouted. And those were Americans! It's not just our people. And it's really nice to see that."

During my fieldwork in 2011–12, the group performed at Mexican Independence Day, Hispanic Heritage Month Family Day at the Anchorage Museum, the Xochiquetzal-Tiqun Ninth Anniversary Performance at the Loussac Library, Día de los Muertos at Out North Contemporary Art House, Christmas Around the World at the Dena'ina Center, Meet the World in Anchorage at the Anchorage Museum (as part of the Fur Rendezvous festival), Kid's Day at the Egan Center, Government Hill School Spring Cultural Festival, and the Anchorage Summer Solstice Festival. They also performed at the Alaska State Fair in Palmer. Ana and Ana carefully decide which performances to do by first ensuring that there are enough dancers available and then checking to make sure that the performance is not too late for the children, not during school hours, not commercial, and not explicitly religious or political. They especially prefer events that promote intercultural cooperation and communication. Ana Del Real said that they have always given careful thought to accepting invitations to perform. "There should always be a cultural reason to participate, never an economic one. The invitations that we accept are from the community, for events that celebrate something culturally."

In this way, the group "freezes the people together" and creates connections with the wider community in Anchorage. It also emphasizes the uniqueness of points within this particular transnational formation. Since there is a high level of ethnic diversity in Anchorage, at community events where Xochiquetzal-Tiqun performs, many other groups perform their traditional dances as well. The group also accommodates the transnational way of life of many of their members: they do not have many performances in the summer, when most of the members of the dance group have gone to Mexico.

In interviews with dance club members, I asked about any performances that were exceptionally memorable for them. Everyone told me about the time the group was invited to perform at Quyana Alaska, a dance celebration that takes place during the Alaska Federation of Natives (AFN) annual convention. Ana Gutiérrez said that they were the only non-Alaska Native group to participate at Quyana that year. She said, "You know, we are also part Indigenous, and we consider ourselves your cousins." And so they were invited to dance at Quyana.

Ana Del Real talked about the importance of dancing at the Quyana event: "It's especially impressive because we were there to perform dances from Mexico, by invitation of the Alaska Native people who themselves dance really professionally. The most amazing moment for me was when they said the name of the group: 'Now we present Xochiquetzal-Tiqun,' and it's something we are very proud of because, imagine, you are dancing in their country, their state, and their culture. I think that was the most memorable moment for me."

This could be seen as a potentially decolonizing moment, as the borders of North America fall away to welcome dancers from across the continent at the Dena'ina Center. But perhaps not. As indicated earlier in the chapter, Xochiquetzal-Tiqun draws on the narrative of Mexican nationalism and *mestizaje* to connect with Alaskan Native dancers. So dancing at Quyana Alaska could instead be seen as a mobilization of Mexican nationalism in Alaska. Nevertheless, in their dances, photographs, and mission statement, Xochiquetzal-Tiqun explicitly brings together Alaska and Mexico. In this way, they work to socialize children within a transnational social field, produce new connections in Anchorage, and unsettle stereotypical representations of space, re-categorizing North America to diminish the sociospatial distance between Mexico and Alaska.

*Postcards from the Mexico in Alaska Restaurant*

One of the most obvious traces of the Mexican presence in the Anchorage cityscape are restaurants. During my fieldwork I counted thirty-two Mexican restaurants, not including national and international chains. Mexican food is commonplace throughout the United States, and most U.S.-Americans are accustomed to the ready availability of margaritas, tacos, and enchiladas. In Anchorage, Mexican migrant-immigrants own many of these restaurants, and some are actually owned by Acuitzences. These are important sites for employment, since restaurants often employ people from their hometowns, including family members, as described in chapter 4. They are important places for migrants to start working upon arrival in Anchorage, and such work often leads to a career in the food industry. Restaurants are also important meeting places for Acuitzences or other groups. Most Mexican restaurants in Anchorage feature a party room that can be rented for celebrating baptisms, birthdays, or other special events. The Migrant Club meets informally at a Mexican restaurant, as discussed earlier in this chapter. These restaurants are also one of the meeting places for people of Mexican background and people of other backgrounds in Alaska. Finally, these restaurants also bring together the flavors and imaginaries of Mexico and Alaska in the food that they serve and the imagery they employ. The food served is a North American creation, cooked by Mexicans who learned some recipes from non-Mexican restaurant owners in Alaska and other recipes from people in their hometowns. They aim to please both Anglo-American palates and Mexican palates. As a result some dishes on the menus are more Mexican American and people from Acuitzio say that the food in many of these restaurants is "not really Mexican." Once cooks from Acuitzio began owning their own restaurants, they introduced dishes important to their community. For example, Miguel told me to attract the Mexican community to your restaurant, "you have to serve a good *menudo*."[21]

This section focuses on one restaurant in particular, named Mexico in Alaska. More specifically, I discuss a set of postcards produced by the restaurant.[22] Mexico in Alaska, located on Old Seward Highway and operated by Maria Elena Ball, claims to be one of the oldest Mexican restaurants in Anchorage; it was recognized as "One of the Nation's 50 best Hispanic Restaurants" as featured in *Hispanic Magazine*; and its interior was used as a stand-in for a Mexican restaurant in Barrow for the filming of the movie *Big Miracle* starring Drew Barrymore.[23] The restaurant also brings Mexico and Alaska together in its name, in its logo, and in a set of images produced as postcards and sold at the restaurant.[24] Bringing Mexico and Alaska together visually creates a spatial fold that draws on recognizable images from Mexico and Alaska to create a representation of a Mexican Alaska. This representation is also a claim to space, visually placing Mexico *in* Alaska.

According to Maria Elena, her restaurant was the third Mexican restaurant in Anchorage when she opened it in 1972, four years after she arrived in Anchorage from Zitácuaro, Michoacán.[25] When we met in 2010, she said that even before she knew what kind of business she would have, she knew it would be called Mexico in Alaska. She said: "I came to that name because I am from Mexico, I'm proud of what I am, and I knew that's what I was going to call it. But I didn't know that it was going to be a restaurant."

She opened the first location of the Mexico in Alaska restaurant in the Anchorage neighborhood of Mountain View in 1972 and then moved to its present and much larger location on Old Seward Highway in 1983. The building features custom-made stained glass windows with symbols of Michoacán, like dancers performing "Los Viejitos" and the aqueduct in Morelia.[26]

Maria Elena said she had the idea for a series of images to visualize "Mexico in Alaska" around the same time that she thought of the name for the restaurant. Decades later, her cousin married Bart Roberts, whose hobby is photography. Maria Elena visited them at their home, where they showed her their album of wedding pictures. Bart Roberts told me how it happened: "We were meeting with Maria Elena one day, and she was talking about the mountains that she loves here in Alaska and how much she loves Mexico. I ran downstairs and pulled up a picture of Chichén Itzá and then I pulled up a picture of the Chugach Mountains here near Anchorage. I did a quick Photoshop job on it, and pow! There's the first one. She just loved them, so she said please make some more. I want to make postcards out of them."

Maria Elena's idea was to create an image whereby Mexico and Alaska were seamlessly integrated together into the same frame. Bart Roberts made five images that superimpose Mexican structures over the Alaska landscape. There are a set of four images that show buildings from the Chichén Itzá archaeological site in Yucatán, Mexico, superimposed against the Chugach Mountains, which are located to the east of Anchorage. One image shows the ball court at Chichén Itzá; another shows El Caracol, or the observatory; and a third shows El Castillo, the largest pyramid at the Chichén Itzá archaeological sites and probably one of the most well-known pyramids in Mesoamerica, if not the world (fig. 7). Another postcard depicts the columns of the Temple of a Thousand Warriors, also at Chichén Itzá, superimposed over the tundra near the North Slope of Alaska, where a caribou grazes serenely to one side, and the Trans-Alaska Pipeline cuts across the background (fig. 8). There is another image that shows the plaza in Zitácuaro, Michoacán, with the Chugach Range in the background (fig. 9). And another image, not yet produced as a postcard, depicts a statue of the Mexican independence hero El Pípila, again superimposed against the Chugach Mountains.

The images are striking, and all but the one featuring El Pípila are sold as postcards at Mexico in Alaska restaurant. They measure four inches by six inches, and on the back list the name and address of the restaurant, the recognition as one of the fifty best Hispanic restaurants, the locations of the images, and a copyright for the photographer, Bart Roberts. Maria Elena also has enlarged, framed versions hanging in her restaurant.[27]

Maria Elena has learned from customers that these postcards have been sent to many locations in the United States and around the world. The postcards themselves do not give any information about the country or state location of the image; it just says, for example "Chugach Mountains—Chichén Itzá." Maria Elena says that she tries to tell people where those places are, because otherwise they do not understand: "The postcard doesn't give you a country, and it doesn't give you a state, it just says Chugach Mountains, Chichén Itzá. Okay? So if you have no idea where Chichén Itzá is, which could be possible, then you'll never find these places. I tell my customers or whoever buys the postcards, this is in Mexico, the peninsula of Yucatan, this is Mayan, and you know I go through the whole thing, and this is the mountain close to Alyeska and so forth, and I try to tell everybody, I do!"

Even so, these are postcards and have the capacity to travel and gather meaning as they move. For example, she said: "Once I got a telephone call from the Lower 48, from this lawyer who had one of our postcards. He said, 'Where in the world is this place?' He thought it was a real place!"

She continued: "A lot of people think it's in South America because of the pyramids and the mountains. But there's no place like that! I also

FIG. 7. Chichén Itzá—Chugach. © Bart Roberts.

FIG. 8. Chichén Itzá—North Slope. © Bart Roberts.

FIG. 9. Zitácuaro—Chugach. © Bart Roberts.

received a letter from a gentleman who sent me a picture of the postcard and very nicely asked me if I could tell him where the place was. Somehow it doesn't register that it's Mexico in Alaska. Even though it says Mexico in Alaska Restaurant on it. Right there you would think that people would know it is advertising or it belongs to the restaurant somehow."

She also told a story about a young couple who came into the restaurant. To her it seemed obvious that the young man was interested in impressing his girlfriend. She said:

> As customers pass by the front of the restaurant there they see the pictures sometimes. One day, this couple came in, and she said, "Oh what a beautiful place," talking about the postcards, right? And he says, "Oh yeah it is, I've been there." I didn't want to embarrass him or anything, so I said, "Yeah, they're really nice, aren't they?" talking about the postcards. But I never told him anything, even though he was talking about it as if he had been there. I didn't say anything at all. I normally do tell them when [customers] try to guess where those places are.

But not everyone is so confused, especially those who recognize the places. As Maria Elena says, "Some of my customers know the names of those buildings in Chichén Itzá, they have been there, and that is really neat. They just mention that there are no mountains like that over there."

What does it mean that the location represented in these images is difficult for people to place? Even though Maria Elena tries to explain to people where the locations are, the postcards were intentionally made without listing the state or nation on the back where the location of a postcard usually appears. Mountains are used here as key emblems of Alaska, particularly in its "sublime wilderness" form. Indeed, all of the Alaska parts of the images center on the landscape—mountains, tundra, and caribou. As with the series of photos taken by Xochiquetzal-Tiqun in front of the painting of Denali at the Anchorage Museum, these images rely on an intentional juxtaposition to unsettle this wilderness setting, to play with it, encourage the viewer to look at Alaska as a place that includes aspects of Mexico even as it is also a spectacular wilderness space. In these images mountain-as-wilderness is deliberately unsettled by juxtaposing the mountain with something that does not quite fit—

Mayan ruins with the Alaska pipeline running past, for instance, or an everyday scene of a plaza in a small town in Mexico. The plaza image is from Maria Elena's hometown and therefore may most closely represent her own experience of transnationality.

Independence heroes and pre-Columbian Aztec and Mayan ruins have become symbols of Mexico writ large. Chichén Itzá signifies Mayan cultures, a reified "Museum of Maya culture and civilization" produced out of the interplay between local Maya society, tourism, and anthropology.[28] Maria Elena and Bart's choice to use Chichén Itzá on the postcards is in part coincidence—Bart and his wife went to the Yucatán for their honeymoon, and he had photos available of the archaeological site. However, there is no question that Chichén Itzá is intended to stand in one of the ancient Indigenous civilizations that are today associated with the image of Mexico writ large. By juxtaposing Chichén Itzá with the Alaskan landscape, viewers are encouraged to ask: where is this? And they thereby rethink and reconsider previously held notions about what Alaska is like.

Relocating Mexico, in the form of Chichén Itzá, El Pípila, or the plaza in Zitácuaro, to Alaska is also a way of placemaking and a way of claiming belonging in Alaska. These postcards are visual representations of Mexican Alaska, a transnational space produced through the movements and everyday practices of people of Mexican background in Alaska. An Alaska vitally interconnected to elsewhere, yet at the same time produced as extremely separate. These images fold the continent and diminish the distance across it, visually placing Mexico *in* Alaska. As postcards, these images can be sent to friends and family as a souvenir from Mexican Alaska. That images of Mexican Alaska are difficult to place or are even seen as unexpected is analogous to how many people react to the idea that there are Mexicans in Alaska. By putting these places into the same frame, Maria Elena Ball and Bart Roberts categorize back, and instead of Mexico being "out of place" in Alaska, the two locations come together in one image.

*The Mexican Consulate in Alaska*

Mexicans!
Long live the heroes that gave us the Fatherland!
Long live Hidalgo!
Long live Morelos!

Long live Josefa Ortiz de Domínguez!
Long live Allende!
Long live Galeana and the Bravos!
Long live Aldama and Matamoros!
Long live National Independence!
Long live Mexico! Long live Mexico! Long live Mexico!

I sat in the crowd at the AT&T Center in south Anchorage as the consul general of Mexico in Alaska, Javier Abud Osuna, waved the Mexican flag and passionately shouted the *Grito de Dolores* in front of the audience. The president of Mexico performs the *Grito* each year on the evening of September 15 to commemorate the beginning of the Mexican War of Independence. The *Grito* is also shouted in cities and towns all over Mexico and in Mexican embassies and consulates worldwide, including in Anchorage.

I attended this Independence Day event in September 2011, after arriving in Alaska two weeks before. At the door I received a piece of paper with a poster of the event on the back and the Mexican national anthem on the front, "so you can sing with us," said the woman who gave it to me. There were *papel picados* in red, green, and white strung across the room and on tables at the back. Rows of seats faced a stage decorated with an arc of red, green, and white balloons.

I recognized one of the masters of ceremonies as a young woman whom I had met in Acuitzio over the summer and the other one as the middle-aged cohost of a local television program called *Latinos en Alaska*. They delivered the whole program in Spanish and English and began the events by asking everyone to stand as the flags of the United States, Mexico, and Alaska were carried to the stage. Next, the consul of Mexico spoke, and he began by citing statistics from the 2010 U.S. census. He told us that "Mexicans are the most numerous foreign-born group in Alaska, and the group which is increasing the fastest." Meanwhile Juana Bravo and her children, Toño, Verónica, and Sophia, arrived. Juana sat in the seat next to me that I had saved for her.

Xochiquetzal-Tiqun then danced two dances, first a *jarabe* with the smallest children and then a second number that had the entire group on stage dancing to "El Cascabel." Next the Mariachi Agave Azul group performed, dressed in *charro* suits. As they sang "Viva México," some people in the audience joined in, shouting out *"Viva, viva!"* After the mariachi performance, there was a theater piece about the war of independence and a performance of a regional dance of Michoacán by another dance group, this one affiliated with Our Lady of Guadalupe Church. Finally there was a performance by a dance group from Oaxaca. Juana said there are many Oaxacans in Anchorage now, and some do not speak any Spanish at all.[29]

Many people at the event were wearing traditional Mexican clothes: women in embroidered tops, *rebozos*, with ribbons in their hair; men in *charro* suits. In fact, the consul himself was dressed in a *charro* suit, and his wife was wearing an embroidered floral dress that Juana told me was from Chiapas. Many others were dressed in casual everyday style, in jeans and T-shirts and baseball caps. Those in attendance were mostly families with young children, but there were a few older people and some teenagers and young adults.

Finally, it was time for the ceremony. A group of three young men in the row behind us had brought their own Mexican flag, and they unrolled it and held it up in front of them. The consul began by introducing all of the dignitaries who were there: the state commissioner of health, a representative for the mayor of Anchorage, a representative of Canada in Alaska, a representative of the FBI, a professor at University of Alaska Anchorage (UAA), a representative of Telemundo in Alaska, someone from the office of Mark Begich (then a U.S. senator for the state of Alaska), and someone else from UAA. Then they thanked the sponsors and restaurants that were selling food at the rear of the room.

Juana, still sitting next to me, said, "Once I went to see the president give the *Grito de Hidalgo*."

"Do they do it in Acuitzio too?" I asked. She said that they do, and that they also celebrate September 1, the Día de San Nicolás, because the church in Acuitzio is named for him.

"*Pura fiesta*," I said. "Nothing but parties."

Juana laughed, "*Sí, Sarita, así es.*" She continued, "We are having Mexican food for lunch tomorrow to celebrate our Independence Day. I work with a lot of other Mexican women, and we're all making something to bring. I made a flan, and that's why I was late tonight."

Next, the singer from Mariachi Agave Azul sang the American national anthem. Some people had their hands over their hearts, and a few people sang along. Juana hummed along beside me. Then another Mexican flag was brought in, and most people in the crowd and on the stage turned to face the flag and raised their arm and held it perpendicular to their chest like I had seen people do at official events in Mexico. A group of students in uniforms marched the flag to the stage, handed the flag to the consul, and he held it while he led the *Grito*, which opened this section. The *Grito* itself was very moving. "A powerful claim to space," I wrote in my field notes afterward. The consul then led the singing of the "Himno Nacional," the Mexican national anthem. I sang along following the handout, with Juana pointing out where we were on the page. Afterward the MC encouraged everyone to "cheer loud enough that they can hear us in Mexico!" Before the Mariachi Agave Azul performed their next song, one of the musicians spoke and said, "We need to teach our children about the richness of Mexican culture."

A few weeks later, I walked downtown to the offices of the Consulate of Mexico in Alaska, which was established in Anchorage in February 2009 when the Mexican government realized that one was necessary due to the increasing numbers of Mexican nationals in Alaska. Before that, a volunteer worked as an honorary consul in Anchorage, but the services she could perform were limited, and Mexican nationals in Alaska had to go to Seattle for access to many services. Unfortunately, the consulate in Alaska was closed in 2015 despite significant opposition from the Spanish-speaking community in Anchorage. The Mexican government cited budget constraints and diminishing demand for consular services in Alaska. Mexican nationals in Alaska once again have to travel to Seattle or access consular services whenever the mobile consulate visits the state.[30]

When I did fieldwork in Anchorage in 2011 and 2012, however, the consulate was open and active in the community. When I visited the building to interview the consul, I was shown immediately to Consul Abud's office, where he shook my hand and greeted me warmly. In the interview, Consul Abud talked about the official functions of the consulate and the services they provided to Mexican nationals in Alaska. "I can tell you that basically we do the same things as any other Mexican consulate in the United States, or anywhere else in the world. Our principal functions are consular assistance and protection. We also have the *emisión de documentación,* and we work to promote trade between Mexico and Alaska. Moreover, we forge cultural relations and educational cooperation between Mexico and Alaska."

The consul emphasized consular assistance and protection because many members of the Mexican community have problems that require legal assistance in terms of immigration or labor law. The consulate partnered with a legal firm in Anchorage to provide access to legal services for Mexican nationals and dual citizens. The most common form of consular assistance and protection they provided was related to deportations, and Consul Abud described deportations as the *"pan nuestro de cada día,"* or their daily bread. They had a fluid agreement with local Immigration and Customs Enforcement (ICE) so that every time ICE detains someone, the consulate is notified. Consular staff interview the deportee and offer all the assistance that they can. "Most people that we interview ask that we contact their families because they have been unable to communicate with them, and so we contact their families to tell them that the person is fine, in good health, their civil rights have been respected, but that, unfortunately, they have been deported, and in a few days they will be with you there in Mexico."

In terms of documentation, they issued passports, consular identification, power of attorney, dual nationality, and so on. Consul Abud said, "we also have birth registration and death registration functions. And this is something that I haven't done yet, but as consul I am able to perform marriages between Mexican nationals." In other words, he can act as a judge of civil registration for marriages and births.

The consulate in Anchorage thus represented an official presence of the Mexican state in Anchorage. In fact, in 2013 President Enrique Peña Nieto of Mexico stopped in Alaska on his return from Asia, when he was in Indonesia for APEC meetings. And since the consulate served the entire state, it did a lot of *mobile* consular work. Its reach therefore extended throughout the state, wherever Mexican nationals reside. When I met with the consul, he explained that the jurisdiction for the consulate is all of Alaska and is situated in Anchorage because it is the largest city in the state, and there are the largest number of Mexicans there. To reach other areas, he explained, they form a mobile consulate. "The last mobile consulate that we did was in Fairbanks for two days at the end of June this year. Even though Fairbanks is far north, there are Mexicans there as well, and we provided some services to them there."

Consul Abud and his staff used location alongside the results of the 2010 U.S. census to decide where to send the mobile consulate.[31] Fairbanks was the best choice for a mobile consulate not only because it has the second-largest population of Mexican nationals in the state, but because it is far from Anchorage, located about six hours away along the Parks Highway. The Matanuska-Susitna Valley, on the other hand, has the third-highest population of Mexicans but is located only seventy kilometers away, and those living in the Mat-Su Borough, in towns like Palmer or Wasilla, could more easily come to Anchorage to access consular services. This is why Consul Abud prioritized Fairbanks over the Mat-Su Valley for a mobile consulate.[32]

Census data is one way to find out the number of people of Mexican background in different areas of Alaska, but another way is to document where people who contact the consulate are located. Consul Abud said, "If someone telephones to ask us a question, we ask them where they are calling from. This is how we learned that there were many people phoning from Juneau who need our services, or in Dutch Harbor, where we have also visited to provide our services." Consular services are only needed seasonally in Dutch Harbor, however, "only when the fish-processing plants are operating, which is normally from the end of the spring and throughout the summer."

Earlier chapters discussed how citizenship requires mobility as a matter of procedure. Becoming a U.S. permanent resident or U.S. citizen requires the ability to travel to get documents and paperwork completed outside of the United States and to reenter with a new status. The mobile consulate, however, traveled to points throughout Alaska to make sure that Mexican nationals in the state have an ID, are aware of their rights, and know how to contact the consulate if they require assistance. In this case it was the state bureaucracy that traveled to facilitate the paperwork of individuals.

Consul Abud was previously stationed in Laredo, Texas, on the U.S.-Mexican border. I asked him to describe the difference in his role as consul in Alaska and Laredo. He described the difference in terms of scale and distance. By scale, he meant that there were so many more cases, and so much more trade between the United States and Mexico along the border with Texas. By distance, he meant the distance between consulates. In Laredo there are consulates located in nearby cities, such as McAllen, Texas, located about 150 miles along the U.S.-Mexican border to the southeast or Eagle Pass or Del Rio, Texas, located along the border to the northwest. In total, there are eleven Mexican consulates in Texas, reflecting the larger population and the increased intensity of consular activities in the border region.

In contrast, the Mexican consulate in Anchorage was responsible for a very large and sparsely populated state. Consul Abud said that because of this, although the role of consul is basically the same, "there are fundamental differences between the functions of a border consulate and a consulate in the north of the United States." Other ways that their work was different related to the specifics of the Alaskan economy and the seasonal employment that many Mexicans experience: "We have to take special care to track those Mexicans who come here to work temporarily, for example in fish processing plants, as well as those who come to work in tourism and all of the seasonal jobs related to the tourism economy. So many of the jobs here are seasonal. All of the outdoor jobs, like construction, they start working in May and stop in September, because even now, at the end of September, it's starting to feel cold, and it's impossible for people working to withstand the cold of Alaska." Finally, he talked about how the trade between Mexico and the United States along the border region is immense, and the work of the consulate along the border was to facilitate that trade. This is not so in Alaska. Work in a border consulate like Laredo and a northern consulate like Anchorage are therefore quite different, according to Consul Abud.

An important consular function in Anchorage was to celebrate Mexican culture and bring together people of Mexican background in Alaska. The consulate was involved with the Independence Day event that I attended, and they were involved with many other events that promote and celebrate Mexican culture in the city. During fieldwork in 2011–12, some examples of other events in which the consulate participated include the Day of the Dead, a food festival commemorating the 150th anniversary of the Battle of Puebla on 5 de Mayo, Hispanic Heritage month, the Government Hill School culture fair, *las posadas* at the Our Lady of Guadalupe church,[33] two events put on by Anchorage Bridge Builders (Police Navidad and Meet the World), a special program of Mexican cinema at the Anchorage International Film Festival, and an exhibit of maps from the era of Spanish exploration in Alaska. I asked Consul Abud about the consulate's role in these events when I interviewed him in his office. He spoke about how these activities are intended to bring people together: "Our priority has been that the Mexican community participate in some of the activities of the consulate, and not just because this is in the laws guiding the Mexican Foreign Service. One of my priorities [as consul] was to *unify* the Mexican community. For example, the Independence Day celebration is an ideal opportunity to be able to *link* all the Mexicans or Mexican Americans who live in Alaska, and in Anchorage in particular."

But events like this were not only intended to bring together people of Mexican background in Alaska: they were also intended to build connections with other groups in Alaska: "Through the consulate, our intent is to rescue our traditions and demonstrate and share them with other communities living in Alaska." Further, the Mexican consulate came to represent and provide services to the "Hispanic" community writ large in Anchorage. For example, the events of the Semana Binacional de Salud, or Binational Health Week, are open to all *"hispanos"* in Alaska. "And why for all Spanish speakers?" Consul Abud asks, and then responds, "Simply because this effort nationwide involved various consulates from Spanish-speaking countries. *Hispanos* in general, and we are talking about Guatemala, El Salvador, Argentina."

"Ah, and they don't have consulates in Alaska," I said.

"Exactly, there are no consulates here. Being the only Hispanic consulate in Alaska, we have been given the task of hosting the Binational Health Week for all *hispanos* in Alaska, whatever their nationality of origin."

Another event in which the consulate participated creates links between *"hispanos"* in Alaska and extends the boundaries of Latin America to Alaska is the celebration of Hispanic Heritage Month at the Anchorage Museum, described earlier in the section about Xochiquetzal-Tiqun.

In 2011 it was held on October 2, the weekend after I met with Consul Abud, who said, "We were invited to participate as the only Hispanic consulate here in Anchorage, and I was invited to give some words of welcome as I did last year. As well, Mexican American singers and dancers will unite with all of the Hispanic nationalities here in Alaska, and we will celebrate that way."

And so, the larger Spanish-speaking community expressed support for a consular presence before its closure in 2015. Consular activities in the city not only produced a new representation of space as "Mexican Alaska," but they also extended the boundaries of all of Latin America northward into Alaska.

The actions of the Mexican consulate are important because they represent the spatial expansion into the geography of Alaska by the Mexican state. This is certainly what embassies and consulates of all nations do all over the world. The events and activities organized by the consulate also show how the everyday practices of *mexicanos* in Alaska are often entangled with official narratives encouraged by Mexican officials in Alaska. Local-to-local connections made by individuals between hometowns of Acuitzio and Anchorage are also wrapped up with nation-to-nation narratives of Mexico and the United States. The image of Consul Abud shouting the *Grito de Dolores* at the AT&T Center in Anchorage amid hundreds of Mexican people living in the city was emblematic of this entanglement. A few hours later the president of Mexico did the same thing. This happened all over the United States and wherever there is a Mexican consular presence in the world. All of these locations become united by the same act performed publicly every September 15.

The Consulate of Mexico in Anchorage therefore added another institutional presence to the making of connections between Mexico and Alaska and makes a further claim to space there. Like Xochiquetzal-Tiqun and the Mexico in Alaska restaurant, these activities produce a new representation of space that once again brings Mexico and Alaska together. Other researchers have documented the reach of the U.S. nation-state across the border into Mexico and how the power of nation-states shapes everyday lives of transnational or transborder migrants on both sides of the border.[34] As well, despite the clear power asymmetry between the two nations, the Mexican state has also expanded its borders by having a presence wherever there are substantial numbers of Mexican nationals living. The consulate provided services to Mexican nationals throughout the state and thereby recognized them *as Mexican nationals in Alaska* and facilitated any paperwork they may have needed. The consulate also took an active role in "freezing the people together," or as Consul Abud put it, linking together the Mexican community in Anchorage and shaping a sense of community. In this way, like the Migrant Club, the consulate explicitly attempted to keep people invested in and linked to Mexico.

## "They Take Their Culture with Them"

Back on the plaza bench in Acuitzio with Lola, we continued our conversation. Thunder rumbled as the clouds rolled in, threatening afternoon rain. I asked her what she liked the most about living in Anchorage. Lola replied,

> I think for me, the nicest thing has been to take the culture with us, and work to support and rescue our culture because nobody else will do it for us. That's the important thing. That they take their culture with them and that they maintain it. *Que lleven su cultura y que la mantengan.* That they don't lose their identity. Because it's possible to get confused, or feel we don't belong anywhere, *que no nos ubicamos en ningún lugar.* Knowing clearly who you are and where you're from helps you settle yourself in the place where you live.

In this chapter I have discussed different sites where a "Mexican Alaska" is produced and analyzed the strategies and practices that are used to "freeze the people together" as Mexicans in Alaska. Mexicans in Alaska intervene in dominant representations of space where Alaska and Mexico are exceptionally separate and distant from one another. The organizations, places, and institutions examined here all draw on a sense of unexpectedness, work to make new connections, and claim local spaces to produce a collective transnationality in Alaska. These practices and events make the connections between Mexico and Alaska visualizable and tangible in everyday life in Anchorage by giving structure to lived space for people who are living transnationally and by encouraging others to consider alternative representations of Alaska.

The dance group, the postcards, and the activities of the consulate all draw on nation-state narratives of Mexican nationalism that render the specificities of culture and dance from Acuitzio or even Michoacán and the contemporary culture of Indigenous people and Afro-descendent peoples in Mexico totally invisible. Although representations of Mexico in Alaska re-categorize space and produce a Mexican Alaska, such representations draw on the same logics of nationalism and patterns of erasure used by the state. These are entangled with more local-to-local connections, such as those made between Acuitzio and Alaska as discussed in previous chapters.

In the following, concluding chapter I describe Acuitzences who have "moved back," leaving Alaska to live in Mexico. As I have shown, people orient their lives and mobilities to the transnational space that extends between Mexico and Alaska. But as circumstances change for individuals or families along the life course, as social life shifts within Acuitzio and Anchorage, and changes in the North American or global political economy emerge, people are able to be flexible and to expand or contract the network as necessary.

# Conclusion

FREEDOM TO MOVE

I hear the phone ring on the other end of the line, and Claudia picks up, "*Bueno.*"

"Claudia, it's Sarita! How is Mexico so far? How was your trip?"

Claudia and her husband Iván and their two children decided to move back to Mexico in 2013. Claudia and Iván met in high school in Acuitzio, and Claudia had lived in Anchorage as a young girl, and again as a teenager. When they married, they needed money to pay for the wedding and start their lives together, so they moved to Alaska, where Claudia's grandfather had worked, and her parents, siblings, aunts, uncles, and cousins had built their lives. Iván's great-uncle also worked in Alaska for many years, and they could both list a large number of relatives in Anchorage.

As time went on, both Claudia and Iván were less sure that they wanted to stay in Anchorage. Iván was having trouble finding work, and the long, cold winters were draining. They were concerned because their children weren't very proficient in Spanish. Even though Claudia tried to speak only Spanish to them at home, she is bilingual and found herself slipping easily into English.

In an interview in Anchorage Claudia told me that she felt at home in Anchorage and that the idea of moving again scared her. "I don't know why, but I just know the city and I know people I guess, I don't know. I guess it's my comfort zone," she said, before laughing nervously. Even so, Claudia said they were thinking about moving to Mexico to seek other opportunities for their family and to be close to her in-laws. "I always want to be where my family's better, and I want to move for

Iván too. He has not been with his parents for a long time. You know, nineteen years. I've been with my parents here, and I see them all the time. I can see that he's not very happy. Well, he's happy, but the winter is too long, and I can see that in him. So I think it's the right time for us to move."

I also talked to Iván about moving back to Mexico when I interviewed him in Anchorage. He said, "Like I told you, having been born and raised in Mexico, your roots are there, and you are always tempted to go back." He continued, explaining that he wants to go back to teach his children what he learned growing up in Mexico, to teach them about their roots and their Mexican heritage. But he wants to able to return to Alaska with his children in the future: "I would like to go back to Mexico someday and live there. Live there and have the opportunity to come here even if it's only for vacation, to spend time where my children were born, because they were born here in Alaska. They have the right to come and visit the place where they were born. So that they know their roots, more than anything. But yes, we are tempted to move back to Mexico one day and retire over there." Although Iván wants to reorient his primary residence to another point within the Mexico-Alaska transnational social field, he wants to keep moving within it.

Claudia also wanted to leave the door open to ongoing mobility between Mexico and the United States. "We would come back for visits for sure. Especially if my parents are still over here in Alaska. So if we do move I will try to come every year with the whole family to see my mom and my dad." Claudia explained how they would keep a house in Anchorage so that they would have options. "I told Iván it's better just to keep it, you never know. In the future if your kids want to come over here, or if something happens in Mexico, then we have a place. Then we can just kick the tenants out and go move in or whatever, you know?"

They considered moving somewhere further south, closer to the border and still within the boundaries of the United States, but by the summer I finished fieldwork and returned to Canada, they had chosen to relocate to a medium-sized city in central Mexico. They visited the city in advance, and Claudia told me about the nice houses available for sale and the good schools, some of which even feature bilingual instruction in both English and Spanish.[1] Her husband wanted to leave immediately, but they decided to take their time to sell another property they owned in Anchorage, pack up or sell their possessions, and allow the kids to finish their school year. Claudia also wanted to help her mother start a business over the next year. She said she "wants to have something on both sides," meaning on both sides of the border, in Anchorage and Mexico. "I want to keep something here," she said.

When I talked to Claudia on the phone after they moved back to Mexico, she told me about their new home, their new city, and invited me to visit as soon as I could. The children liked their school, and she and Iván were selling clothes at the weekly outdoor market, called a *tianguis* in Mexico. Her youngest son's Spanish was improving, and her daughter had made lots of friends. But Claudia seemed torn and told me that she missed Alaska, and she missed her family. She often posted status updates on Facebook of the northern lights in starry skies or rows of salmon fishermen on the Kenai River alongside candid snapshots of their new life in Mexico. By the time this book went to press, the family had moved back to Anchorage together.

Over time, Acuitzences have oriented their lives and mobilities to a transnational social field that extends between Mexico and Alaska. Even though many of them often feel "neither here nor there,"[2] I show that through uneven spatial practices such as travel between Acuitzio and Anchorage, family networks, ways of "getting used to" new places, and new representations of space in Alaska, Acuitzences in Alaska live both here *and* there. Increasingly, it is the uneven experience of life in *both* places and mobility between them out of which a sense of belonging is built. As circumstances change along the life course, within Acuitzio and Anchorage, in North America, or globally, people are able to be flexible and to expand or contract the network as necessary. In fact, some Acuitzences reoriented their primary residence to Mexico but kept a house in Alaska so that they can visit or return there to live. Again, the possibility of mobility is always there. The ideal transnational life, the North American Dream, is lived in both Anchorage and Acuitzio and along routes between them, and identities are built that draw on these multiple spatial points of reference. This way of life is precarious and can easily fail as things change. Furthermore, this way of life is only possible for a very specific group of multigenerational migrants who are now dual citizens or U.S. permanent residents. The opportunity to live between the United States and Mexico is closed without a path to citizenship. For the Acuitzences in this book, it took generations.

In this conclusion I focus on two main threads. First, I analyze the future that Acuitzences envision. I show that people want the ability to move between the United States and Mexico and can build lives within a transnational social field that contribute to both nation-states.[3] Many Acuitzences in Alaska structure their lives to leave their options open, and for them freedom is the freedom to move. Second, although we are presently witnessing a hardening of the boundaries between people and places, I advocate for a transnational framework that reconfigures expectations about people and places and criticizes the increasingly commonplace production of boundaries and walls, both symbolic and literal, that restrict mobility and separate peoples and places from one another. Instead, a transnational frame embraces the multiplicity of place and the multiple trajectories that construct all places. How might taking a North American continental view on migration reconfigure expectations about people and places? And how might it shift policy and public opinion about migrant-immigrants in North America to accommodate the freedom to move?

*Transnational Futures*

Acuitzences in Alaska have built a social world and way of life that includes both Acuitzio and Anchorage, and they imagine their futures transnationally as well. In interviews I asked Acuitzences in Anchorage directly where they imagine themselves in the future, and in most of their responses, like Claudia and Iván, Acuitzences illustrate that they hope to keep living between Anchorage and Acuitzio, perhaps changing their main residence over time but continuing to travel between the two. Even though deciding where to live is a fraught decision, Acuitzences in Alaska wish to keep moving within the transnational social field, even if they change their primary residence within it.

For example, Claudia's mother, Alina, also wants to move back to Mexico: "We could rent our house like Claudia, maybe wait until my youngest daughter graduates from high school and then go to Mexico.

But I don't know." She paused. "I don't know what's going to happen, but I don't want to be in Alaska anymore."

Alina's husband, Ernesto, wants to come and go:

> Maybe someday we will move back, but I want to be realistic. I think my best option isn't to totally move back to Mexico. I think the best option for at least another fifteen years, I think, would be to split the time between the two. For example, I would go to Mexico for January, February and March, come back to Anchorage in April. I would be there for three months, or I could even stay for four or five months, no? But I could spend a bit more time there and enjoy our homeland while continuing to come back to Alaska as well. Because my grandchildren are here, my children, my sons-in-law, you know, they have married and built their lives here in Alaska.

Others say the same thing, that they would like to continue to come and go. For example, Joaquín told his wife that in ten years "we're going to Mexico" where he's got his house, his ranch, and his horses. They can come to Alaska in the summertime, stay in a holiday trailer, kayak, hike, and fish, before returning to Mexico. Octavio plans to retire soon, and when he does he intends to split his time between a home in Anchorage, a condo on the Pacific Ocean in Mexico, and a house in Acuitzio.

In chapter 3 I analyzed the experience of the Bravo children and where they see their futures as third-generation members of a multigenerational family unit that has spatially extended between Mexico and Alaska. They can imagine potential futures in both Anchorage and Acuitzio and are not entirely sure where they will end up. They, even more than their parents and grandparents, are best positioned to remain oriented to the transnational social field as they move between Alaska and Mexico. Their parents also say they are not sure where they will live. Luis Bravo would like to move back because he feels *a gusto*, or comfortable, in Acuitzio. If he has the chance to move back to Mexico, he says he will raise livestock for sale like he did the last time he moved back to Mexico, but this time he will not rely on loans to do it. He told me he has already installed all the pens for the animals. They could sell their house in Anchorage and go. However, Juana wants to stay close to her children. As she said,

For me it will be difficult. Like right now I can't leave my children here and go back to Mexico. Maybe if they married and moved away, to another state, well, then I could go. Luis says we're going to go, but I don't know. Because as long as my children need me here, I'm going to be here. Like I told you, I was always really close to my parents. And I think that even though you are grown up, you always need your parents. Moreover, another thing that I've noticed is that in comparison to other cities in the United States, Anchorage is *tranquilo*, and it's better to stay here than move elsewhere in the Lower 48.

Once again, where people imagine their futures depends on familial, economic, and political considerations, but always along established trajectories within the transnational social field.

Many families that I met talk about similar negotiations. For example, Efrén said, "Soledad already wants to go back!" Soledad said, "I'd like to go back, but not to Acuitzio or to Mexico City. I'd like to live somewhere else in Mexico. But I don't think we will go back soon, we'll move back when we're older. But then again, we're already old," she laughs. "Who knows, we were only supposed to live here for five years, and it's been thirteen years already!" She said that over time you start to make your life in Anchorage, and moreover the political and economic situation in Mexico is bad. It is safer in Anchorage, and there is work.

Renata also talked about her plans in an interview: "Before I graduated from high school my dream was to take a year off, to go to Mexico, and spend it with my family and everything. But that didn't come true." When I spoke to her about her future plans, her hopes were to finish her postsecondary training in Anchorage. She said, "I don't see myself living in Mexico. I'd rather just go there to visit." After we spoke, Renata did live in Mexico for a time, studying there for a few months, before returning to Anchorage to live.

I asked Renata's mother, Gloria, where she thinks she will live. She sighed and said,

> At first my husband and I were thinking that when we retire, we will go to live in *el pueblo*. That's why we built the house there, right? With air conditioning and everything. But Mexico is in a sad state right now, and we're afraid, honestly. It's especially sad because when we

grew up in Acuitzio, and in all of Michoacán, at midnight or whatever time, you could be *tranquilo* without any fear. But now the situation makes you afraid. It makes you afraid, what if something happens to you, and no, well, honestly we don't know. My husband's parents and my parents are in Mexico, but we appreciate the health care benefits we receive from working in the United States. So, the truth is, we don't know. That is what keeps us here most of all.

For Gloria, the decision is fraught, especially within a context where some people describe their town as *tranquilo* while others fear for their safety on trips to Michoacán. In the end Gloria reiterates Juana's sentiment: "If Renata gets married someday, we are going to be where she is, to be close to her. So we don't know. We don't know what's going to happen."

Humberto was similarly conflicted about where he sees his future. He had been working in Anchorage in landscaping for the summer, then spending the winter in Mexico, but at seventy-eight years old, he was not sure how much longer he would carry on. I asked him, "Do you want to go back to Mexico permanently or carry on in Anchorage?"

He replied, "It depends," and went on to explain that the ideal is to return to *su tierra*, your land. "But Alaska is my second choice." In Mexico, he said, there have been many political problems, meaning that one doesn't have the *tranquilidad* that one needs to live in peace, "as you should be able to."

The desire for peace and security and the perceived lack of it in Michoacán is a major consideration for Acuitzences as they imagine their future. Although Acutizences highlighted the safety and tranquility of both sites, personal lives across the continent are sometimes broken and fractured due to violence, drugs and alcohol, delinquency (in Alaska or Michoacán), or deportation from the United States. Indeed, not everyone is able to build a life across the continent, such as Diego (chapter 4) and Jaime (chapter 3).

The need for work is another major consideration. For example, although Leonardo said he has not thought about where he imagines his future, he said, "Why would we go somewhere else when we are doing well here? I want to be realistic. In other states further south there are lots of problems with work, the economy is bad, it's worse." Oscar said he is thinking of moving elsewhere in the United States because, "like I told you, if I see that the economy in Acuitzio is still really bad, I want to start my own company in the U.S." Tomás says that he would like to live in Anchorage forever. It's *tranquilo,* he likes it, and more than anything, it is safe. Safer than in the Lower 48, and the economy is a little better too.

This too could change. It depends on what happens within the United States and Mexico and how these national economies and political spheres interact with each other, including how the U.S. War on Drugs unfolds in Mexico. I argue that people will continue to move within the transnational social field to wherever they perceive conditions to be best for themselves and their families. Some will move back to Acuitzio, others will stay in Anchorage, and others will relocate to new points in Mexico or the United States. As Miguel Bravo says, "*a ver qué pasa,* see what happens."

To put his statement into context, Miguel's initial plan upon coming to Alaska for work was to go back to Acuitzio when he could not work any more and it was time to retire. For that reason he invested in an avocado orchard, so that they would have some income when they lived in Acuitzio. "But now with the violence in Mexico it's become very difficult. I wanted to live there someday, but it depends. Every day it seems worse, and there's no point thinking about being there when you would suffer from the violence and the cartels. No, I wouldn't be *a gusto,* I wouldn't be comfortable there right now." Moreover, his children were born in Anchorage and grew up there, and Miguel assumes they will not want to live in Mexico. "Maybe we could buy a house in another state," he says, "somewhere with a less extreme climate, where it is neither too hot nor too cold. Here the main thing is the snow; you just have to be able to stand the cold, right?" For all of these reasons, Miguel says, "We'll have to see what happens, *a ver qué pasa.*"

So, people orient their lives within the transnational social field. As circumstances change along the individual life course, within the family, in the economy, and politically within Acuitzio and Anchorage, in North America, or globally, people are flexible and expand or contract the network as necessary. For example, when things were not going well in Alaska and they wanted to spend more time with family in Mexico, Claudia and Iván moved themselves and their children back to Mexico. A few years later, they moved back to Anchorage. When the *autodefensas* in Michoacán began using violence to reclaim territory under control of the cartels, Juana and Luis Bravo and their family debated whether or not to go to Acuitzio for the summer. They ended up going, only later than usual and for a shorter length of time. When Gonzalo Calderón decided to retire, he first moved to his *rancho* near Michoacán, but health problems led him to move back to the United States, where he could access high-quality medical care near his home. Lola moved to Anchorage in 2012 after she had returned to Acuitzio to live over ten years before. When she returned to Anchorage, she opened a restaurant with her husband. In 2014 they sold the restaurant and moved back to Acuitzio to run in the following year's elections. By 2016 Lola was back in Anchorage again. People thus orient their lives around both locations, never moving to either location permanently, rather shifting primary residence to a different node in the network for the time being.

As described by anthropologist Deborah Boehm, many Mexicans in the United States want the ability to *come and go*, to develop their own patterns of temporary settlement between the United States and Mexico over the life course and within family and kin networks, without fear of arrest and deportation or the danger of illicit border crossing.[4] Immigration policy in the United States is fundamentally at odds with the freedom to move. Specifically, and as described in the introduction, the rules and regulations laid out by the Immigration and Nationality Act in the United States and the kind of abstract space that it produces is in tension with the lived experience and spatial practice of many migrant-immigrants.[5] Indeed, "visible boundaries, such as walls or enclosures in general, give rise for their part to an appearance of separation between spaces, where in fact what exists is an ambiguous continuity."[6] This is true of the U.S.-Mexican border where although a visible boundary may exist, more people from Mexico than anywhere else continue to cross it to make a space for themselves. This "ambiguous continuity" extends throughout the continent all the way to Alaska. As well, U.S. immigration policy and the U.S. border are relatively recent historical products: there is a long history of mobility between what is now the United States and Mexico, and, of course, a very large part of the United States was once part of Mexico.

Mexican policy toward its diaspora already better accommodates the desire to come and go, likely because government officials are motivated to maintain the flow of remittances and investments back to Mexico. Through federal, state, and municipal programs, Mexican governments have managed to keep migrants engaged in their home country through participation in federal elections, the 3x1 Program, migrant clubs, and consular activities.[7] In contrast, it is clear that the balance between rights to movement and rights to containment is still being negotiated in the United States.[8] This is the double imagining of space—of the bounded space created by the state and the more open space characterized by immigrant movement—an imagining "that *in the very fact of its doubleness . . . works in favor of the already-powerful.*"[9] If we accept a world of originally separate and culturally distinct bounded places, then immigration policy becomes a question of how hard we should try to maintain this order.[10] As Akhil Gupta and James Ferguson state, "If, on the other hand, it is acknowledged that cultural difference is produced and maintained in a field of power relations in a world always already spatially interconnected, then the restriction of immigration becomes visible as one of the main means through which the disempowered are kept that way."[11] Acuitzences in Alaska, however, structure their lives to leave their options open. Freedom is the freedom to move and live between places. Earlier I asked how immigration policy and public discourse about migrant-immigrants in North America might shift to accommodate the freedom to move, and it remains an open question. Given the present context of increased border security and restriction of migration policies that enforce spatial segregation between nation-states and peoples, freedom to move appears to be an impossibility, at least for most people. But all people should be free to move, regardless of passport, citizenship, or the "shoes we have to run in."[12]

*North American Lives*

Transnational life between Mexico and Alaska reworks expectations about the North, Alaska, and Mexicans in the United States to include the multiplicity of trajectories that cross the continent. This book interrupts histories of expectation about the Circumpolar North and Alaska in particular and about Mexicans in the United States.[13] The lives of Acuitzences in Alaska show a different picture of U.S.-Mexican migration. In contrast to studies of illegal or undocumented migration in the Lower 48 states, I documented and analyzed how legal migrants with dual citizenship or U.S. permanent residency move between Acuitzio and Anchorage and construct class, family, community, and national identities through relationships and cultural practices. I analyzed what life is like for those who are able to "come and go" and live the North American Dream across the continent. Throughout, I intended to interrupt expectations of Mexicans in the United States as a group of people and of Alaska as a place. Indeed, the mobility of white, western people appears as a historical given, while Mexicans in Alaska are considered "surprising." The lives of those who live across the continent and who create roots in both places show that attempts to produce sharp divisions and build walls between Mexico and the United States are ultimately futile. The lives of Acuitzences in Alaska tangle up stories across the continent, both "here" and "there."

In this view Mexico and the United States are profoundly entangled geographies, and not only along the U.S.-Mexican border or in southern regions more traditionally associated with Mexican immigration, culture, and transnationality, but all the way to Alaska. Alaska, and the Circumpolar North more generally, can and should be conceptualized as uniquely situated but interconnected to elsewheres. Rather than situating my work as a regional ethnography of either the Circumpolar North or Latin America, I argue that these regions can be productively analyzed through their *crossings*, the links and mobilities that produce them. I show that over time Acuitzences in Alaska build a transnational social field and orient themselves more to the field as a whole than to any one location in it. Acuitzio, Anchorage, and the common experience of mobility between the two are necessary to feel at home in the world. By focusing on Acuitzences in Alaska and their trajectories that cross the North American continent, I encourage the production of analytical links that connect north and south. Indeed, I show that this is something that Acuitzences themselves do in their everyday lives.

For example, during the 2014 World Cup in Brazil, a research contact posted a photo on social media of himself and other Acuitzences in Brazil before the Mexico-Portugal game. The men in the photo smiled in front of the crowds outside the stadium, and all of them were dressed in Mexican national colors, wearing national team Mexico jerseys and hats that said *"Viva México,"* carrying green and red horns with which to make noise inside the stadium. One of the men was dressed in a novelty Aztec costume with a Mexican flag as a cape. Clearly, everyone was planning to cheer for Mexico. However, in front of them they held a navy blue Alaska flag, with a twist. In addition to the gold stars that trace out the Big Dipper and North Star on the Alaskan flag were the words "Alaska, USA" across the top, and "Acuitzio del Canje, Mich., Mex." across the bottom. Clearly, making this flag and then taking it all the way to Brazil for display at the game indicate how strongly these men felt that they come from both places. But, it should be pointed out, when it came to the soccer game, they were cheering for Mexico.

I also think of a wedding that was celebrated in Anchorage. In Mexico a couple might have both a civil ceremony, for marriage in the eyes of the state, and a religious ceremony, where they are married in the eyes of God. But this couple is a transnational one: she lived in Anchorage most of the time but traveled back to Acuitzio with her family every year. He lived in Acuitzio, and they met there on one of her trips home. They had a long-distance courtship, followed by a long-distance engagement. They decided to have their civil marriage ceremony in Anchorage, followed by a church wedding and fiesta in Acuitzio. At the civil ceremony their cake had a bride and groom balanced on a globe, with a Mexican flag on one side, and the Alaska flag on the other. An important moment in the lives of these people and their families is celebrated at both sites within the transnational social field, symbolically connecting Acuitzio and Anchorage as part of marriage. Mobilities are entangled with life stages within the transnational social field. However, the couple followed the tradition of the civil ceremony being the smaller of the celebrations and celebrated with a larger, more festive church marriage in Acuitzio.

Stories like these lead me to adopt a transnational frame and a continental view on social life.[14] In both of these examples, Acuitzences draw on multiple spatial reference points to build a sense of belonging, as is evident at the World Cup, at the wedding, and in multiple and more everyday spatial practices described throughout this book. Acuitzences are already living, working, and imagining their futures across the continent, and anthropologies of the United States, Canada, and Mexico should look across borders to see how larger structural conditions operate both within and across national boundaries, as well as how these are lived by all of us.[15] Taking a transnational frame allows for the opportunity to reimagine space outside of nation-state borders, to decolonize the continent, and to draw attention to the crossings that work as a counterpoint to more rigid spatial imaginings and expectations.[16] I aim to intervene by simultaneously critiquing the boundary effects of area studies topics that separate circumpolar studies from Latin American studies from migration studies, for example, and interrupt and reconfigure expectations about people and places. This minimizes the ability to distance problems and locate them elsewhere, among other groups in faraway locations such as "violence in Mexico" or "destructive resource exploitation in Alaska." Indeed, other researchers have shown that moving toward a transnational analysis allows for better understanding of the dynamics of migration-immigration between Mexico and the United States, as well as other processes, such as analyses of the U.S.-led War on Drugs, and the production of indigeneity across international borders.[17]

Viewing a location, region, or area through its crossings doesn't completely reject area studies as a useful paradigm for academic or applied research.[18] Indeed, the Circumpolar North is a unique geography, positioned vis-à-vis the world economy in a particular way. Rather, it is most productive to understand *all* places as meeting points for multiple trajectories and "stories so far."[19] Attention to the multiplicity of places enriches our understanding of them. Indeed, in this book common Alaska narratives of adventure, wilderness, strategic Cold War location, the Alaska earthquake, and Alaska Native cultures are viewed from a different vantage point. I also introduce other perspectives to northern spaces, perspectives that have heretofore been ignored, erased, or dismissed as not authentically northern. The challenge for area studies, such as circumpolar studies, Arctic studies, or even Latin American studies, is balancing attention to the crossings with the boundary making inherent to the process of marking off a spatial frame for analysis.

More research needs to be done to examine the production of North America in historical perspective outside of U.S.-Mexican migration, and with care to include circumpolar spaces and perspectives within this frame, as uniquely geographically and historically positioned spaces within it. In some ways global attention looks north, as climate change, resource exploration, and Indigenous land claims continue to have repercussions further south. Even so, northern spaces still suffer from the production of distance and an expectation of isolation and wilderness. But what happens to our understanding of North America if we start with the North, with northern spaces and the perspectives of northern people? Northern Indigenous and newcomer voices already analyze these global processes and opportunities from a different and unique perspective. So do scholars of circumpolar spaces who analyze the specific ways in which colonialism and globalization play out in the North.[20] There is also an opportunity to better understand what it means to be an immigrant in Indigenous territory, in places like Anchorage, or Vancouver (where I studied), or Edmonton (where I now live and work), and all across the continent. In all of these ways, the characteristics of northern spaces and the experiences of circumpolar peoples *interrupt* representations of the North as distant and isolated.[21] Instead the North is an important region for the development of knowledge, theory, and practice across North America.

This project has benefited immensely from a focus on Acuitzences who live, work, and move between Acuitzio and Anchorage, but as a result it lacks insight from those who do not or cannot move between Mexico and the United States. Other researchers have explored Acuitzio as a migratory town,[22] and I do not present analysis here of my interactions with family members, friends, and townspeople who watch Acuitzences come and go but never leave themselves. For Acuitzences who do not live in Alaska, their perceptions of their town and of those who come and go are very different. Indeed, a focus on those who leave may run the risk of implying that the only option in Acuitzio is to migrate. This became an issue for some town residents after a Mexican newspaper published two reports about Mexicans in Alaska in September 2014. In one article the author cited a paper in which I wrote about Gonzalo Calderón arriving in Acuitzio with his new car, and how after that, "everyone wanted to go to Alaska." That is how Gonzalo told me the story, and how I reported it. One woman who lives in Acuitzio resented the characterization of the town as a *hormiguero*, or anthill, a word chosen by the reporter, with the implication that the people are ants with nothing to do but migrate to the United States.[23] Some Acuitzences in Alaska were upset with the reporting because it made it seem as though everyone in Alaska made lots of money or were even millionaires.[24] This made some people uneasy, considering that many already fear returning to Mexico, as I describe below, given the context of cartel intimidation and violence in Michoacán and lack of work opportunities cited for encouraging people to resort to kidnapping and crime. Obviously, an implication that everyone who goes to Alaska is rich poses a risk to those who wish to travel back and forth.

Indeed, my focus here has been on one group of people who move between Alaska and Mexico, and who make up something of a town elite. While their experiences contribute to our understanding of mobility, the production of distance, transnationality between the United States and Mexico, and of places like rural Mexico and urban Alaska, it also elides other perspectives from Acuitzio. But Acuitzio has long been a migrant town, with many residents who have lived and worked in the United States and Canada. All Acuitzences, whether they migrate or not, live with the effects—ranging from inflated property values as migrants have purchased homes and property in Acuitzio to the need to provide support for extended family members "left behind" in Mexico.

Similarly, I did not conduct research with Mexicans in Alaska in general, a diverse group including Triqui refugees from Oaxaca, highly educated professionals, temporary workers in salmon canneries and greenhouses, and undocumented workers in the restaurant industry, janitorial services, landscaping, and construction. It is therefore with caution that any of my findings be generalized to the larger community of Mexicans in Alaska. All of these groups would experience life there very differently. I also did not conduct research among Anchorageites outside of the Spanish-speaking community there, or the links between Acuitzences and others in Anchorage. Acuitzences do have non-Mexican friends, however, and there are many opportunities for people of diverse backgrounds to meet each other in Anchorage, especially for those who work, parents with children in the public school system, and those who engage with groups such as Xochiquetzal-Tiqun.

Since I began this project, people have come to me with stories about migration and immigration elsewhere in the circumpolar world. Had I heard of the large number of Filipino workers in Whitehorse, Yukon? Do I know the story of Jim Fiji, the Pacific Islander who boarded the wrong boat and wound up near Paulatuuq, Northwest Territories, in the early twentieth century and went on to work for the 1917 Canadian Arctic Expedition?[25] Even my mother sent me a news story about Palestinian refugees in Iceland. As with Acuitzences in Alaska, all of these stories interrupt expectations about the Circumpolar North and provide insight into the multiplicity of trajectories that produce northern spaces. In this regard, my findings relate only to a very particular transnational social field, produced by a small group of Acuitzences who live between Michoacán and Alaska. These findings cannot be extended to other mobilities and locations within the Circumpolar North, and further comparative research would be required to understand those trajectories and livelihoods on their own terms, as well as how such "unexpected" mobilities change our ideas about the Circumpolar North. Comparative research would also shed light on what is uniquely *northern* about migratory trajectories, transnational lives, and urban arctic spaces that connect northern spaces with elsewhere. Moreover, comparative historical research rejects the framing of northern spaces as newly or surprisingly cosmopolitan and emphasizes that north and south have always been interconnected and defined in relation to each other and linked by a multiplicity of mobilities.[26] Indeed, emptying, frontier-making, and boundary-making practices facilitate ongoing land dispossession and capitalist accumulation in the Circumpolar North and make it so that diverse mobilities like Mexicans in Alaska, Filipinos in Yukon Territory, a Pacific Islander in the Canadian North, and Palestinians in Iceland seem novel, anomalous, and unexpected.

*To Come and Go*

Many people told me that they left Acuitzio with the hope to return someday. This is what Ernesto said, from the comfortable living room couch in his Anchorage townhouse, the day I interviewed him: "Sarita, what brought me to Alaska was economic necessity. I was in debt, and I saw coming to Alaska as a good way to solve this problem. I came here with a lot of sorrow and pain, because I left my family, my land, my things, my solutions, and my plans. But I always had the hope and the dream to come back, *con la ilusión de volver*."

People build a life between Acuitzio and Anchorage based on the uneven and fraught development of a transnational habitus and the common experience of mobility between these points. Some people do move back to Mexico, or imagine their futures there, but Anchorage still remains important. Acuitzences who have lived and worked in Alaska require both locations within the transnational social field and the ability to *come and go*, to move between Acuitzio and Alaska in order to feel at home in the world. The lives of Acuitzences in Alaska confound expectations about Mexicans in the United States and about places like Acuitzio, Alaska, and the relationship between them. Rather than understanding the lives and mobilities of Acuitzences in Alaska as anomalous, I show how people live their everyday lives across the continent. Places are continually produced through connection with other geographies, and Alaska, Mexico, and North America are all products of interrelations. Throughout this book I shift the discussion from anomaly to unexpectedness by focusing on the crossings between Mexico and Alaska, specifically those crossings between Acuitzio, Michoacán, Mexico, and Anchorage, Alaska, United States, made by multigenerational families who re-categorize North America.

Immigration policy throughout North America, and especially in the United States, needs to be reconfigured to allow more people to *come and go*, to *echarle vueltas*, to allow them to realize their dream to return to their hometowns, their *ilusiones de volver*. Anthropologists and activists might take a transnational frame to see how distance, difference, and inequality are produced within the continent, and how people live within it. It is time to deconstruct expectations about people and places and to work to build theory and policy that fits with the actual everyday lives and dreams of people at both ends of the continent, and at the multiplicity of points in-between.

# Notes

*Introduction*

1. All names of research participants are pseudonyms except Consul Javier Abud Osuna, the directors of Xochiquetzal-Tiqún, Ana Gutiérrez-Scholl and Ana Del Real, the owner of Mexico in Alaska restaurant Maria Elena Ball, photographer Bart Roberts, my friend Edgar Calvillo López, and Gonzalo Calderón, who requested that his real name be used in this book.
2. Similarly, Leah Schmalzbauer opens her book with a vignette describing her surprise at encountering Latino men at the grocery store in Bozeman, Montana. Yes, there are Mexicans in Montana, too! See Schmalzbauer, *Last Best Place?*
3. In Alaska, a sourdough is an old-timer, someone with many years of experience in the North. The term apparently dates back to the Klondike Gold Rush, where experienced miners carried sourdough starter with them. This term is still in use today in northern North America, and especially in Alaska and Yukon Territory. A newcomer to Alaska is colloquially called a *cheechako*, a Chinook jargon term that also dates to the Klondike. For a work that explores the North in terms of a Settler-Native dichotomy, see Thompson, *Settlers on the Edge*.
4. The term "Outside" is commonly used by Alaskans to refer to any location outside the state boundaries.
5. Deloria, *Indians in Unexpected Places*.
6. Douglas, *Purity and Danger*.
7. Gupta and Ferguson, "Beyond 'Culture,'" 6.
8. Malkki, "National Geographic," 56; See also Anderson, *Imagined Communities*; Gupta and Ferguson, "Beyond 'Culture.'"
9. Malkki, "National Geographic," 65.
10. Lefebvre, *Production of Space*.
11. Immigration and Nationality Act, U.S. Citizenship and Immigration Services, September 20, 2013, http://www.uscis.gov/laws/immigration-and-nationality-act, accessed October 31, 2014.

12. Gupta and Ferguson, "Beyond 'Culture,'" 7.
13. Gupta and Ferguson, "Beyond 'Culture,'" 7.
14. Lefebvre, *Production of Space*, 37.
15. Lefebvre, *Production of Space*, 33.
16. De Certeau, *Practice of Everyday Life*, 122.
17. Foucault, *Discipline and Punish*, 219.
18. Sedentary space is striated "by walls, enclosures, and roads between enclosures" (Deleuze and Guattari, *Thousand Plateaus*, 384). Like the Great Wall of China, the U.S.-Mexican border fence is a particularly spectacular example of the striation of space.
19. Deleuze and Guattari, *Thousand Plateaus*, 385.
20. Deleuze and Guattari, *Thousand Plateaus*, 386; see also Virilio, *Speed and Politics*.
21. Simpson, *Mohawk Interruptus*.
22. Trouillot, *Global Transformations*, 34.
23. See Gordillo, *Landscapes of Devils*; Gupta and Ferguson, "Beyond 'Culture'"; Massey, *For Space*; Rockefeller, *Starting from Quirpini*; Tsing, *Friction*.
24. Simpson, *Mohawk Interruptus*.
25. Deloria, *Indians in Unexpected Places*.
26. Malkki, *Purity and Exile*, 8.
27. See also Komarnisky, "To Come and Go."
28. Striffler, "Neither Here Nor There"; Zavella, *I'm Neither Here nor There*.
29. Passel and Cohn, *Overall Number*. There are important differences between these statuses, and especially the requirement to actually reside in the United States to maintain permanent residency there. This requirement does not recognize that people may "reside" in both places even while being physically absent from the country. The bureaucratic rules and regulations around permanent residency therefore do not allow for the same flexibility of residence as dual citizenship does.
30. Boehm, *Intimate Migrations*; Cohen, *Culture of Migration*; De Genova, *Working the Boundaries*; Rouse, "Mexican Migration to the United States"; Rouse, "Mexican Migration and the Social Space"; Stephen, *Transborder Lives*; Striffler, "Neither Here nor There."
31. Boehm, *Intimate Migrations*, 3.
32. Boehm, *Intimate Migrations*, 3.
33. Boehm, *Intimate Migrations*, 4.
34. Boehm, *Intimate Migrations*, 3 (my emphasis).
35. Malkki, "National Geographic," 72.
36. Appadurai, "Sovereignty without Territoriality."

37. Striffler, "Neither Here nor There"; Basch, Glick Schiller, and Blanc, *Nations Unbound*; Glick Schiller, Basch, and Blanc-Szanton, "From Immigrant to Transmigrant."
38. Bourdieu, *Outline of a Theory*; Bourdieu, *Logic of Practice*; Bourdieu, *Pascalian Meditations*; Lefebvre, *Production of Space*; Lefebvre, *Rhythmanalysis*.
39. Here, I draw primarily on Bourdieu's writing in *Pascalian Meditations*. In it, he adds a spatial analysis to his theory of habitus so that "everyone is characterized by the *place* where he is more or less permanently domiciled" in addition to one's social position (135, my emphasis). Acuitzences in Alaska live within a transnational social field, and this is the "place" that their habitus is aligned to. As I show in the following chapters, it is from this transnational habitus that their practice and strategy generate, and it is this transnational field that shapes certain possibilities.
40. Rouse, "Mexican Migration to the United States," 32.
41. Rouse, "Mexican Migration to the United States."
42. Bourdieu's theory conceptualizes a harmony between the habitus and the field. For example, "being at home . . . arises from the quasi-perfect coincidence between habitus and habitat" (*Pascalian Meditations*, 147). As I show, for Acuitzences with a transnational habitus, being at home requires both locations and the common experience of mobility between them. This habitus is not "mismatched," but it is experienced as contradictory, conflicted, and tension-filled—as well as rewarding in many ways.
43. Soccer is also a field where the division between migrant and nonmigrant is literally played out in Acuitzio. Acuitzio celebrates January 2 as the Day of the Northerners, and at least once they have held a migrant vs. nonmigrant soccer match.
44. Rouse, "Mexican Migration to the United States."
45. Stephen, *Transborder Lives*.
46. Malkki, "National Geographic."
47. I analyze the experiences of two multigenerational families in this book: the Bravo family and the Cárdenas family. Both names are pseudonyms, taken from street names in Acuitzio del Canje.
48. Glick Schiller, Basch, and Blanc-Szanton, "Towards a Definition."
49. Appadurai, "Disjuncture and Difference."
50. Law, "Home Cooking," 280.
51. Komarnisky, "Eating Transnationally"; Komarnisky, "Suitcases Full of *Mole*."

## 1. Tracing Mexican Alaska

1. Overmyer-Velázquez, *Beyond La Frontera*.

2. For example, Alvarez, "Mexican-US Border"; Boehm, *Intimate Migrations*; Cohen, *Culture of Migration*; De Genova, *Working the Boundaries*; Gomberg-Muñoz, *Labor and Legality*; Heyman, *Life and Labor*; Hirsch, *Courtship after Marriage*; Kearney, *Changing Fields of Anthropology*; Lattanzi-Shutika, *Beyond the Borderlands*; Rouse, "Mexican Migration and the Social Space"; Stephen, *Transborder Lives*.
3. García Castro and Velázquez Verdugo, "Mexico in Its Newest Frontier"; Brooke Binkowski, "Alaska's Hottest Mariachi Band," *Atlantic*, August 12, 2014.
4. Langdon, "Efforts at Humane Engagement"; Olson, *Through Spanish Eyes*.
5. The earliest Declaration of Intention or Petition for Citizenship made by a Mexican national at the National Archives was dated 1901.
6. Paredes, *Folklore and Culture*.
7. De Genova, *Working the Boundaries*.
8. Cornelius, "From Sojourners to Settlers."
9. Durand, Massey, and Zenteno, "Mexican Immigration."
10. Lattanzi-Shutika, *Beyond the Borderlands*; Schmalzbauer, *Last Best Place*; Striffler, "Neither Here nor There."
11. Massey, Rugh, and Pren, "Geography of Undocumented Mexican Migration."
12. Massey, Rugh, and Pren, "Geography of Undocumented Mexican Migration."
13. Massey, Rugh, and Pren, "Geography of Undocumented Mexican Migration."
14. Massey, Rugh, and Pren, "Geography of Undocumented Mexican Migration."
15. Striffler, "Neither Here nor There," 675.
16. Lattanzi-Shutika, *Beyond the Borderlands*, 4.
17. Schmalzbauer's framing of Montana as "The Last Best Place" for Mexican migrant-immigrants resonates with reasons why Acuitzences prefer life in Anchorage as well—better work, a rural lifestyle, and access to nature. There are also similarities in the spatialized, gendered, and racial contours of life in Montana and Alaska—both framed as masculine, white, rural, and geographically dispersed (Schmalzbauer, *Last Best Place*). However, as I outline throughout this book, aspects of Alaska's history, economy, government, migrant-immigrant communities, framing as Indigenous territory, and location as spatially discontinuous with the rest of the United States make the migrant experience in the "Last Frontier" very different from that of the "Last Best Place" (Schmalzbauer, *Last Best Place*).
18. U.S. Census Bureau, "Hispanic or Latino by Type, Anchorage Municipality," 2010, http://factfinder2.census.gov/faces/tableservices/jsf/pages/productview.xhtml?pid=DEC_10_SF1_QTP10&prodType=table, accessed October 20, 2011.

19. De Genova, *Working the Boundaries*, 98.
20. Beasley-Murray, *Posthegemony*; Kearney, *Changing Fields of Anthropology*; Rouse, "Mexican Migration and the Social Space."
21. Price, *Dry Place*, 45.
22. Arsenio Rey-Tejerina, "Spanish Place Names on the Face of Alaska," ExploreNorth: An Explorer's Guide to the North, http://www.explorenorth.com/library/yafeatures/bl-Spanishindex.htm, accessed September 22, 2014.
23. Boehm, *Intimate Migrations*, 15. See also De Genova, *Working the Boundaries*; Gomberg Muñoz, *Becoming Legal*; Stephen, *Transborder Lives*.
24. Boehm, *Intimate Migrations*, 15.
25. Boehm, *Intimate Migrations*, 15; see also Gomberg Muñoz, *Becoming Legal*.
26. Deloria, *Indians in Unexpected Places*; Gordillo, "Longing for Elsewhere"; Simpson, *Mohawk Interrupus*.
27. Komarnisky, "Reconnecting Alaska."
28. Ganapathy, "Imagining Alaska."
29. Ganapathy analyses these translocal spatial formations in tension with the more grounded and culturally meaningful placemaking of Gwich'in Athabascan people ("Imagining Alaska").
30. Buchholdt, *Filipinos in Alaska*; Dombrowski, *Against Culture*; Feldman, "Applied Cultural Anthropology"; Fitzhugh and Crowell, *Crossroads of Continents*; Friday, *Organizing Asian-American Labor*; Haycox and Mangusso, *Alaska Anthology*; Kollin, *Nature's State*; Kurtz, "Ruptures and Recuperations"; Langdon, "Efforts at Humane Engagement"; Luehrmann, *Alutiiq Villages*; Norris, *North to Alaska*; Olson, *Through Spanish Eyes*; Willis, *Alaska's Place*.
31. This section draws on archival documents from the following sources: Federal Court Records in the holdings of National Archives and Records Administration, Anchorage (Record Group 21); Naturalization Case Files, Alaska State Archives, Juneau, Alaska; and Alaska Juneau Gold Mining Company's employee record index, 1914 to 1944, Alaska State Library Historical Collections, Juneau, Alaska. A potential direction for future research is documentation and analysis of the Mexican experience in Alaska before statehood.
32. I am not sure which Santa Rosalía—there are many.
33. Barman, "Packing in British Columbia."
34. In mining, a mucker is someone who shovels broken ore or waste rock into tramcars or buckets.
35. Norris, *North to Alaska*.
36. Langdon, "Efforts at Humane Engagement"; Olson, *Through Spanish Eyes*.

37. The exhibit was held at the Wells Fargo Alaska Heritage Museum, located in the entrance to the Wells Fargo building in midtown Anchorage.
38. Olson, *Through Spanish Eyes*.
39. Abud Osuna, "Historic and Social Links Between Mexico and Alaska."
40. Buchholdt, *Filipinos in Alaska*.
41. For "categorize back," see Malkki, *Purity and Exile*. For "crossings," see Alexander, *Pedagogies of Crossing*.
42. The census category of "Hispanic/Latino" has changed over time, as have the definitions and social meanings of terms used to describe people, such as "Hispanic" and "Latino." For more on changing census categories in the United States, see Rodriguez, *Changing Race*. For more on terminology within the Mexican diaspora, see Rinderle, "Mexican Diaspora." I use "Hispanic" and "Latino" in this section because that is how these data are reported. My participants preferred to call themselves "Mexicans" or "*mexicanos*." U.S. Census Bureau, "Hispanic or Latino by Type, Anchorage Municipality."
43. U.S. Census Bureau, "Hispanic or Latino by Type, Anchorage Municipality."
44. García Castro and Velázquez Verdugo, "Mexico in Its Newest Frontier"; Velázquez Verdugo, "'Mexico's Last Frontier.'"
45. García Castro and Velázquez Verdugo, "Mexico in Its Newest Frontier."
46. Hunsinger, "Alaska's Hispanic Population."
47. Hunsinger, "Alaska's Hispanic Population."
48. Immigration Policy Center, "New Americans in Alaska."
49. Immigration Policy Center, "New Americans in Alaska."
50. Passel and Cohn, *Unauthorized Immigrant Population*.
51. Jonasson, "Visions of Community."
52. Wiest, "Wage-Labor Migration and the Household"; Wiest, "Impressions of Transnational Mexican Life."
53. INEGI, *Censo de población y vivienda 2010*.
54. Arenas García, *Acuitzio del Canje*. An *escuela normal* or normal school is a teacher's college. In Mexico the system of normal schools was created after the Mexican revolution, and today the schools maintain some of the revolutionary ethos of that era in the focus on educating and uplifting the rural poor.
55. Bienvenidos a Acuitzio del Canje: Lugar del Canje de Prisioneros Belgas y Franceses por Mexicanos 1865.
56. Jonasson, "Visions of Community."
57. In the region around Acuitzio, there are many natural thermal springs, and some of these have been developed into water parks, called *balnearios*. During the hottest time of the year, these are popular places to go for a day trip, to swim and enjoy a picnic or *carne asada* (grilled beef) at the park.

58. P'urhépecha are an Indigenous group of Michoacán. They and their language are also sometimes referred to as Tarascan.
59. Tapia, *Acuitzio*.
60. Arenas García, *Acuitzio del Canje*, 9.
61. Arenas García, *Acuitzio del Canje*.
62. Wiest, "Wage Labor Migration and Household Maintenance," 11.
63. Arenas García, *Acuitzio del Canje*; Garibay Sotelo, *Acuitzio*; Tapia, *Acuitzio*.
64. Wiest, "Wage Labor Migration and Household Maintenance," 12.
65. *Huaraches* are a Mexican sandal with pre-Columbian origins.
66. Wiest, "Wage Labor Migration and Household Maintenance"; Wiest, "Wage-Labor Migration and the Household."
67. Wiest, "Wage Labor Migration and Household Maintenance," 12.
68. Wiest, "Wage Labor Migration and Household Maintenance," 12.
69. For research about labor migration from Acuitzio, see Wiest, "Wage Labor Migration and Household Maintenance"; Wiest, "Wage-Labor Migration and the Household"; Wiest, "Implications of International Labour Migration"; Wiest, "Interrelationship of Rural, Urban"; Wiest, "External Dependency"; Wiest, "Impressions of Transnational Mexican Life."
70. Wiest, "Wage Labor Migration and Household Maintenance," 12.
71. Jonasson, "Visions of Community."
72. Jonasson, "Visions of Community."
73. U.S. Census Bureau, "Hispanic or Latino by Type, Anchorage Municipality."
74. Demographer Chad Farrell told me that based on data from the 2010 U.S. census, one of the largest concentrations of people with Mexican ancestry in Anchorage is on Joint Base Elmendorf-Richardson. He believes that this points to the role of institutions like the military in contributing to localized diversity (Farrell, personal communication, 2014). Through archival research I also found that during the 1940s and 1950s many Mexican-born air force and army personnel became U.S. citizens while stationed at military facilities in Alaska (National Archives and Records Administration, Anchorage, Record Group 21).
75. For example, the neighborhood I lived in, Fairview, had a bad reputation, partly due to its low socioeconomic status but perhaps also because many people were seen walking around in the neighborhood. Many were Alaska Native people visiting Anchorage from rural communities and therefore didn't have a car in which to get around. Hanging out in Fairview and walking around on foot was considered "sketchy" by middle-class Anchorageites, but I liked the neighborhood, its walkability, and its proximity to downtown.

76. Although the name of the Tordrillo Range appears Spanish, it may be an adaptation of a Dena'ina (Athabascan) place-name (Bright, *Native American Place Names*, 508).
77. For example, in 2014 the *Atlantic* reported that the top two most diverse counties in the United States are in the Alaskan Aleutian Islands due to the commercial king crab fishery there (Svati Kirsten Narula, "The 5 U.S. Counties Where Racial Diversity Is Highest—and Lowest," *Atlantic*, April 29, 2014). Potential oil development would increase labor migration to the islands (Lauren Rosenthal, "Remote Alaska Fishing Town Braces for Oil Development," *Al Jazeera America*, January 15, 2014).
78. Feldman, "Applied Cultural Anthropology."
79. English Language Learners Program, "Languages Spoken at ASD," Anchorage School District, http://www.asdk12.org/aboutasd/languages/, accessed October 31, 2014.
80. Farrell, "Changing City."
81. Farrell, "Changing City."
82. Farrell, "Changing City."
83. In Anchorage there are also many migrant-immigrants with a long-term connection to communities in Jalisco and Zacatecas. Here I focus only on Acuitzio.
84. *Alaska Dispatch News* reporter Theriault Boots writes that immigration raids were especially common in the 1990s, but during Obama's presidency they were much less frequent (Theriault Boots, "Alaska's Federal Immigration Agents Used to Be Known for Raids. Will They Be Again?," *Alaska Dispatch News*, March 3, 2017). Deborah Brevoort wrote a screenplay called *Mexico in Alaska* about the raids in Mexican restaurants in Anchorage during the 1990s. She explained: "The authorities would round up the illegal workers and deport them in these raids. It was almost a ritual—they would do this about once a year. But it never worked. The workers would be back in a few days time and everything would go back to normal until the next raid. 'Mexico in Alaska' is the name of a well known Mexican restaurant in Anchorage. The events of my screenplay are fictional—they are not based on actual things that happened at that restaurant. They are loosely based on what happened in numerous restaurants around Alaska in the 1980–90s" (Brevoort, personal communication, 2012). As I write this in 2017, under the anti-immigration administration of Donald Trump there has already been at least one major Immigration and Customs Enforcement operation in the Northwest Region, which includes Washington, Oregon, and Alaska.

85. Marcus, "Ethnography in/of the World System," 105.
86. Boehm, *Intimate Migrations*; Lattanzi-Shutika, *Beyond the Borderlands*; Stephen, *Transborder Lives*.
87. Clifford, *Routes*, 31.
88. Clifford, *Routes*, 31.
89. Striffler, "Neither Here nor There."

## 2. Migration of the Traveling Swallows

1. Golondrinas viajeras / vamos sin descanzar / añorando quimeras / pero buscando siempre donde anidar. Joan Sebastian, with Lucero, "Golondrinas Viajeras," *Huevos Rancheros*, compact disc, Universal Music Latin Entertainment, 2011.
2. Terminology from Rouse, "Mexican Migration and the Social Space"; Striffler, "Neither Here nor There"; Kearney, *Changing Fields of Anthropology*; De Genova, *Working the Boundaries*; Stephen, *Transborder Lives*, in that order.
3. Rouse, "Mexican Migration and the Social Space."
4. In 2014 Airports Council International (ACI) reported that Ted Stevens International Airport in Anchorage was the sixth-busiest airport in the world for cargo traffic. It did not rank in the top thirty for passenger traffic (ACI, "Preliminary World Airport Traffic and Rankings," http://www.aci.aero/News/Releases/Most-Recent/2014/03/31/Preliminary-World-Airport-Traffic-and-Rankings-2013—High-Growth-Dubai-Moves-Up-to-7th-Busiest-Airport-, accessed October 1, 2014). The globe has a smaller circumference near the poles, so the distance of a flight from Asia to Alaska is much less than a flight that travels around the wider parts of the globe. Consumer goods are routed from points in Asia, through Ted Stevens International Airport in Anchorage, then to points in the Lower 48 states. Fed Ex and UPS each have major warehouses at the Anchorage airport.
5. Sure enough, we did get together to make Oaxacan-style tamales shortly after my arrival in Anchorage. As we made them, we reminisced about our time in Mexico City and the tamales we bought there.
6. This is a major international airport, located in Mexico City. Originally built as a military airport in 1928, it was converted into a commercial airport in 1939 (Aeropuerto Internacional de la Ciudad de México [AICM], "Marco Histórico," http://www.aicm.com.mx/wp-content/uploads/2013/08/Marco-Historico.pdf, accessed October 31, 2014). In 2006 it was renamed after Benito Juárez, who served as president of Mexico for five terms from 1852 to 1872.

7. My colleague Erin Jonasson outlined some other strategies for using and maximizing cell phone credit among Acuitzences in her MA thesis ("Visions of Community").
8. In Acuitzio, the usual type of *mole* people eat is *mole poblano*. Although the sauce is famously from Puebla, many people in Acuitzio make it to sell, and many Acuitzences buy mole sauce in town to take to Alaska with them. It can be purchased either *en polvo*, dried as a powder, or *en pasta*, as a paste. I write about mole as a "traveling food" in chapter 5, in Komarnisky, "Suitcases Full of *Mole*," and Komarnisky, "Eating Transnationally." *Pinole* is toasted and lightly sweetened corn meal. It can be made into a thick beverage, similar to *atole*, or eaten like porridge. Juana bought bags of small crispy churros, not the large soft ones with which that the reader might be more familiar.
9. Research participants told me that permanent residents are allowed to be outside of the United States for only three months per year, meaning that for those who wish to spend more time with families in Mexico, U.S. citizenship is an attractive option, as is bringing their families to the United States. Many people do both. As I understand it, although there is now no such restriction on time spent outside the United States for permanent residents, being away for more than six months (180 days) leads to scrutiny upon reentry. Those wishing to spend more than a year outside of the United States must apply for a reentry permit and prove that they have maintained ties to the United States. It is up to the individual Customs and Border Protection Agent to determine whether a longer stay outside of the country is "temporary" and whether to allow the permanent resident to reenter the United States. This is an important reminder that immigration law and perceptions of it shift and change over time.
10. The town's Día del Canje falls on December 5, Día de Guadalupe on December 12, and then there are the posadas, Christmas, and finally Three Kings Day on January 6.
11. As of 2015, the lowest amount was $331.29 in 1984, and the highest was $2,069 in 2008. In most years, residents received between $800 and $1,000, enough for a return ticket from Anchorage to Mexico City or Guadalajara (Alaska Permanent Fund Corporation, "The Permanent Fund Dividend," http://www.apfc.org/home/Content/dividend/dividendamounts.cfm, accessed March 30, 2015; Alaska Department of Revenue, Permanent Fund Dividend Division, http://pfd.alaska.gov, accessed October 31, 2014).
12. Harvey, *Condition of Postmodernity*.

13. Appadurai, "Disjuncture and Difference"; Appadurai, *Modernity at Large*; Appadurai, "Sovereignty without Territoriality"; Tsing, *Friction*, 5.
14. Gordillo, *Rubble*.
15. Gastón Gordillo, "Opaque Zones of Empire," *Space and Politics*, June 25, 2013, http://spaceandpolitics.blogspot.ca/2013/06/opaque-zones-of-empire_25.html, accessed October 31, 2014.
16. Tsing, *Friction*.
17. Massey, *Space, Place, and Gender*.
18. Hellman, "Pedro P. Coyote."
19. Stephen, *Transborder Lives*.
20. Deleuze and Guattari, *Thousand Plateaus*; Gordillo, "Longing for Elsewhere."
21. Alvarez, "Mexican-US Border."
22. I elaborate on the concept of "traction" in chapter 3, and on how people *acostumbrarse*, "get used to," transnational life this way in chapter 4.
23. Of course, it depends on where you have citizenship and where you are traveling. Citizenship from the United States, for example, means that you can travel without a visa to many countries around the world. However, to visit other countries (Russia, for example), someone traveling on a U.S. passport would need a visa.
24. I observed something similar when traveling from Mexico with two young dual-citizen Acuitzences. One traveled with both a Mexican and a U.S. passport, and the other traveled with only a U.S. passport. When entering Mexico, all visitors (i.e., those traveling without Mexican passports and returning as Mexican nationals) are required to fill out an Entry Registration form (Forma Migratoria Múltiple). Upon entry, the border guard keeps one portion and gives the person a certain number of days on the visa. Upon exit, the traveler is required to return the other portion. If the traveler does not have that slip of paper, he or she must fill out a new form and pay a fee to have the visa reissued.
25. My participants used the Spanish term *residencía*, "residency," most of the time and infrequently the English term "Green Card." I use the term "residency" in English to mean Green Card or U.S. permanent residency. Gomberg-Muñoz, "Juárez Wives Club."
26. Gomberg-Muñoz, "Juárez Wives Club"; Gomberg-Muñoz, *Becoming Legal*.
27. There are exceptions to the state building highways, of course. Private property owners may build a road to their home, and roads are built by corporations for access to resources. The roads that Gonzalo travels along were built by the state, although to facilitate economic and military access to territory. Harvey and Knox, *Roads*; Wilson, "Towards a Political Economy."

28. Arguonova-Low, "Roads and Roadlessness."
29. DEW stands for Distant Early Warning, and the DEW Line was a Cold War–era series of radar stations built across the North American Arctic to detect a Soviet invasion by air, sea, or land. Military projects like this, along with resource extraction projects and tourism, required a particular infrastructure that brought workers to Alaska and produced connections to elsewheres. Although people came to Alaska from many parts of the world seeking work and fortune, the typical narrative of Alaskan settlement does not include much diversity, and certainly not the stories of Mexican migrants working on Cold War–era military projects (like Gonzalo Calderón) or the Trans-Alaska Pipeline (like Ernesto Cárdenas Sr.) or roads and railways throughout the state (like Luis Bravo). I discuss this further in chapter 3.
30. In a previous publication, I said that Gonzalo's car was a convertible (Komarnisky, *Reconnecting Alaska*). More recently, he corrected me: it was a 1958 Chevrolet Bel Air.
31. Wiest, "Wage Labor Migration and Household Maintenance," 12.
32. Raymond E. Wiest, personal communication, 2014.
33. Raymond Wiest wrote in his dissertation, "Wage Labor Migration and Household Maintenance," in 1970 that the road between Presa (reservoir) Cointzio to Villa Madero had not yet been paved. Wiest's personal correspondence with his friend and research participant Carlos shows that the road from Morelia to Lagunillas was nearly completed in March 1970, and the road from Lagunillas to Tiripetio was nearly finished a year later. In November 1971 Carlos said that the road to Acuitzio might be completed as early as 1972, and plans were to continue paving the road to Villa Madero (Wiest, personal communication, 2014). Wiest and several grad students returned to Acuitzio from May through August 1972, and he remembers taking pictures of the very muddy road just outside La Colonia at the southern end of Acuitzio. Wiest's student John Ames later wrote that "Acuitzio is connected to Morelia by paved road as of 1972" ("Mexican Plaza"). Past Acuitzio, the road to Villa Madero remained unpaved as of 1972. In a book about Acuitzio published in 1988, Carlos Arenas García writes about the completion of the Tiripetio-Acuitzio-Villa Madero road under the administration of Governor Chávez Hernández, whose term ran from 1974 to 1980 (Arenas García, *Acuitzio del Canje*).
34. Around 1975 PROFORMICH (Productos Forestales de Michoacán) began major lumber extraction for the new sawmill in Villa Madero and the furniture factory in Acuitzio. Leading up to this, in 1972 and 1973 Carlos reported to Raymond Wiest that the Independiente Company, who had

offices in Acuitzio, was working on the road to Villa Madero (Wiest, personal communication, 2014).
35. This account draws on both the spoken version, as Gonzalo told it to me in Long Beach, and the written version, typed into the computer, printed, and sent to me in Edmonton.
36. "La Pajerera" (meaning "the birdcage") is a popular Mexican song that narrates the story of a man and his sweetheart who catch birds in the wild and then go to Mexico City to sell them.
37. A *rancho* in Mexico is a small farm, usually with humble accommodations and plot of land, where people may keep livestock as well as grow corn and other produce for their own use. Some Acuitzences have a house in town and a rancho outside of town. Other municipality residents live full-time on their *ranchos*. The rural hamlets outside of the town of Acuitzio del Canje are also called *ranchos*, for example. Gonzalo is from the *rancho* of Huajumbo. I believe here Gonzalo is referring to *rancho* in both ways—as his own farm and as the *rancho* of Huajumbo where he is from.
38. Technically the Alaska Highway does not go all the way to Vancouver, but many people refer to the whole route as the Alaska Highway, a highway to Alaska.
39. Cruikshank, *Do Glaciers Listen?*
40. The first 987 kilometers of the Alaska Highway are in British Columbia, traveling in a northwesterly direction to the Yukon Territory border near Watson Lake. From there the highway continues through 929 kilometers of Yukon Territory to Port Alcan on the Alaska border. From the border, it is about 320 kilometers to Delta Junction, the official end of the highway and 476 kilometers to Fairbanks, the unofficial end of the highway (*Milepost*).
41. Willis, *Alaska's Place*.
42. Willis, *Alaska's Place*.
43. Willis, *Alaska's Place*, 72.
44. Willis, *Alaska's Place*.
45. Willis, *Alaska's Place*.
46. Willis, *Alaska's Place*, 72.
47. Cruikshank, "Alaska Highway."
48. Cruikshank, "Alaska Highway."
49. Cruikshank, "Alaska Highway."
50. Arguonova-Low, "Narrating the Road."
51. My colleague Ana Vivaldi alerted me to the wider significance of *golondrinas* as a metaphor in Latin America. For example, in Argentina there is an almost formal concept of *migrantes golondrinas* that people use to name

the temporary rural workers who travel from harvest to harvest (Vivaldi, personal communication, 2014).

52. Deje también / mi patria idolatrada / esa mansion / que me miró nacer / mi vida es hoy / errante y angustida / y ya no puedo / a mi mansión volver / Ave querida / amada peregrina / mi corazón / al tuyo acercare / voy recordando / tierna golondrina / recordare / mi patria y lloraré.

### 3. "My Grandfather Worked Here"

1. A *tejano* is a Texan of Spanish or Mexican heritage but not a migrant or immigrant.
2. *Hija* means "daughter"; it is also used as an expression of affection.
3. *Compadrazgo* means "co-parenthood" and refers to the tie between the parents and godparents of a child.
4. Boehm, *Intimate Migrations*; Cohen, *Culture of Migration*; Rouse, "Mexican Migration to the United States"; Stephen, *Transborder Lives*; Wiest, "Wage-Labor Migration and the Household."
5. Much like the family analyzed by Rouse, I do not envision the Bravo family as acting in sync as a coherent entity. Instead, individual family members across generations have disparate projects and differing perspectives on events (Rouse, "Mexican Migration to the United States").
6. Moore, *Suffering for Territory*, 282.
7. Lefebvre, *Rhythmanalysis*.
8. Stephen, *Transborder Lives*.
9. Glick Schiller, Basch, and Blanc-Szanton, "Towards a Definition."
10. I was unable to reach some men who were part of this group, and there were other Acuitzences who traveled between Acuitzio and Alaska at this time, but they have since passed away.
11. Discovery of oil and rising oil prices prompted intense corporate pressure to clarify land claims, and the Alaska Native Claims Settlement Act (ANCSA) was passed in 1971 to settle and extinguish all outstanding land claims of Alaska Native peoples. Cash payments of $980 million and 40 million acres of land were transferred to twelve Alaska Native Regional Corporations and many village corporations. A thirteenth corporation was later created for Alaska Native peoples no longer residing in the state. The rest of the land became property of the state (Dombrowski, *Against Culture*).
12. Overmyer-Velázquez, *Beyond La Frontera*.
13. The 1964 earthquake was the most powerful ever recorded in North American history and was followed by tsunamis that wreaked additional destruction along the West Coast of North America.

14. Allen, *Trans Alaska Pipeline*.
15. Willis, *Alaska's Place*, 124.
16. Willis, *Alaska's Place*, 124.
17. Between 1965 and 1971, the U.S. Atomic Energy Commission carried out three underground nuclear tests on Amchitka Island, a small island in the Aleutian Island chain of Alaska. These tests were done in the context of the nuclear arms race during the Cold War. During World War II, due to the Japanese occupation of Kiska and Attu Islands, also in the Aleutian chain, the U.S. military occupied Amchitka Island and built facilities there (Kohlhoff, *Amchitka and the Bomb*).
18. Gonzalo is here talking more about numbers of Acuitzences in Anchorage, and not about people living in a spatially defined area or neighborhood. In fact, one of the notable characteristics of city life in Anchorage is that people do not seem to live in ethnic enclaves as they do in bigger cities in the Lower 48 states, such as Chicago or Los Angeles. Instead, demographers found that the neighborhood of Mountain View in Anchorage was the single most diverse census tract in the entire United States in 2010, even surpassing the highest diversity tracts in Seattle and New York City (Farrell, personal communication, 2012).
19. "*Siempre con la ilusión de regresar.*" Many people used this phrase in my conversations with them to express that they left Acuitzio with the intention to go back to Mexico someday.
20. Wiest, "Wage Labor Migration and Household Maintenance."
21. Wiest, "Wage Labor Migration and Household Maintenance," 211–12.
22. Wiest, "Wage Labor Migration and Household Maintenance."
23. Wiest, "Wage Labor Migration and Household Maintenance," 216.
24. Wiest, "Wage Labor Migration and Household Maintenance," 216.
25. Wiest, "Wage Labor Migration and Household Maintenance," 217.
26. Wiest, "Wage Labor Migration and Household Maintenance," 215.
27. Wiest, "Wage Labor Migration and Household Maintenance," 216 (emphasis in the original).
28. So many Acuitzences work in Costco, in fact, that it is known to be a source of town gossip. People joke that you can hear all the news from *el pueblo* in Costco sooner than you can in the town itself. One woman who lives in Acuitzio and has two children living in Anchorage told me that she hears gossip from her Alaskan children before she hears it from anyone in town. So, the town *chisme* spans the continent.
29. Earlier I wrote that Alaska is different as a receiving region, and perhaps the many Mexican-owned businesses in Anchorage illustrate that. Dayra Velázquez completed a master's thesis about the Mexican community in

Anchorage, reporting high levels of entrepreneurship (Velázquez Verdugo, "'Mexico's Last Frontier'").

30. Massey, *Space, Place, and Gender*.
31. Massey, *Space, Place, and Gender*.
32. Hogan and Pursell, "'Real Alaskan.'"
33. For the role of gender in the migrant experience, see Constable, "Transnational Perspective"; Gamburd, *Kitchen Spoon's Handle*; Hirsch, *Courtship after Marriage*; Massey, *Space, Place, and Gender*; Stephen, *Transborder Lives*; Zavella, *I'm Neither Here nor There*.
34. Boehm, *Intimate Migrations*, 124; Striffler, "Neither Here nor There."
35. Later in this chapter I discuss a *quinceañera* where travel is in the opposite direction—to celebrate her coming-of-age, Sophia traveled from Anchorage to Acuitzio, where her party was held with friends and family in Acuitzio. Many of her closest relatives traveled from Alaska to be there.
36. Luis calls Octavio his uncle, reflecting the common use of "uncle" to refer to a male relative of an older generation. For example, someone is an uncle if they are your mother's or father's brother, or if they are your grandmother's and grandfather's nieces and nephews.
37. Luis actually said *"uno se junta de la misma gente,* one gets together with the same kind of people," but I think it fits his personality and way of speaking to use a more colloquial phrase.
38. Bloch, "Intimate Circuits."
39. Bloch, "Intimate Circuits"; see also Boehm, *Intimate Migrations*; Hirsch, *Courtship after Marriage*.
40. Luis had a hard time finding work in Alaska that summer, and during this time he not only worked in Anchorage but also worked at a Mexican restaurant in Barrow and at a restaurant in Homer. Until it closed, Acuitzences continued to work at the restaurant in Barrow, which was featured (under a different name) in the 2012 movie *Big Miracle* starring Drew Barrymore. In a funny coincidence, the restaurant where they actually filmed the scenes is called Mexico in Alaska (chapter 6), where some Acuitzences also worked during my fieldwork.
41. *Casi siempre voy y vengo, ya ves.*
42. Rouse wrote about the impact of the currency devaluation and recession on Aguilillan migrant projects at the time: "The recession in the United States impeded the ability of children north of the border to acquire the savings they considered necessary for a definitive return, and the crisis in Mexico further discouraged them from returning soon while also making it more difficult for [already returned migrants] to re-establish [themselves] in Aguilila" (Rouse, "Mexican Migration to the United States," 160–61).

43. Many Acuitzences told me about going to Ciudad Juarez for medical exams and immigration interviews before their applications are approved. This is called consular processing and is how the families of U.S. citizens receive their visas while living in Mexico (Gomberg-Muñoz, "Juárez Wives Club"). No matter where people are planning to live in the United States, it seems they must spend a few days in Ciudad Juarez for exams, interviews, and paperwork.
44. Many Acuitzences that I interviewed recall the exact date that they came to the United States.
45. See also Wiest, "Impressions of Transnational Mexican Life," 33–34.
46. One example is Claudia Cárdenas, who went to elementary school in Anchorage, then high school in Acuitzio, and then moved back to Alaska after graduation. Gloria's daughter Renata also relocated multiple times as she was growing up and might move again as she is living in Anchorage but recently married someone who lived in Acuitzio before they wed.
47. Orellana et al., "Transnational Childhoods," 587; see also Boehm, "'For My Children'"; Boehm, *Intimate Migrations*; Cole and Durham, *Generations and Globalization*; Dreby, "Honor and Virtue"; Parreñas, *Children of Global Migration*.
48. Orellana et al., "Transnational Childhoods," 587.
49. The young woman celebrating her *quinceañera* selects formal escorts. *Chambelanes* are male escorts and *damas* are female. The number of *chambelanes* and *damas* in a young woman's court can vary. At the *quinceañera* I went to in 2011, there were four escorts and no *damas*. All of the escorts but one were family members (brother and maternal cousins), and the final one was a friend of another maternal cousin.
50. On my first fieldwork trip to Acuitzio in 2005, I lived with a family who owns a grocery store and rents a party room and supplies such as tables, chairs, and tablecloths for fiestas. They told me that the summer months and December are the busiest times for their rental business.
51. Johnson-Hanks, "On the Limits"; Mazzucato, Kabki, and Smith, "Transnational Migration"; Olwig, "Wedding in the Family."
52. I am not sure how rigidly this gender divide is enforced, since I have never gone to a *caballgata* myself. Juana told me that she went once in place of her husband, who had already paid but could not go. She said, "Honestly Sarita, it was quite boring."
53. In fact, the two older Bravo siblings did go to Acuitzio without their parents for the first time in December 2013. Vero, Toño, and Sophia are all adults now, and they have traveled alone to Acuitzio and other locations in Mexico and the United States.

54. Striffler, "Neither Here nor There."
55. Bourdieu, *Outline of a Theory*, 86.
56. Olwig, *Caribbean Journeys*, 12.
57. Boehm, *Intimate Migrations*; Kearney, *Changing Fields of Anthropology*; Ong, *Flexible Citizenship*; Stephen, *Transborder Lives*; Wiest, "Implications of International Labour Migration"; Wiest, "Impressions of Transnational Mexican Life."

## 4. "You Have to Get Used to It"

1. The North Slope is a region of Alaska located in northern Alaska between the Brooks Range to the south and the Arctic Ocean to the north. The area includes the Arctic National Wildlife Refuge as well as large and productive oil fields. It is also the ancestral and present-day home of Iñupiat people. Utqiaġvik (formerly Barrow) is the northernmost city in the United States and is accessible by air or sea.
2. Some Acuitzences would disagree, saying that money invested by individuals in the town only benefits themselves and their families, and not the town in general or the poorest or most needy townspeople. The Acuitzio migrant club that I discuss in chapter 6 takes a different approach to community development, soliciting contributions from migrants for community projects. However, many people fear government corruption and believe that they know best how to spend their money.
3. Boehm, *Intimate Migrations*; Ong, *Flexible Citizenship*.
4. I wrote about this in chapter 3 from the perspective of Alina's daughter, Claudia.
5. Ernesto explained the process like this: first he sent in the paperwork, then he was interviewed, then he attended the naturalization ceremony at the courthouse, then later the official certificate arrived in the mail, and then he could get his U.S. passport.
6. Ernesto and his family didn't have to wait very long for their papers compared to some other families for whom the process took many years. For example, Ernesto's father lived and worked in California for most of his life. He became a U.S. permanent resident and got his Green Card, and eventually he applied for papers for all seven of his children. Ernesto said that his own papers took eight or nine years to arrive.
7. Some women from Acuitzio say that having a hairdresser that knows how to cut hair "like in Mexico" is important.
8. Lattanzi-Shutika, *Beyond the Borderlands*.
9. Wiest, "Wage-Labor Migration and the Household."
10. Wiest, "Wage Labor Migration and Household Maintenance," 216.

11. Wiest, "Wage Labor Migration and Household Maintenance," 216.
12. Rouse, "Mexican Migration to the United States."
13. The region is known for its avocado production. Uruapan, located approximately a hundred kilometers away from Acuitzio, calls itself the "Avocado capital of the world." The green fruit is harvested on contract and shipped to locations throughout North America. Indeed, avocadoes also *move*, albeit through significantly different channels than the food in suitcases I talk about in the next chapter.
14. Seiler, *Republic of Drivers*.
15. For analysis of the spatial dynamics and social importance of the plaza in Latin America, see Ames, "Mexican Plaza"; Low, "On the Plaza"; Richardson, "Being-in-the-Market."
16. *Calle* literally means "street," but people use it to mean "out" or "out of the house."
17. *Comida* means "food" but also refers to the main meal of the day. It is also used to refer to a social event organized around a meal, and it was at this kind of event where Soledad and Efrén met.
18. Similarly, Rouse wrote that age of children and attendance at school was a major consideration in decisions about whether or not to return to Mexico for members of the Delgado Morales family in Redwood City, California. Migrants wanted their children socialized to life in Mexico, and part of this implied attending school in Mexico (Rouse, "Mexican Migration to the United States," 282).
19. In schools in Acuitzio there is usually a morning schedule and an afternoon one, and children attend one of them. Claudia and her siblings attended both daily sessions for a while after moving back to Mexico.
20. *Charrería* is a competitive event, similar to the North American rodeo.

## 5. The Stuff of Transnational Life

1. Komarnisky, "Eating Transnationally"; Komarnisky, "Suitcases Full of *Mole*."
2. Binford, "Migrant Remittances and (Under)Development"; Cohen, "Remittance Outcomes and Migration"; Rubenstein, "Migration, Development, and Remittances." See also Instituto de Mexicanos en el Exterior, "Reporte de remesas cifras al cierre de 2014," June 24, 2016, http://www.gob.mx/ime/acciones-y-programas/remesas, accessed August 15, 2016.
3. Appadurai, "Disjuncture and Difference."
4. Ferry, *Minerals, Collecting, and Value*.
5. Muehlmann, *When I Wear*.
6. De León, "'Better to Be Hot.'"
7. De León, "'Better to Be Hot.'"

8. De León, "'Better to Be Hot.'"
9. Food is important as nourishment in a biological sense, but it is also profoundly cultural and connected with the formation of social and cultural identities. Cuisines, ingredients, specific dishes, and raw materials that become food can be studied in terms of their social and cultural importance and analyzed in terms of food production, exchange, and consumption. For this reason, I analyze food as material culture in this chapter and elsewhere (Komarnisky, "Suitcases Full of *Mole*"). See Mintz and Du Bois, "Anthropology of Food and Eating," for a review of approaches to food and eating in anthropology and De Solier, *Food and the Self*, for analysis of food as material culture specifically.
10. Komarnisky, "Eating Transnationally"; Komarnisky, "Suitcases Full of *Mole*."
11. Law, "Home Cooking," 277.
12. Komarnisky, "Eating Transnationally"; Komarnisky, "Suitcases Full of *Mole*."
13. I wrote about a similar experience cooking and eating *buñuelos* (a crispy, sweet snack traditionally served with *atole blanco* in the plaza in Acuitzio) at different points in the transnational social field elsewhere (Komarnisky, "Suitcases Full of *Mole*").
14. Ong, *Flexible Citizenship*, 4.
15. U.S. Customs and Border Protection, "Travelers Bringing Food into the U.S. for Personal Use," https://help.cbp.gov/app/answers/detail/a_id/3619/~/travelers-bringing-food-into-the-u.s.-for-personal-use, accessed October 1, 2014.
16. U.S. Customs and Border Protection, "Travelers Bringing Food."
17. Friday, *Organizing Asian-American Labor*; Hébert, *Enduring Capitalism*; Lowe, "Impact of Industrialized Fishing."
18. Not everyone is able to travel with food like this. For many Mexican migrants without U.S.-recognized status, it is risky to travel back and forth across the border and additionally risky to travel with food. These migrants are unlikely to be able to use their mobility to "eat transnationally" in this way. There is a link to food sovereignty and food justice movements here, where "all people have the right to healthy and *culturally appropriate* food produced through ecologically sustainable methods, and their right to define their own food and agriculture systems" (Alkon and Mares, "Food Sovereignty").
19. Wiest, "Impressions of Transnational Mexican Life," 32–33.
20. In fact, when I traveled from Anchorage to Acuitzio in 2006, I carried a backpack full of clothes and other gifts on behalf of a research participant. Juana Bravo said that she used to take things to Acuitzio for people, but she doesn't do that as much anymore.

21. Juana also purchased handicrafts from Mexico to take to Alaska to give to friends there, and the link between Juana and Mexico was likely emphasized when she gave those gifts away to her Alaskan coworkers and friends.
22. I've seen the same sticker on vehicles in both Mexico and in Anchorage. Luis Bravo got his made in Acuitzio and took it back to Anchorage for his pickup truck there. Luis's truck fits in well in Anchorage, where people emblazon their vehicles with multiple bumper stickers and messages. I am not sure if this is an "Alaska" or a "U.S." practice, but it is a notable aspect of the car culture in Anchorage. In fact, one friend in Anchorage who was called up for jury duty told me that as part of the process everyone was asked to describe the bumper stickers that they had on their cars, since that would likely indicate what strong opinions or alliances a person had.
23. Wiest, "Implications of International Labour Migration," 95.
24. Wiest, "Implications of International Labour Migration," 95.
25. In the following chapter I write about the Migrant Club and how, as a group, members have coordinated the purchase of blankets and jackets from Alaska to donate to impoverished families in the municipality of Acuitzio. These blankets and jackets are associated with Alaska in terms of climate (Alaska is cold, and hence it is appropriate for blankets and jackets to be brought from there) and price (consumer goods like jackets and blankets are cheaper in Alaska than in Mexico.

## 6. "It Freezes the People Together"

1. In her interview Lola said that she moved back to Acuitzio in part so that her children could go to school there. She wanted to be sure they finished university, and to her, they had the best chance to do so in Mexico. She believes the quality of education is much higher in Mexico. Moreover, Lola said that no one from Acuitzio has graduated from university in Alaska, something she attributes to multiple factors, including the tendency to prioritize working over studying in migrant families, the inability for Spanish-language speaking and high school–educated parents to help their children navigate the English university system, the inability for parents to afford the high tuition, and the tendency for young people to get married or move in together and not complete their studies. Her assertion that the best chance for her children's education lies in Mexico is unique and in contrast to most other Acuitzences, who say that the best education is in the United States.
2. Abu-Lughod, "Writing against Culture."
3. De Genova, *Working the Boundaries*, 7.

4. De Genova, *Working the Boundaries*.
5. De Genova, *Working the Boundaries*; Paredes, *Folklore and Culture*.
6. *De coperacha* is informally used to refer to the creation of a collective fund, similar to the idea of "chipping in" in English.
7. *Carnitas* are braised pork; they are often served at special events in Acuitzio and are sold every Sunday in the plaza. Buying *carnitas* on Sunday in the plaza is something that many Acuitzences living abroad look forward to on visits to their hometown.
8. The 3x1 Program matches contributions made by Mexicans in the United States via Hometown Associations to improve the infrastructure of so-called sending communities like Acuitzio in Mexico. The program provides $3 in federal, state, and local funds for every $1 contributed by migrants through their Hometown Associations. The money can be used for "social infrastructure and productive projects" (Secretaría de Desarrollo Social, "Programa 3x1 para Migrantes," http://www.3x1.sedesol.gob.mx/, accessed August 29, 2016).
9. The Danzantes Tradicionales de Acuitzio group has since revived a traditional dance called "Los Frasicos," or "Los Carboneros" after extensive consultation with older community members.
10. National Hispanic Heritage Month in the United States is observed from September 15 to October 15 by celebrating the histories, cultures, and contributions of American citizens whose ancestors came from Spain, Mexico, the Caribbean, and Central and South America. President Lyndon Johnson established Hispanic Heritage Week in 1968, and in 1988 President Ronald Reagan expanded it to cover a thirty-day period starting on September 15 and ending on October 15 (National Hispanic Heritage Month, http://hispanicheritagemonth.gov/about/, accessed October 15, 2014).
11. The dance group has also been photographed in front of a large painting by Tlingit artist Jim Schoppert. Although here I focus on the photos of the group in front of the Denali painting, I believe that taking a photo in front of the Schoppert painting produces a similar re-categorization of space, bringing contemporary Native Alaska and Mexican folk dance together.
12. See the website for Xochiquetzal-Tiqun at http://anadenmar.com/aboutthegroup.htm, accessed August 8, 2014.
13. This is also true of the postcards produced by the Mexico in Alaska restaurant, discussed later in this chapter. The postcards use Mayan ruins and images of the Alaskan landscape to re-categorize space, but they could also be critiqued on the same grounds: that these images use mestizo nationalism in transnational nation-building, reinforcing ethnoracial inequality in the same way that the Mexican and U.S. nation-states do.

14. Bonfil Batalla, *Mexico Profundo*; Fienup-Riordan, *Eskimo Essays*.
15. Alonso, "Conforming Disconformity," 481.
16. Many Acuitzences in Anchorage have been involved with the group from the beginning, including Juana Bravo and her family, and Esteban and Laura and their family; many Acuitzences dance with the group today including Soledad and her children and Serefina and her young son. However, the group is open to anyone of any background, as long as they are willing to perform. Ana Gutiérrez told me that they have had Athabascan Mexican, Puerto Rican American, Albanian, Croatian Mexican, and African American Mexican participants. When I was in Anchorage for fieldwork in 2011–12, all of the participants were of Mexican background.
17. Nájera-Ramírez, "Staging Authenticity."
18. Nájera-Ramírez, "Staging Authenticity," 283.
19. Masayo Doi, *Gesture, Gender, Nation*.
20. Nájera-Ramírez, "Staging Authenticity."
21. *Menudo* is a spicy Mexican soup made of tripe, the edible lining of the stomach of cattle, pig, or sheep.
22. I first encountered these postcards in 2005 when I was in Anchorage for fieldwork for the first time (Komarnisky, "Eating Transnationally"). As a result of my research focus on food, restaurants were a key field site for me, and I visited as many Mexican restaurants and Mexican-run restaurants as I could. The Mexico in Alaska restaurant was one of these, and I purchased a set of postcards there when I visited in 2005. In 2010 I visited Anchorage and met with and interviewed both Maria Elena Ball, the owner of Mexico in Alaska, and Bart Roberts, the photographer. During fieldwork in 2011–12 I met with Bart and Maria Elena informally and visited the restaurant occasionally.
23. Pepe's North of the Border was likely the northernmost Mexican restaurant in the world, located in Barrow, Alaska. Diego (chapter 4), Luis Bravo Jr. (chapters 2 and 3), and other Acuitzences worked in the kitchen there, extending the network all the way to the edge of the Arctic Ocean. Unfortunately I read that Pepe's burned down in 2013.
24. The Mexico in Alaska logo depicts the shape of the state of Alaska in blue, with a gold Aztec calendar in the middle, set across a diagonal tricolor ribbon (green, white, and red). Maria Elena gave me a business card with this logo on it, but it is also found on the restaurant's line of prepared salsas and burritos that are sold in such grocery stores in Anchorage as Carrs-Safeway and Costco.
25. According to Maria Elena Ball, "La Cabaña is the oldest Mexican restaurant in Anchorage, and then it's La Mex, which used to be La Mexicana.

But everybody would just pronounce La Mex, with emphasis on the x; they wouldn't say La Mexicana. Eventually they did change the name. And Mexico in Alaska was opened next."

26. "Los Viejitos," the old men, is a dance from Michoacán where the dancers, dressed as old men, start out hunched over with restricted movements, play-acting as elderly people. However, as the music speeds up, so does the dancing of the *viejitos*.
27. I exhibited the images at the Liu Institute at UBC in the spring of 2011 and gave them to Maria Elena when I arrived in Alaska for fieldwork that fall. She hung them in the restaurant's banquet room.
28. Castañeda, *In the Museum*; Gordillo, *Rubble*.
29. I found out later that many of these Oaxacans are Trique (Triqui), an Indigenous people from the western part of Oaxaca, who have come to the United States seeking political asylum. How and why they came to Alaska and their experience as compared to Acuitzences is a topic for potential future research.
30. Devin Kelly, "Mexican Consulate in Anchorage to Close," *Alaska Dispatch News*, September 25, 2015.
31. U.S. Census Bureau, "Hispanic or Latino by Type, Anchorage Municipality," 2010, http://factfinder2.census.gov/faces/tableservices/jsf/pages/productview.xhtml?pid=DEC_10_SF1_QTP10&prodType=table, accessed October 20, 2011.
32. Consul Abud said that the Kenai Peninsula has the fourth-highest population of *hispanos* and *mexicanos*, and Juneau has the fifth-largest population of Mexicans in the state.
33. *Las posadas* is a nine-day celebration beginning December 16 and ending December 24. It reenacts Mary and Joseph's search for lodging before the birth of Jesus Christ. Those hosting the *posada* play the role of the innkeepers, and the guests play the role of the pilgrims. At the door these groups sing verses to each other before being welcomed inside to celebrate.
34. Boehm, *Intimate Migrations*; De Genova, *Working the Boundaries*; Gomberg Muñoz, *Becoming Legal*; Stephen, *Transborder Lives*.

### Conclusion

1. As I describe in chapters 3 and 4, Claudia moved back and forth between Mexico and Alaska as a child and knew firsthand the difficulties of getting used to the different school systems and languages in these countries.
2. Striffler, *Neither Here nor There*; Zavella, *I'm Neither Here nor There*.
3. Boehm, *Intimate Migrations*.
4. Boehm, *Intimate Migrations*.

5. I refer here and elsewhere in the book to the Immigration and Nationality Act in terms of the general spatial orientation of this set of laws. Even though this body of law has changed many times since 1952, the spatial form it produces persists. See U.S. Immigration and Nationality Act, http://www.uscis.gov/laws/immigration-and-nationality-act, accessed October 31, 2014.
6. Lefebvre, *Production of Space*, 87.
7. See my discussion of groups and organizations that "freeze the people together" in chapter 6, as well as Gutiérrez, "Fostering Identities."
8. Massey, *For Space*. It is also being negotiated along categories of ethnicity, age, socioeconomic status, and gender. For example, the proposed DREAM Act would have given a period of permanent residency to "illegal" immigrants in the United States who were brought there as children, are of good moral character, and have completed postsecondary education or military service. President Obama talked about ending deportations for those already living, working, and contributing to the United States while unaccompanied minors from Central America were sent home. Under the Trump administration, policy and rhetoric are increasingly anti-immigrant, and instead of debating paths to citizenship the U.S. administration plans to build more walls along the U.S.-Mexican border.
9. Massey, *For Space*, 86 (emphasis in the original).
10. Gupta and Ferguson, "Beyond 'Culture,'" 17.
11. Gupta and Ferguson, "Beyond 'Culture.'" 17.
12. Tsing, *Friction*, 5.
13. Deloria, *Indians in Unexpected Places*; Simpson, *Mohawk Interruptus*.
14. Shukla and Tinsman, *Imagining Our Americas*.
15. Audra Simpson writes about the articulations between the juridical and discursive history of the imposed, international U.S.-Canadian border and a Mohawk community's efforts to formalize membership in ways that might or might not enable it to exercise rights that guarantee passage across that border. Simpson reminds us to focus on the production and experience of other borders besides the extensively researched U.S.-Mexican border, as well as how these borders articulate with one another (Simpson, *Mohawk Interruptus*).
16. Alexander, *Pedagogies of Crossing*.
17. Boehm, *Intimate Migrations*; Cohen, "Transnational Migration"; Cohen, *Culture of Migration*; De Genova, *Working the Boundaries*; Hirsch, *Courtship after Marriage*; Kearney, *Changing Fields of Anthropology*; Rouse, "Making Sense of Settlement"; Rouse, "Mexican Migration and the Social Space"; Stephen, *Transborder Lives*; Striffler, "Neither Here nor

There." For War on Drugs, see Muehlmann, *When I Wear*; for indigeneity across international borders, see Muehlmann, *Where The River Ends*, and Simpson, *Mohawk Interruptus*.
18. Alexander, *Pedagogies of Crossing*.
19. Massey, *For Space*.
20. On the specifics of global processes and ongoing colonialism in the Canadian North, see Bell, "Diamonds as Development"; Christensen, *No Home*; Fraser, "Long Ago"; Todd, "You Never Go Hungry."
21. See Komarnisky and Bell, "North, Interrupted," and the collection of papers in "Arctic Interruptions: Reshaping the Northern Imaginary" (*Northern Public Affairs* 4, no. 1).
22. Ames, "Mexican Plaza"; Jonasson, "Visions of Community"; Komarnisky, "Eating Transnationally"; Komarnisky, "Suitcases Full of *Mole*"; Komarnisky, "To Come and Go"; Wiest, "Wage Labor Migration and Household Maintenance"; Wiest, "Wage-Labor Migration and the Household"; Wiest, "Implications of International Labour Migration"; Wiest, "Interrelationship of Rural, Urban"; Wiest, "External Dependency"; Wiest, "Impressions of Transnational Mexican Life."
23. Victor Hugo Michel, "Qué magia hay en el Árctico que hace hombres ricos?," *El Milenio*, September 6, 2014.
24. Victor Hugo Michel, "Dicen que como México no hay dos; pues como Alaska, tampoco," *El Milenio*, September 5, 2014.
25. Canadian Museum of History, The People of the Canadian Arctic Expedition, "James Asaela (Jim Fiji)," http://www.historymuseum.ca/cmc/exhibitions/hist/cae/peo614e.shtml, accessed September 22, 2014. Thank you to Zoe Todd for telling me about Jim Fiji.
26. Brooke Binkowski, "Alaska's Hottest Mariachi Band," *Atlantic*, August 12, 2014; Emily Ridlington, "The New North: Arctic Multiculturalism," CBC *News North*, March 12, 2012; Brooke Warren, "'I Am Alaskan': The Surprising Diversity of the 50th State, through Brian Adams' Lens," *High Country News*, February 2, 2015.

# Bibliography

Abud Osuna, Javier. "Historic and Social Links between Mexico and Alaska." Presentation at the University of Alaska, Anchorage, October 24, 2012.

Abu-Lughod, Lila. "Writing against Culture." In *Recapturing Anthropology: Working in the Present*, edited by Richard G. Fox, 137–62. Santa Fe NM: School of American Research Press, 1991.

Alexander, M. Jacqui. *Pedagogies of Crossing: Meditations on Feminism, Sexual Politics, Memory, and the Sacred*. Durham: Duke University Press, 2006.

Alkon, Alison, and Teresa Mares. "Food Sovereignty in US Food Movements: Radical Visions and Neoliberal Constraints." *Agriculture and Human Values* 29, no. 3 (2012): 347–59.

Allen, Lawrence J. *The Trans Alaska Pipeline: The Beginning*. Seattle: Scribe, 1975.

Alonso, Ana María. "Conforming Disconformity: 'Mestizaje,' Hybridity, and the Aesthetics of Mexican Nationalism." *Cultural Anthropology* 19, no. 4 (2004): 459–90.

Alvarez, Robert R., Jr. "The Mexican-US Border: The Making of an Anthropology of Borderlands." *Annual Review of Anthropology* 24 (1995): 447–70.

Ames, John R. "A Mexican Plaza: Social Accumulation and Its Relation to Vending Patterns." MA thesis, University of Manitoba, 1973.

Anderson, Benedict. *Imagined Communities: Reflections on the Origin and Spread of Nationalism*. New York: Verso, 1991.

Appadurai, Arjun. "Disjuncture and Difference in the Global Cultural Economy." *Public Culture* 2, no. 2 (1990): 1–24.

———. *Modernity at Large: Cultural Dimensions of Globalization*. Minneapolis: University of Minnesota Press, 1996.

———. "Sovereignty without Territoriality: Notes for a Postnational Geography." In *The Anthropology of Space and Place: Locating Culture*, edited by Setha M. Low and Denise Lawrence-Zúñiga, 337–49. London: Blackwell, 1996.

Arenas García, Carlos. *Acuitzio del Canje: 1888–1988*. Morelia: Ediciones Casa de San Nicolás, 1988.

Argounova-Low, Tatiana. "Narrating the Road." *Landscape Research* 37, no. 2 (2012): 191–206.

———. "Roads and Roadlessness: Driving Trucks in Siberia." *Journal of Ethnology and Folkloristics* 6, no. 1 (2012): 71–88.

Barman, Roderick J. "Packing in British Columbia: Transport on a Resource Frontier." *Journal of Transport History* 21, no. 2 (2000): 140–67.

Basch, Linda, Nina Glick Schiller, and Cristina Blanc, eds. *Nations Unbound: Transnational Projects, Postcolonial Predicaments, and Deterritorialized Nation-States*. London: Routledge, 1994.

Beasley-Murray, Jon. *Posthegemony: Political Theory and Latin America*. Minneapolis: University of Minnesota Press, 2010.

Bell, Lindsay A. "Diamonds as Development: Suffering for Opportunity in the Canadian North." PhD diss., University of Toronto, 2013.

Binford, Leigh. "Migrant Remittances and (Under)Development in Mexico." *Critique of Anthropology* 23, no. 3 (2003): 305–36.

Bloch, Alexia. "Intimate Circuits: Modernity, Migration and Marriage among Post Soviet Women in Turkey." *Global Networks* 11, no. 4 (2011): 1–20.

Boehm, Deborah A. "'For My Children': Constructing Family and Navigating the State in the US-Mexico Transnation." *Anthropological Quarterly* 81, no. 4 (2008): 777–802.

———. *Intimate Migrations: Gender, Family, and Illegality among Transnational Mexicans*. New York: NYU Press, 2012.

Bonfil Batalla, Guillermo. *Mexico Profundo: Reclaiming a Civilization*. Austin: University of Texas Press, 1996.

Bourdieu, Pierre. *The Logic of Practice*. Cambridge: Polity Press, 1990.

———. *Outline of a Theory of Practice*. Cambridge: Cambridge University Press, 1977.

———. *Pascalian Meditations*. Stanford CA: Stanford University Press, 2000.

Brevoort, Deborah. "Mexico in Alaska." Unpublished screenplay, 1999.

Bright, William. *Native American Place Names of the United States*. Norman: University of Oklahoma Press, 2004.

Buchholdt, Thelma. *Filipinos in Alaska: 1788–1958*. Anchorage: Aboriginal Press, 1996.

Castañeda, Quetzil E. *In the Museum of Maya Culture: Touring Chichén Itzá*. Minneapolis: University of Minnesota Press, 1996.

Christensen, Julia. *No Home in a Homeland: Indigenous Peoples and Homelessness in the Canadian North*. Vancouver: University of British Columbia Press, 2017.

Clifford, James. *Routes: Travel and Translation in the Late Twentieth Century*. Cambridge MA: Harvard University Press, 1997.

Cohen, Jeffrey H. *The Culture of Migration in Southern Mexico*. Austin: University of Texas Press, 2004.

———. "Remittance Outcomes and Migration: Theoretical Contests, Real Opportunities." *Studies in Comparative International Development* 40, no. 1 (2005): 88–112.

———. "Transnational Migration in Rural Oaxaca, Mexico: Dependency, Development, and the Household." *American Anthropologist* 103, no. 4 (2001): 954–67.

Cole, Jennifer, and Deborah L. Durham, eds. *Generations and Globalization: Youth, Age, and Family in the New World Economy*. Bloomington: Indiana University Press, 2007.

Constable, Nicole. "A Transnational Perspective on Divorce and Marriage: Filipina Wives and Workers." *Identities* 10, no. 2 (2003): 163–80.

Cornelius, Wayne A. "From Sojourners to Settlers: The Changing Profile of Mexican Migration to the United States." In *U.S.-Mexico Relations: Labor Market Interdependence*, edited by Jorge A. Bustamante, Clark W. Reynolds, and Raúl A. Hinojosa. Stanford CA: Stanford University Press, 1992.

Cruikshank, Julie. "Alaska Highway: Beyond the Gravel Magnet." Presentation at the International Congress of Arctic Social Sciences VIII, University of Northern British Columbia, Prince George, May 25, 2014.

———. *Do Glaciers Listen? Local Knowledge, Colonial Encounters, and Social Imagination*. Vancouver: University of British Columbia Press, 2005.

De Certeau, Michel. *The Practice of Everyday Life*. Berkeley: University of California Press, 1984.

De Genova, Nicholas. *Working the Boundaries: Race, Space, and "Illegality" in Mexican Chicago*. Durham NC: Duke University Press, 2005.

De León, Jason. "'Better to Be Hot Than Caught': Excavating the Conflicting Roles of Migrant Material Culture." *American Anthropologist* 114, no. 3 (2012): 477–95.

Deleuze, Gilles, and Felix Guattari. *A Thousand Plateaus: Capitalism and Schizophrenia*. Minneapolis: University of Minnesota Press, 1987.

Deloria, Philip J. *Indians in Unexpected Places*. Lawrence: University Press of Kansas, 2004.

De Solier, Isabelle. *Food and the Self: Consumption, Production, and Material Culture*. London: Bloomsbury, 2013.

Dombrowski, Kirk. *Against Culture: Development, Politics, and Religion in Indian Alaska*. Lincoln: University of Nebraska Press, 2001.

Douglas, Mary. *Purity and Danger: An Analysis of the Concepts of Pollution and Taboo*. New York: Praeger, 1966.

Dreby, Joanna. "Honor and Virtue: Mexican Parenting in the Transnational Context." *Gender & Society* 20, no. 1 (2006): 32–59.

Durand, Jorge, Douglas S. Massey, and Rene M. Zenteno. "Mexican Immigration to the United States: Continuities and Changes." *Latin American Research Review* 36, no. 1 (2001): 107–27.

Farrell, Chad R. "A Changing City, a Changing State: Diversity in the North." Presentation at the Alaska Press Club Conference, Anchorage, April 25, 2014.

Feldman, Kerry D. "Applied Cultural Anthropology in Alaska: New Directions." *Alaska Journal of Anthropology* 7, no. 1 (2009): 1–19.

Ferry, Elizabeth Emma. *Minerals, Collecting, and Value across the US-Mexico Border*. Bloomington: Indiana University Press, 2013.

Fienup-Riordan, A. *Eskimo Essays: Yup'ik Lives and How We See Them*. New Brunswick NJ: Rutgers University Press, 1990.

Fitzhugh, W. W., and A. Crowell, eds. *Crossroads of Continents: Cultures of Siberia and Alaska*. Washington DC: Smithsonian Books, 1988.

Foucault, Michel. *Discipline and Punish: The Birth of the Prison*. New York: Vintage Books, 1995.

Fraser, Crystal. "Long Ago Will Be in the Future: Interruptus, Residential Schools Research, and Gwich'in Continuities." *Northern Public Affairs* 4, no. 1 (2016): 20–22.

Friday, Chris. *Organizing Asian-American Labor: The Pacific Coast Canned-Salmon Industry*. Philadelphia: Temple University Press, 1995.

Gamburd, Michelle Ruth. *The Kitchen Spoon's Handle: Transnationalism and Sri Lanka's Migrant Housemaids*. Ithaca NY: Cornell University Press, 2000

Ganapathy, Sandhya. "Imagining Alaska: Local and Translocal Engagements with Place." *American Anthropologist* 115, no. 1 (2013): 96–111.

García Castro, Ismael, and Dayra L. Velázquez Verdugo. "Mexico in Its Newest Frontier: Mexican Immigrants in Anchorage (Alaska): Migratory Networks and Social Capital." *Mexico and the World* 18, no. 1 (2013): 1–23.

Garibay Sotelo, Salvador. *Acuitzio: Estudio socioeconomico*. Dirección de Servicio Social y Ejercicio Profesional, Gobierno del Estado de Michoacán, 1980.

Glick Schiller, Nina, Linda Basch, and Cristina Blanc-Szanton. "From Immigrant to Transmigrant: Theorizing Transnational Migration." *Anthropological Quarterly* 68, no. 1 (1995): 48–63.

———. "Towards a Definition of Transnationalism." *Annals of the New York Academy of Sciences* 645, no. 1 (1992): ix–iv.

Gomberg-Muñoz, Ruth. *Becoming Legal: Immigration Law and Mixed-Status Families*. New York: Oxford University Press, 2017.

———. "The Juárez Wives Club: Gendered Citizenship and US Immigration Law." *American Ethnologist* 43, no. 2 (2016): 339–52.
———. *Labor and Legality: An Ethnography of a Mexican Immigrant Network*. Oxford: Oxford University Press, 2011.
Gordillo, Gastón. *Landscapes of Devils: Tensions of Place and Memory in the Argentinean Chaco*. Durham NC: Duke University Press, 2004.
———. "Longing for Elsewhere: Guaraní Reterritorializations." *Comparative Studies in Society and History* 53, no. 4 (2011): 855–81.
———. *Rubble: The Afterlife of Destruction*. Durham NC: Duke University Press, 2014.
Gupta, Akhil, and James Ferguson. "Beyond 'Culture': Space, Identity, and the Politics of Difference." *Cultural Anthropology* 7, no. 1 (1992): 6–23.
Gutiérrez, Carlos G. "Fostering Identities: Mexico's Relations with Its Diaspora." *Journal of American History* 86, no. 2 (1999): 545–67.
Harvey, David. *The Condition of Postmodernity*. Oxford: Blackwell, 1990.
Harvey, Penny, and Hannah Knox. *Roads: An Anthropology of Infrastructure and Expertise*. Ithaca NY: Cornell University Press, 2015.
Haycox, Stephen W., and Mary Childers Mangusso. *An Alaska Anthology: Interpreting the Past*. Seattle: University of Washington Press, 1996.
Hébert, Karen. "Enduring Capitalism: Instability, Precariousness, and Cycles of Change in an Alaskan Salmon Fishery." *American Anthropologist* 117, no. 1 (2015): 32–46.
Hellman, Judith P. "Pedro P., Coyote." In *The Mexico Reader*, edited by Gilbert M. Joseph and Timothy J. Henderson, 717–27. Durham NC: Duke University Press, 2002.
Heyman, Josiah M. *Life and Labor on the Border: Working People of Northeastern Sonora, Mexico, 1886–1986*. Tucson: University of Arizona Press, 1991.
Hirsch, Jennifer S. *A Courtship after Marriage: Sexuality and Love in Mexican Transnational Families*. Berkeley: University of California Press, 2003.
Hogan, Maureen P., and Timothy Pursell. "The 'Real Alaskan': Nostalgia and Rural Masculinity in the 'Last Frontier.'" *Men and Masculinities* 11, no. 1 (2008): 63–85.
Hunsinger, Eddie. "Alaska's Hispanic Population." *Alaska Economic Trends* 33, no. 2 (2013): 4–6.
Immigration Policy Center. *New Americans in Alaska: The Political and Economic Power of Immigrants, Latinos, and Asians in the Last Frontier*. Washington DC: Immigration Policy Center, 2015.
Instituto Nacional de Estadística y Geografía (INEGI). *Censo de población y vivienda 2010: Acuitzio*. Morelia: Instituto Nacional de Estadística y Geografía, 2010.

Johnson-Hanks, Jennifer. "On the Limits of Life Stages in Ethnography: Toward a Theory of Vital Conjunctures." *American Anthropologist* 104, no. 3 (2002): 865–80.

Jonasson, Erin D. "Visions of Community: Mexican Community Identity in a Transnational Context." MA thesis, University of Manitoba, 2008.

Kearney, Michael. *Changing Fields of Anthropology: From Local to Global*. Lanham MD: Rowman & Littlefield, 2004.

Kohlhoff, Dean W. *Amchitka and the Bomb: Nuclear Testing in Alaska*. Seattle: University of Washington Press, 2002.

Kollin, Susan. *Nature's State: Imagining Alaska as the Last Frontier*. Chapel Hill: University of North Carolina Press, 2001.

Komarnisky, Sara V. "Eating Transnationally: Mexican Migrant Workers in Alaska." MA thesis, University of Manitoba, 2006.

———. "Reconnecting Alaska: Mexican Movements and the Last Frontier." *Journal of Ethnology and Folkloristics* 6, no. 1 (2012): 107–22.

———. "Suitcases Full of *Mole*: Traveling Foods and the Connections between Mexico and Alaska." *Alaska Journal of Anthropology* 7, no. 1 (2009): 41–56.

———. "To Come and Go: Transnational Life between Mexico and Alaska." PhD diss., University of British Columbia, 2015.

Komarnisky, Sara, and Lindsay Bell. "North, Interrupted." *Northern Public Affairs* 4, no. 1 (2016): 19.

Kurtz, Matthew. "Ruptures and Recuperations of a Language of Racism in Alaska's Rural/Urban Divide." *Annals of the Association of American Geographers* 96, no. 3 (2006): 601–21.

Langdon, Stephen J. "Efforts at Humane Engagement: Indian-Spanish Encounters in Bucareli Bay, 1779." In *Enlightenment and Exploration in the North Pacific, 1741–1805*, edited by Stephen Haycox, James Barnett, and Caedmon Liburd, 187–97. Seattle: University of Washington Press, 1997.

Lattanzi-Shutika, Debra. *Beyond the Borderlands: Migration and Belonging in the United States and Mexico*. Berkeley: University of California Press, 2011.

Law, Lisa. "Home Cooking: Filipino Women and Geographies of the Senses in Hong Kong." *Ecumene* 8, no. 3 (2001): 264–83.

Lefebvre, Henri. *The Production of Space*. Oxford: Blackwell, 1991.

———. *Rhythmanalysis: Space, Time, and Everyday Life*. London: Continuum Books, 2004.

Low, Setha M. *On the Plaza: The Politics of Public Space and Culture*. Austin: University of Texas Press, 2000.

Lowe, Marie E. "The Impact of Industrialized Fishing on Localized Social and Environmental Change in Alaska's Aleutian Islands." PhD diss., Columbia University, 2006.

Luehrmann, Sonja. *Alutiiq Villages under Russian and US Rule*. Fairbanks: University of Alaska Press, 2008.

Malkki, Liisa. "National Geographic: The Rooting of Peoples and the Territorialization of National Identity among Scholars and Refugees." *Cultural Anthropology* 7, no. 1 (1992): 24–44.

———. *Purity and Exile: Violence, Memory, and National Cosmology among Hutu Refugees in Tanzania*. Chicago: University of Chicago Press, 1995.

Marcus, George E. "Ethnography in/of the World System: The Emergence of Multi-Sited Ethnography." *Annual Review of Anthropology* 24, no. 1 (1995): 95–117.

Masayo Doi, Mary. *Gesture, Gender, Nation: Dance and Social Change in Uzbekistan*. Westport CT: Bergin and Garvey, 2002.

Massey, Doreen. *For Space*. London: Sage, 2005.

———. *Space, Place, and Gender*. Minneapolis: University of Minnesota Press, 1994.

Massey, Douglas S., Jacob S. Rugh, and Karen A. Pren. "The Geography of Undocumented Mexican Migration." *Mexican Studies* 26, no. 1 (2010): 129–52.

Mazzucato, Valentina, Mirjam Kabki, and Lothar Smith. "Transnational Migration and the Economy of Funerals: Changing Practices in Ghana." *Development and Change* 37, no. 5 (2006): 1047–72.

*The Milepost: All-the-North Travel Guide*. 63rd ed. Augusta GA: Morris Communications, 2011.

Mintz, Sidney, and Christine DuBois. "The Anthropology of Food and Eating." *Annual Reviews of Anthropology* 31 (2002): 99–117.

Moore, Donald S. *Suffering for Territory: Race, Place, and Power in Zimbabwe*. Durham NC: Duke University Press, 2005.

Muehlmann, Shaylih. *When I Wear My Alligator Boots: Narco-Culture in the US-Mexico Borderlands*. Berkeley: University of California Press, 2014.

———. *Where the River Ends: Contested Indigeneity in the Mexican Colorado Delta*. Durham NC: Duke University Press, 2013.

Nájera-Ramírez, Olga. "Staging Authenticity: Theorizing the Development of Mexican *Folklórico* Dance." In *Dancing across Borders: Danzas y Bailes Mexicanos*, edited by Olga Nájera-Ramírez, Norma E. Cantú, and Brenda M. Romero, 277–92. Urbana: University of Illinois Press, 2009.

Norris, Frank. *North to Alaska: An Overview of Immigrants to Alaska, 1867–1945*. Anchorage: Alaska Historical Commission, 1984.

Olson, Wallace M. *Through Spanish Eyes: Spanish Voyages to Alaska, 1774–1792*. Auke Bay AK: Heritage Research, 2002.

Olwig, Karen F. *Caribbean Journeys: An Ethnography of Migration and Home in Three Family Networks*. Durham NC: Duke University Press, 2007.

———. "A Wedding in the Family: Home Making in a Global Kin Network." *Global Networks* 2, no. 3 (2002): 205–18.
Ong, Aihwa. *Flexible Citizenship: The Cultural Logics of Transnationality*. Durham NC: Duke University Press, 1999.
Orellana, Marjorie F., Barrie Thorne, Anna Chee, and Wan Shun Eva Lam. "Transnational Childhoods: The Participation of Children in Processes of Family Migration." *Social Problems* 48, no. 4 (2001): 572–91.
Overmyer-Velázquez, Mark. *Beyond La Frontera: The History of Mexico-US Migration*. Oxford: Oxford University Press, 2011.
Paredes, Américo. *Folklore and Culture on the Texas-Mexican Border*. Austin: University of Texas Press, 1995.
Parreñas, Rhacel Salazar. *Children of Global Migration: Transnational Families and Gendered Woes*. Stanford CA: Stanford University Press, 2005.
Passel, Jeffrey S., and D'Vera Cohn. *Overall Number of U.S. Unauthorized Immigrants Holds Steady since 2009*. Washington DC: Pew Hispanic Center, 2016.
———. *Unauthorized Immigrant Population: National and State Trends, 2010*. Washington DC: Pew Hispanic Center, 2011.
Price, Patricia L. *Dry Place: Landscapes of Belonging and Exclusion*. Minneapolis: University of Minnesota Press, 2004.
Richardson, Miles. "Being-in-the-Market versus Being-in-the-Plaza: Material Culture and the Construction of Social Reality in Spanish America." *American Ethnologist* 9, no. 2 (1982): 421–36.
Rinderle, Susana. "The Mexican Diaspora: A Critical Examination of Signifiers." *Journal of Communication Inquiry* 29, no. 4 (2005): 294–316.
Rockefeller, Stuart A. *Starting from Quirpini: The Travels and Places of a Bolivian People*. Bloomington: Indiana University Press, 2010.
Rodriguez, Clara E. *Changing Race: Latinos, the Census, and the History of Ethnicity in the United States*. New York: New York University Press, 2000.
Rouse, Roger. "Making Sense of Settlement: Class Transformation, Cultural Struggle, and Transnationalism among Mexican Migrants in the United States." *Annals of the New York Academy of Sciences* 645, no. 1 (1992): 25–52.
———. "Mexican Migration and the Social Space of Postmodernism." In *The Anthropology of Globalization: A Reader*, edited by J. X. Inda and R. Rosaldo, 155–71. Oxford: Blackwell, 2002.
———. "Mexican Migration to the United States: Family Relations in the Development of a Transnational Migrant Circuit." PhD diss., Stanford University, 1989.
Rubenstein, H. "Migration, Development, and Remittances in Rural Mexico." *International Migration* 30, no. 2 (1992): 127–53.

Schmalzbauer, Leah. *The Last Best Place? Gender, Family and Migration in the New West*. Stanford CA: Stanford University Press, 2014.

Seiler, Cotten. *Republic of Drivers: A Cultural History of Automobility in America*. Chicago: University of Chicago Press, 2008.

Shukla, Sandhya, and Heidi Tinsman, eds. *Imagining Our Americas: Toward a Transnational Frame*. Durham NC: Duke University Press, 2007.

Simpson, Audra. *Mohawk Interruptus: Political Life across the Borders of Settler States*. Durham NC: Duke University Press, 2014.

Stephen, Lynn. *Transborder Lives: Indigenous Oaxacans in Mexico, California, and Oregon*. Durham NC: Duke University Press, 2007.

Striffler, Steve. "Neither Here nor There: Mexican Immigrant Workers and the Search for Home." *American Ethnologist* 34, no. 4 (2007): 674–88.

Tapia, Isidro L. *Acuitzio: Sus Tradiciones y Leyendas y Ligeros Apuntes para la Historia Moderna*. Villa de Acuitzio del Canje, Michoacán, 1945.

Thompson, Niobe. *Settlers on the Edge: Identity and Modernization on Russia's Arctic Frontier*. Vancouver: University of British Columbia Press, 2008.

Todd, Zoe. "'You Never Go Hungry': Fish Pluralities, Human-Fish Relationships, Indigenous Legal Orders, and Colonialism in Paulatuuq, Canada." PhD diss., University of Aberdeen, 2016.

Trouillot, Michel-Rolph. *Global Transformations: Anthropology and the Modern World*. New York: Palgrave Macmillan, 2003.

Tsing, Anna L. *Friction: An Ethnography of Global Connection*. Princeton NJ: Princeton University Press, 2005.

Velázquez Verdugo, Dayra. "'Mexico's Last Frontier': Mexican Communities in Anchorage, Alaska—Their History Settlement, Work, Entrepreneurship, Networks, and Social Capital." MA thesis, Universidad Autónoma de Sinaloa, 2007.

Virilio, Paul. *Speed and Politics*. Los Angeles: Semiotext(e), 2006.

Wiest, Raymond E. "External Dependency and the Perpetuation of Temporary Migration to the United States." In *Patterns of Undocumented Migration: Mexico and the United States*, edited by Richard C. Jones. Totowa NJ: Rowman & Allanheld, 1984.

———. "Implications of International Labour Migration for Mexican Rural Development." In *Migration across Frontiers: Mexico and the United States*, edited by Fernando Camara and Robert Van Kemper. State University of New York at Albany: Contributions of the Latin American Anthropology Group (AAA) and the Institute for Mesoamerican Studies, 1979.

———. "Impressions of Transnational Mexican Life in Anchorage, Alaska: Acuitzences in the Far North." *Alaska Journal of Anthropology* 7, no. 1 (2009): 21–40.

———. "The Interrelationship of Rural, Urban, and International Labour Markets: Consequences for a Rural Michoacán Community." *Papers in Anthropology* 21, no. 1 (1980): 39–46.

———. "Wage Labor Migration and Household Maintenance in a Central Mexican Town." PhD diss., University of Oregon, 1970.

———. "Wage-Labor Migration and the Household in a Mexican Town." *Journal of Anthropological Research* 29, no. 3 (1973): 180–209.

Willis, Roxanne. *Alaska's Place in the West: From the Last Frontier to the Last Great Wilderness*. Lawrence: University Press of Kansas, 2010.

Wilson, Fiona. "Towards a Political Economy of Roads: Experiences from Peru." *Development and Change* 35, no. 3 (2004): 525–46.

Zavella, Patricia. *I'm Neither Here nor There: Mexicans' Quotidian Struggles with Migration and Poverty*. Durham NC: Duke University Press, 2011.

# Index

*Some research participants are identified by the family pseudonyms Bravo and Cárdenas. Other participants are identified by pseudonyms without a last name. Pseudonyms are alphabetized by first name; real names are alphabetized by last name. Page numbers in italics refer to illustrations.*

Abud Osuna, Javier, 25, 187, 189–95. See also Consulate of Mexico, Anchorage
Abu-Lughod, Lila, 166
Acuitzio (municipality), Michoacán, 28, 29, 86, 168–71, 227n37, 232n2, 235n25. See also schools in Acuitzio
Acuitzio del Canje: about, 28–34, *29*; celebrations and events in, 32–33, 34, 99, 170, 188, 224n10; churches in, 30; climate in, 40; clothing norms in, 131–33; comparison of, with Anchorage, 37–40, 126; corruption in, 169, 171–72, 232n2; demographics of, 28; history of, 29, 32–34; maps and location of, 29, 34, *49*; origin of name of, 32; out-migration from, 33–34, 210–11, 217n43; peace and security in, 28, 30–31, 39; pedestrian culture in, 35; public spaces in, 30, 38, 126; roads in, 65–66, *67*, 226n33; scholarship on, 85, 226n33; as seat of Acuitzio municipality, 28; soccer in, 12–13, 45, 208, 217n43; springs in, 31, 38, 39, 220n57; wilderness, 38–40
Acuitzio del Canje economy: and avocados, 31, 39, 233n13; comparison of, to Anchorage, 110, 111–12; and exchange rate (USD/MXN), 111–12, 113; and forestry industries, 31, 39, 66, 226n34; history of, 33–34; and housing costs, 111–12; impact of migrants on, 85–86, 92, 110, 121, 162–63, 211; and labor mobility, 33–34; and things that travel, 160–62; and wage labor, 111–12. See also everyday economics
Adán (nephew of Luis Jr., Miguel, and Gloria Bravo), xxiii, 155–56, 160
agriculture: and avocados, 31, 120, 121–22, 233n13; impact of U.S. migrants on, 86, 92; large-scale industries of, 86; and restrictions on travel with food, 148–49; and small farms (*ranchos*), 86, 227n37
Aguililla, Michoacán, 10

251

Alaska: bureaucratic processes in, 108; earthquake in (1964), 80, 82, 228n13; history of, 21–26, 34, 36; as international crossroads, 48, 50, 78–79, 81, 212, 223n4; Lower 48 as separate from, 4; maps of, 36, 49; military projects in, 226n29; political climate in, 40; racial and spatial categories in, 3–4; schools in, 37, 129, 235n1; stereotypes of, 23–24; undocumented immigrants in, 28, 39, 222n84; wilderness, 38–40, 185. *See also* Alaska Highway; Anchorage; Indigenous peoples, Alaska; Mexican Alaska; Trans-Alaska Pipeline

Alaska Airlines, 53, 55–56, 57

Alaska demographics: about, 27–28, 187; and census categories, 220n42; and diversity, 37, 221n74, 222n77, 229n18; of Fairbanks, 27, 191; of Juneau, 238n32; of Kenai Peninsula, 238n32; and military bases, 35, 221n74; and population, 21, 27, 28; and socioeconomic levels, 27; terminology of, 220n42; and undocumented immigrants, 28. *See also* Anchorage demographics

Alaska economy: comparison of, to Acuitzio, 111–12; and military bases, 35, 221n74; and oil and gas, 232n1; and permanent fund dividends, 56, 224n11; and resource extraction, 23; and salmon, 35–36, 150; and seasonal employment, 192; and tourism, 35–36. *See also* Anchorage economy

Alaska Federation of Natives (AFN), 180

Alaska Highway: about, 71–72, 227n40; into Anchorage, 34–35; and borders and boundaries, 49, 60, 72; and Gonzalo's trips, 67–71; and Indigenous peoples, 70, 71–72; route of, 49, 227n38, 227n40; and sociospatial distance, 72

Alaska Native Claims Settlement Act (ANCSA), 79, 228n11

Alaska Natives. *See* Indigenous peoples, Alaska

Alaska Permanent Fund Dividend (PFD), 56, 224n11

Aleutian Islands, 27, 36, 81, 83, 222n77, 229n17

Alina Cárdenas (wife of Ernesto Jr., mother of Claudia): about, xxii, 113–14; border crossing of, 59–61, 114; children of, 102, 129; citizenship of, 113–14; concerns of, 31; and food, 146, 149, 150, 157–58; future plans of, 200–201; and languages, 129, 131

Amchitka Island, 36, 81, 229n17

Ames, John, 226n33

Ana Bravo (wife of Miguel, mother of Araceli): about, xx, 78; citizenship of, xx; and food, 142, 146; future plans of, 122; homes of, xx, 78, 95; and industrial food preparation, 91; and love of outdoors, 39

Anchorage: about, 34–40; archives in, 24; car culture in, 35, 235n22; climate in, 40; comparison of, with Acuitzio, 37–40, 126; and earthquake (1964), 80, 82, 228n13; and highways, 34–35; as international crossroads, 37, 48, 50, 78–79, 81, 223n4; languages in, 37, 128–29; map and location of,

34, 36; and military base, 35, 221n74; and peace and security, 12, 38, 203–4; public spaces in, 126; schools in, 37, 129, 235n1; wilderness, 35, 38–40
Anchorage demographics: and diversity, 37, 40, 179, 221n74, 229n18; and Indigenous peoples, 37; and population, 26, 34, 35; and residential areas, 27; and temporary foreign workers, 26
Anchorage economy: and airports, 36–37, 48, 223n4; comparison of, to Acuitzio, 111–12; and military base, 35, 36–37; and oil, 35; and salmon fishing, 35–36; and tourism, 35–36. *See also* Alaska economy; everyday economics
Anchorage Museum, 172–73, *174*, 193
Antonio (Toño) Bravo. *See* Luis Antonio (Toño) Bravo (son of Luis Jr. and Juana)
Araceli Bravo (daughter of Miguel and Ana), xx, 119
Arenas García, Carlos, 33, 226n33
automobiles. *See* car culture in Alaska; car culture in Mexico; travel by road
avocados, 31, 120, 121–22, 233n13
Aztecs, 31, 173, 175, 237n24

Ball, Maria Elena, 181–82, 185–86, 237n22, 237nn24–25
baptisms, 94
Barrow AK (now Utqiaġvik), *36*, 107, 230n40, 232n1, 237n23
belonging: places needed for, 12–14, 104–5, 213; re-categorization of, in images, *184*, 186, 236n11, 236n13; transnational frame for, 47, 77–78, 208–9; and travel knowledges, 47. *See also* identity
Bernardo Cárdenas (husband of Ernesto Jr's sister), xxii, 91
*Big Miracle*, 230n40
Binational Health Week, 193
the body, 108, 123–24, 127. *See also* "getting used to" transnational life
Boehm, Deborah, 8–9, 23, 88, 205
border, U.S.-Canadian, *49*, *60*, 68–69
border, U.S.-Mexican: about, 21, 58; and airport checkpoints, 54; Anchorage as site of, 22; and artifacts of desert crossers, 139; entry into Mexico at, 61–62; and ground checkpoints, 58; influence of, on entire continent, 22; and Mexican consulate services, 191–92; and migration, 19–26; and militarization, 21; and striation of space, 216n18; and travel with food, 54, 148–49; and visas, 225n24; and visible boundaries, 21, 205; and workplaces, 58. *See also* Immigration and Nationality Act (INA), U.S.; undocumented migrants
borders: consulates and expansion of, 194–95; as imperial frontiers, 22–23; and mobility, 205–6; and roads and highways, 71–72; scholarship on, 239n15; as spatial categories, 5–6; transnational frame for, 207–9
Bourdieu, Pierre, 10, 217n39, 217n42
boys. *See* children and youth; men
Bravo family: about, xx–xxi, 76–78, 104–5; corridors for future generations of, 86–87, 90–91, 101–2, 121–22; future plans of, 103–4, 201–2; identity of, 75–76; as

INDEX 253

Bravo family (*continued*)
  individuals, 228n5; kinship ties of, 93–94; migration of, first generation, 76, 86–87; migration of, second generation, 87–96; migration of, third generation, 96–104, 201; mobility of, 16, 76–78, 104–5; pseudonyms for, xix, 215n1, 217n47; transnational lives of, 77–78, 103–5
bread, 54, 143, 144, 149, 162
British Columbia, 49, 70–71
bumper stickers, 235n22
bureaucratic processes, 108, 113–20. *See also* citizenship, U.S.

La Cabaña (restaurant), 237n25
Calderón, Gonzalo: about, xxiv, 64–71; citizenship of, xxiv, 68; homes of, xxiv, 67, 205, 227n37; retirement of, xxiv, 67, 87, 205; road trips of, 64–72, 83–84, 210–11; social network of, 83, 84–85; work of, in Alaska, xxiv, 64–65, 81–83, 226n29
California, 20–21, 24, 34, 58, 67, 172
Calvillo López, Edgar, 165, 215n1
Canada: and Alaska Highway, 49, 60, 68–72; border of, 60, 68–69; imperial frontiers of, 22; Indigenous peoples of, 7, 70–72, 239n15; maps of, 36, 49; and Mexican migration, 24
candy, 51, 54, 144
car culture in Alaska, 35, 103, 124–25, 127, 221n75, 235n22. *See also* travel by road
car culture in Mexico, 34, 49, 64–67, 124, 156–57, 235n22. *See also* travel by road

Cárdenas family, xix, xxii–xxiii, 59, 86–87, 215n1, 217n47
*carnitas* (braised pork), 144, 149, 169, 170, 236n7
categories: about, 3–7, 209–12; and anomalies, 4, 6–7; census, U.S., 220n42; and erasure of past, 6–7; and immigration law, 5–6; and mestizo nationalism, 175, 180, 208, 236n13; and Mexican nationalism, 195–96, 208; racial, 3–4; spatial, 3–7, 194–95; and transnational analysis, 209–10
categories, resistance to: about, 7–9, 17–18, 166–67, 209–12; and "categorizing back," 7–9, 17–18, 26; by collective action, 194–95; by dance, 178; in images, 182–86, *184*, 236n11, 236n13; in Mexican Alaska, 17–18, 166–67
Catholic churches, 30, 98, 131, 166, 167, 170, 188
cell phones, 53–54
certifications, 117–20. *See also* education
César (Migrant Club), xxiii, 171
*charro* suits, 132–33, 153, 188
cheese, 54, 142, 143, 148, 150
Chicago IL, 21, 34, 40, 172
Chichén Itzá (Mayan ruins), 182–86, *184*
children and youth: and absent fathers, 87, 89, 92, 93–94, 97; and age and mobility, 102; and dance and culture groups, 170, 176; and freedom, 102; and languages, 128–29, 197–99; and Mexican citizenship, 116; and *quinceañera*, 88–89, 97–99, 230n35, 231n49; and relocations, 233n18, 235n1, 238n1; and

socialization in Mexican culture, 102–3, 176, 180, 189, 197–98; third generation of, 97–100. *See also* education; schools in Acuitzio; schools in Alaska
chiles and chile sauce, 54, 143, 144, 145, 149–50
Christmas traditions (*las posadas*), 238n33
Chugach Mountains, 182–85, 184
Circumpolar North, 23–24, 207–10, 212
citizenship: ambiguous continuity of, 205–6; and mobility, 14, 47, 55, 61–62, 205–6; and systems of inequality, 8–9; and traction, 105; and transnational lives, 7–8, 77–78
citizenship, dual: of children born in Alaska, 116; comparison of, with permanent residency, 216n29; and entrepreneurship, 162; and inequalities, 142; and mobility goals, 9; and social capital, 155–56; and transnational lives, 7–8, 200; and travel with things, 138–42, 148, 150; and visas, 225n24
citizenship, U.S.: about, 14, 47, 58, 61, 113–20; and amnesty (1986), 79; and border crossing procedures, 114; and consular processing, 62–64, 94, 113, 115, 231n43, 232n5; exams and interviews for, 113–14; and mixed-status families, 62–64; and mobility goals, 14, 113–16; and reentry permits, 224n9; and time outside United States, 55, 224n9; and transnational social field, 47, 77–78; and visas, 225n23. *See also* Immigration and Nationality Act (INA), U.S.; permanent residency, U.S.

Ciudad Juarez, Mexico, 62–64, 94, 115, 231n43
class: and Alaska Native peoples, 221n75; and citizenship status, 7–8; and clothing norms, 132; and demographics, 27–28; and multigenerational mobility, 8, 16, 82; and poverty, 27; and systems of inequality, 8–9; and travel with things, 138
Claudia Cárdenas (wife of Iván, daughter of Ernesto Jr. and Alina): about, xxii, 129–30; border crossing of, 59–61, 129; citizenship of, xxii, 59–61, 114; and food, 150; future plans of, 200; and home décor, 152; homes of, xxii, 197–99; and languages, 130; lives of children of, 130, 197, 233n19; multiple relocations of, 129–30, 197–99, 205, 231n46, 238n1; and things that travel, 159–61, 162
climate. *See* weather and climate
closed-in feelings, 124–25, 127
clothes: *charro* suit, 132–33, 153, 188; and gender and class, 132; as gifts, 159, 161; and norms and social rules, 131; and personal identity, 155; price comparisons of, 159–60; for *quinceañera*, 97–98; for resale, 160–62, 199; sandals, 221n65; traditional Mexican, 188; and travel with things, 153
Club de Migrantes de Acuitzio del Canje en Alaska. *See* Migrant Club
Cold War, 35, 65, 81, 221n74, 226n29, 229n17
*comida*, term of, 233n17
*compadrazgo*, term of, 76, 84, 91, 228n3

INDEX    255

Consulate of Mexico, Anchorage: about, 1, 189–95; closure of, 189; and consular services, 189–91, 194–95; and cultural events, 25–26, 186–89, 192–94; and Mexican Alaska, 166–67, 194, 196; and mobile services, 190–91. *See also* Abud Osuna, Javier

Costco, 143, 229n28, 237n24

Cruikshank, Julie, 71

Customs and Border Protection, U.S., 148–49. *See also* border, U.S.-Mexican

dance and culture groups. *See* groups and organizations

Danzantes Tradicionales de Acuitzio, 170, 236n9

Day of the Northerners, 34

De Certeau, Michel, 6

De Genova, Nicholas, 20

De León, Jason, 139–40

Deleuze, Gilles, 6

Deloria, Philip J., 4, 7

Del Real, Ana, 174–79, 215n1

demographics, 27–28. *See also* Alaska demographics; Anchorage demographics

Dena'ina people, 34, 173, 222n76

Denali Mountain, 36, 45, 151, 173, 185, 236n11

deportation, 8–9, 39, 105, 108, 190, 222n84. *See also* Immigration and Nationality Act (INA), U.S.; undocumented migrants

DEW (Distant Early Warning) Line, 65, 81, 226n29

Diego, xxiii, 107–8, 153–54

Douglas, Mary, 4

dual citizenship. *See* citizenship, dual

Dutch Harbor, Aleutian Islands, 81, 191

earthquake (1964), 80, 82, 228n13

economy. *See* Acuitzio del Canje economy; Alaska economy; Anchorage economy; everyday economics

Eduardo, xxiii, 144–45

education: about, 117–20; for both places, 12, 117, 119–20; and certifications, 117–20; and demographics, 27; and gender differences, 89, 117; and languages, 117–19; in Mexico, 119, 125, 126; postsecondary, 220n54, 235n1; second-generation, 89, 90. *See also* schools in Acuitzio; schools in Alaska

Efrén (husband of Soledad), xxiv, 128, 202, 233n17

Elmendorf-Richardson military base, 35, 36–37, 48, 221n74

El Tzintzun, Michoacán, 169

emotional in-betweenness, 52–53, 72–74

English language. *See* language(s)

entrepreneurship, 160–62, 199, 204, 229n29

Ernesto Cárdenas Jr. (husband of Alina, father of Claudia): about, xxiii, 109–10; border crossing of, 59–61; citizenship of, 110, 114–15, 232n5–6; and food, 146; future plans of, 201, 212–13; and "getting used to" lifestyle, 109–10

Ernesto Cárdenas Sr.: about, xxii, 81; citizenship of, 232n6; as first generation, 86–87, 109; homes of, 81, 86–87; retirement of, 86–87; social network of, 84; work of, xxii, 59, 81, 84, 109, 226n29

Esteban (husband of Laura), xxiv, 123–24, 152–53, 237n16

everyday economics: about, 157–63; and first-generation out-migration, 85–87; and food prices, 157–58; and price comparisons, 111–12, 139, 150, 157–60; and resale of things that travel, 160–62, 199. *See also* Acuitzio del Canje economy; Alaska economy; Anchorage economy

Fairbanks AK, 27, 36, 71, 191, 227n40
family and kinship ties: about, 96; and future plans, 202–3; and godparents, 76, 84, 91, 228n3; of second generation, 90–92, 95–97; and support for property owners, 121–22; and work, 90–91
Farrell, Chad, 221n74
feeling at home: about, 9–14; and educational challenges, 119; and food, 145–46, 150; mobility needed for, 9–11, 14, 22, 207; and pets, 137; places needed for, 9–13, 22, 137–38, 207, 213; as a process, 105; and roots, 14; and things that travel, 17, 137–38, 145–46; and uneven attachments, 12–14, 197–99. *See also* "getting used to" transnational life
feeling closed in, 124–25, 127
feeling like yourself, 137, 138, 142. *See also* identity
Ferguson, James, 4, 5, 206
Fernando (husband of Ivonne), xxiii, 143, 144
Ferry, Emma, 139
first generation. *See* multigenerational mobility, first-generation
food, 146, 147, 150, 157–59, 234n9, 234n18. *See also specific foods*
food in Anchorage, 143, 145, 146, 237n24. *See also* restaurants, Mexican
food that travels: about, 17, 51, 142–50; availability and quality of, 143, 145; avocados as, 233n13; and border control, 143, 148, 149; bread as, 54, 142, 143, 144, 149, 162; candy as, 51, 54, 144; cheese as, 142, 143, 148, 150; chiles as, 54, 143, 144; churros as, 54; and citizenship status, 148, 150, 234n18; containers for, 144, 148, 150; and cookware, 149; as gifts, 145, 150, 154–55; *mole* as, 54, 142, 143–44, 146, 148; prices and flavors of, 139, 142–43, 145–47, 150, 157–58; salmon as, 150; tamales as, 51, 144, 147. *See also* things that travel
Foucault, Michel, 6
free trade, 23, 90, 157
future plans, 18, 200–206, 212–13

gender: about, 88; and careers, 118; and clothing norms, 131–33; and educational attainment, 89, 117; and family ties, 95–96; and "getting used to" transnational life, 124–25, 127; and multigenerational migration, 88; and systems of inequality, 8–9; and travel with things, 144, 152–53. *See also* men; women and girls
"getting used to" transnational life: about, 16–17, 105, 108–9, 133–34; in both places, 17, 105, 126; and bureaucratic processes, 108, 113–20; and car culture, 124–25; and certifications, 117–20; and citizenship, 113–17; and clothing norms, 108, 131–32; and education, 126; as embodied process,

"getting used to" (*continued*)
108, 123, 127; and everyday life, 108, 123–33; and feeling closed in, 108, 124–26; and feeling like yourself, 137, 138, 142; and gendered processes, 124–25, 127; and languages, 108, 117, 125, 127–31; and money and salaries, 109–10, 111–12; and property ownership, 120–22; and social and kinship ties, 37–38; as social process, 108; and tension between here and there, 95–97; and territorialization, 108, 120–22; and third generation, 119; and transnational habitus, 10; and weather, 108, 123–24, 126–27, 154. *See also* feeling at home

Gilberto (husband of Mónica), xxiv, 146, 153

girls. *See* children and youth; women and girls

Glenn Highway, 34–35

globalization, 56–57

Gloria Bravo (Luis Sr.'s daughter, mother of Renata): about, xx, 78; children of, 90; citizenship of, xx, 88–89, 90, 91; and education, 89, 90, 119; and feeling at home, 12; first trip of, to Alaska, 85, 88–89; and food, 142; future plans of, 202–3; and "getting used to" life, 113; and home décor, 151–52; homes of, xx, 78, 85, 88; and industrial food preparation, xx, 91; marriage of, 90; mobility of, 57; and peace and security, 12; as second generation, 90

godparents (*compadrazgo*), 76, 84, 91, 228n3

*golondrinas* (swallows), 45–47, 72–73, 227n51

"Golondrinas Viajeras," 46–47

Gomberg-Muñoz, Ruth, 62

Green Card, term of, 225n25

*Grito de Dolores*, 187, 188, 189, 194

groups and organizations: about, 17–18, 166–67; in Acuitzio, 170, 176, 236n9; in Anchorage, 166, 187–89; and Mexican Alaska, 166–67, 176, 195–96, 238n26; and Migrant Club fundraising, 170; and mistrust of authorities, 171–72; and national backgrounds, 237n16; as out of place, 3. *See also specific groups*

Guattari, Felix, 6

Gupta, Akhil, 4, 5, 206

Gutiérrez-Scholl, Ana, 173–80, 215n1, 237n16

hairdressers, 232n7

handicrafts, 54, 151, 235n21

highways. *See* roads and highways

home décor, 54, 151–52, 155

horse parades (*cabalgatas*), 99, 231n52

Humberto Bravo (Luis Sr.'s brother), xx, 203

identity: and careers, 118; of children as Mexican American, 174; and citizenship interviews, 75–76; and clothes, 155; and dance and cultural preservation, 177; and feeling like yourself, 137, 138, 142; and food, 147, 234n9; of Mexican Alaska, 166–67, 195; and multigenerational mobility, 75–76; places needed for, 9, 11–13, 75–76, 213; and social capital, 154–55; and souvenirs, 154–55; and transnational social field, 77–78; and uneven attachments, 13–14, 154–56, 197–99, 213

Immigration and Nationality Act (INA), U.S.: about, 5–6, 205–6, 239n5; and bounded space of state, 5; changes to, over time, 224n9; enforcement of, 6, 190, 222n84; and lived experience, 205–6; and spatial relationships, 5–6, 205–6, 239n5. *See also* border, U.S.-Mexican; citizenship, U.S.; deportation

Independence Day events, 187–89, 194

Indigenous peoples, Alaska: and ANCSA land claims settlement, 79, 228n11; categories of, 26; and dance performances, 180; and demographics in Anchorage, 37; and dichotomy with white settlers, 4; and Indigenous space, 8; and intermarriage, 26; as part of Circumpolar North, 24. *See also specific peoples*

Indigenous peoples, Canada, 7, 70–72, 239n15

Indigenous peoples, Mexico, 173, 175, 178, 180, 182–86, *184*, 208, 236n13. *See also specific peoples*

industrial food preparation, xx, 91

Inés (wife of Salvador), xxiv, 62–63

Iñupiat people, 232n1

Iván Cárdenas (husband of Claudia): about, xxiii, 126–27; citizenship of, xxiii; and feeling at home, 127; future plans of, 127, 198, 200; and "getting used to" transnational life, 126–27; homes of, xxiii, 126;

kinship ties of, 126; and languages, 130, 197; mobility of, 197–99, 205

Ivonne (wife of Fernando), xxv, 143–44, 145

Jaime, xxv, 38–39, 83, 105, 132, 153, 156

Jalisco, Mexico, 20, 176–77, 222n83

Juana Bravo (wife of Luis Bravo Jr., mother of Toño, Verónica, and Sophia): about, xx, 78; citizenship of, xx, 54, 75–76, 92, 94, 115; and dance group, 179, 237n16; and emotional in-betweenness, 52–53; and everyday economics, 159; and feeling at home, 11; and food, 54, 143, 147; future plans of, 96, 103, 201–2; and gifts, 54, 154–55, 159, 235n21; and home décor, 45, 155; homes of, 45–46, *78*, 93, 94–95; identity of, 75–76, 154–55; and Independence Day events, 187–89; and industrial food preparation, xx, 91; and languages, 131; lives of children of, 102; marriage and family life of, 52, 93–95; mobility of, to Anchorage, 45, 48–55, *49*, 52, 72; and peace and security, 205; personal qualities of, 46; and service industry, 55; and travel with things, 54, 143–44, 159, 234n20, 235n21

Juneau AK, 24, 36, 191, 238n32

Kenai Peninsula, 36, 238n32

Kodiak Island, 27, 36

Komarnisky, Sara, 2, 54, 145–46, 224n8, 234n9, 234n13, 237n22

Kotzebue AK, 36, 107

labor migration: about, 226n29; first-generation, 81–82; and fish canneries, 27; history of, 20–21, 24–25; and restaurants, 27; and seasonal work, 192; and temporary foreign workers, 26, 192; and wage comparison, 111–12

language(s): about, 127–31; in Anchorage, 119, 127–29, 176; and bilingualism, 128–31; for certifications, 117, 119; in children's schools, 119, 128–29, 197–99; and demographics, 27; and diversity in Anchorage, 37; and feeling closed in, 124–25; and "getting used to" transnational life, 127–28; at immigration checkpoints, 54; and postsecondary education, 235n1; and second generation, 128; and socialization, 180; and third generation, 97, 119, 128–29, 176

Latin America, transnational analysis of, 209–10

*Latinos en Alaska*, 167, 187

Lattanzi-Shutika, Debra, 21, 120–21

Laura (wife of Esteban), xxv, 12, 13, 38, 123–24, 152–53, 237n16

Law, Lisa, 145

learning. *See* education; schools in Acuitzio; schools in Alaska

Lefebvre, Henri, 5, 10

Leonardo, xxv, 167–72, 203–4

life event(s): about, 89; baptism as, 94; and economic hardships, 90, 92, 93, 109, 230n42; impact of, on mobility, 94; and luck and chance, 82–83; marriage as, 90; mobility needed for, 14; *quinceañera* as, 88–89, 97–99, 230n35, 231n49; and traction, 105; transnational frame for, 98–99, 208–9; wedding as, 208–9

Lola (wife of Gilberto's brother): about, xxv, 125–26, 165–66; careers of, xxv, 125–26, 165, 168, 205; citizenship of, xxv, 125; and dance groups, 166; and feeling closed in, 125; homes of, 125–26, 165, 195; and languages, 125; and Migrant Club, 166–72; and relocation, 125–26, 235n1; as restaurant owner, 120, 125, 126, 165–66, 205

Los Angeles CA, 34, 53–54, 72

"Los Viejitos," 238n26

Lower 48. *See* United States, Lower 48

Luis Antonio (Toño) Bravo (son of Luis Jr. and Juana): about, xxi, 78, 100–101; citizenship of, 75–76, 92, 103–4; future plans of, 103–4; homes of, 78, 103–4; and horse parades, 99, 231n52; mobility of, 100–101, 149–50, 231n53; move of, to Alaska, 92–93, 100; nickname of, 100; and service industry, 55; as third generation, 78, 96–97, 100–101, 103–4

Luis Bravo Jr. (son of Luis Sr., husband of Juana, father of Toño, Verónica, and Sophia): about, xxi, 78; as absent father, 92, 93; citizenship of, xxi, 75–76, 90, 91, 92; and clothing norms, 132; and economic hardships, 92, 93, 109; and education, 90; and everyday economics, 158–59; and feeling at home, 13; and food, 158–59; future plans of, 96, 103, 201–2; and home décor, 45, 151, 155; homes of, 45, 78, 92, 96; identity of, 76, 154–55; and languages, 131; love of, for

Acuitzio, 30; marriage and family life of, 92–94, 101; mobility of, 52, 151; move of, to Alaska, 92–93, 109–10; Octavio as uncle to, 90–91, 230n36; and peace and security, 205; and price and flavor comparisons, 158–59; as second generation, xxi, 90–92, 96; and service industry, xxi, 55; social and kinship networks of, 90–91

Luis Bravo Sr. (father of Yolanda, Gloria, Luis Jr., and Miguel): about, xxi, 78, 79–81; absence of, from family, 93, 101; and avocado orchard, 121–22; citizenship of, xxi, 85; and earthquake (1964), 80, 82, 228n13; family of, 78, 85, 86, 87, 105; as first generation, 79–81, 85, 86; and Gloria's first trip to Alaska, 85, 88–89; and home décor, 79; homes of, 79, 85, 121; and luck and chance, 83; and photographs, 154; repetitive mobility of, 83–84; retirement of, xxi, 85, 87; social networks of, 85, 88–89; work of, xxi, 79–83, 226n29

Malkki, Liisa, 7
manicures, 158
Mariachi Agave Azul dance group, 187–89
marriage and family life, 87, 89, 92–99
masculinity. *See* men
Massey, Doreen, 239n8
Massey, Douglas, 20–21
Matanuska-Susitna Valley, 35, 191
material culture: about, 17, 137–43, 162–63; and deterritorialization, 146; and feeling like yourself, 137, 138, 142; and kinship networks, 138; and link to place, 142–43, 146. *See also* food that travels; things that travel

Mayan ruins, postcards of, 182–86, *184*, 236n13

men: as absent fathers, 87, 89, 92, 93–94; and Alaska as masculine space, 88; and clothing norms, 132–33; and coming of age, 81–82, 88; and horse parades, 99, 231n52; and travel with things, 144, 152–53

*menudo* (tripe soup), 181, 237n21
mestizo nationalism, 175, 180, 208, 236n13
La Mex (restaurant), 237n25
Mexican Alaska: about, 17–20, 166–67, 186, 195–96, 208–9; and Catholic churches, 131, 166, 167, 170, 188; comparison of, with Lower 48 culture, 40; and flags, 208; and Hispanic and Latino community, 193–94; and Independence Day celebrations, 186–87; material culture of, 17; and mestizo nationalism, 175, 180, 208, 236n13; and National Hispanic Heritage Month, 25, 172, 193, 236n10; and national narratives, 166; as out of place, 1–3, 166–67; and postcards as transnational space, 182–86, *184*, 236n11, 236n13; and restaurants, 180–81; and stereotypes, 174–75; and wilderness recreation, 38–40

Mexican consulate. *See* Consulate of Mexico, Anchorage

Mexico: and children's freedom, 102; and consular services, 189–90; corruption in, 127, 169, 171–72; crime and violence in, 31, 109, 122,

INDEX 261

Mexico (*continued*)
127, 202–5, 211; and diaspora policies, 206; economic crises in, 90, 92, 93, 157, 230n42; fiestas in, 176; history of, 22–23, 32–33; maps of, *29*, *49*; and mestizo nationalism, 175, 180, 208, 236n13; and NAFTA, 23, 90, 157; out-migration regions of, 20; in popular imagination, 3–4, 174–75; popular songs of, 46, 73; symbols of, 186; and 3x1 Program, 169, 171, 236n8; and traditional dance groups, 176–77; wilderness, 38–40

Mexico City, 40, 51–52, 63–64, 223n6

Mexico in Alaska (restaurant): about, 181–86; as film setting, 222n84; logo of, 237n24; and Mexican Alaska, 166–67, 180–82, 238n27; and postcards, 181–86, *184*, 237n22; prepared foods in, 237n24; and time in business, 237n25

*Mexico in Alaska* (screenplay), 222n84

Michoacán, Mexico: and first-generation migration, 64–66; map of, *29*; and out-migration, 20; and roads and highways, 65–66; scholarship on, 10; violence in, 31, 39, 203–4, 205, 211; wilderness, 39–40

Migrant Club, 166–72, 232n2, 235n25

*migrantes golondrinas*, 227n51

migration, Mexican-U.S., 5–6, 19–26. *See also* border, U.S.-Mexican; Immigration and Nationality Act (INA), U.S.; multigenerational mobility

Miguel Bravo (son of Luis Sr., husband of Ana, father of Araceli): about, xxi, *78*, 95; and avocado orchard, 116–17, 120, 121–22, 204; citizenship of, xxi, 91, 95, 122; and education, 89; future plans of, 122, 204; homes of, xxi, *78*; ID card of, 116; Octavio as uncle to, 91; and property ownership, 121–22; as restaurant owner, xxi, 91, 120, 121; as second generation, 95, 122

military bases, 35, 36–37, 48, 221n74, 229n17

mobility: about, 8–9, 14–15, 205, 213; barriers to, 8, 15; and citizenship, 14, 47, 55, 61–62, 205–6; common desire for, 8–9, 213; and Indigenous peoples, 71–72; and life events, 89; and property ownership, 120–21; and social class, 8, 16; and social networks, 120; in space, 15, 205–6; and traction and resilience, 77, 78, 83, 105; and transnational social field, 16, 77–78, 213. *See also* multigenerational mobility

*mole* sauce, 54, 143–44, 146, 148, 149, 150, 157, 224n8

Mónica (wife of Gilberto), xxv, 153

Montana, 20, 21, 215n2, 218n17

Morelia, Michoacán, *29*, 29, 31, 65–66

Mount Susitna, 36

Muehlmann, Shaylih, 139

multigenerational mobility: about, 16, 76–78, 91, 104–5, 140–41; and citizenship, 75–76, 85, 104–5; and class mobility, 16; and corridors for future generations, 83, 86–87, 90–91, 104, 121; and economic capital, 84, 85–87; and gender relations, 88; and identity, 75–76; and life events, 98, 105; and luck and chance, 60, 82–83; and marriage and family, 95–97; and social and kinship networks, 82–83, 91, 98; and social capital, 84–85; and statehood and personal maturity, 81–82; and traction and resilience, 77, 78, 83, 105; and transnational lives, 77–78, 104–5

multigenerational mobility, first-generation: about, 78–87, 104–5; and citizenship amnesty (1986), 79; and economic and social capital, 82, 84, 85–87; and educational background, 117; and gender relations, 88; and laborers, 64–66, 80–81, 117; and luck and chance, 82–83; of men alone, 79, 87, 88; and repetitive mobility, 83–84; and sociospatial distance, 64–67; and statehood and personal maturity, 81–82

multigenerational mobility, second-generation: about, 87–96, 104–5; and absent fathers, 87, 89, 92, 93–94; and economic hardships, 90, 92, 93, 230n42; and education, 89, 90, 117; and entrepreneurship, 87; and gender, 88–89, 95–96; and homes, 87, 96; and languages, 128; and marriage and family, 92–96; and social and kinship networks, 84–85, 87, 90–91, 95–97; and tension between here and there, 95–97; and transnational lives, 77–78, 87, 96

multigenerational mobility, third-generation: about, 96–105; and future plans, 97, 102–4, 201, 202; and languages, 97, 119, 128–29; and life events, 97–99; and social and kinship networks, 97–100; and transnational lives, 77–78, 97–98

NAFTA (North American Free Trade Agreement), 23, 90, 157

National Hispanic Heritage Month, 25, 172, 193, 236n10

nations, 4–6, 175, 180, 194–96, 207–10, 236n13. *See also* borders; identity

Native Americans. *See* Indigenous peoples, Alaska

nature. *See* wilderness

North America: economy of, 23, 157–62; as frame of analysis, 15, 48, 208–10; imperial frontiers of, 22–23; map of, *49*; and Mexican economic crises, 90, 92, 93, 157, 230n42; and NAFTA, 23, 90, 157; re-categorizing of, 213; and stereotypes, 23–24; and transnational lives, 77–78, 206–12

North American Dream, 9, 109, 199

North Slope, 36, 80, 183–85, *184*, 232n1

Oaxacans in Anchorage, 188, 211, 238n29

Obama, Barack, 222n84, 239n8

Octavio (uncle to Luis Jr., Miguel, and Gloria Bravo): about, xxvi; citizenship of, 61–62, 115–16; future plans of, 201; homes of, xxvi, 87; and luck and chance, 83; mobility of, while undocumented, 61–62; as restaurant owner, 87, 90; social and kinship networks of, 84, 90–91, 230n36; and statehood and personal maturity, 81–82

oil and gas industry, 228n11, 232n1. *See also* Trans-Alaska Pipeline

INDEX 263

organizations. *See* groups and organizations

Oscar (rooster breeder): about, xxvi, 135–38, *136*; citizenship of, xxvi; and feeling like himself, 137, 142; future plans of, 204; and home décor, 152; homes of, xxvi, 135; mobility of, 136–37, 142, 152; as rooster breeder, 135–37, *136*, 142, 152, 161–62, 204; as taxi driver, 135–36, 137

Our Lady of Guadalupe Church, Anchorage, 131, 166, 167, 170, 188

out of place: about, 1–4, 166–67; and anomalies, 4, 6–7; and cars, 156–57; and erasure of past, 6–7; and first generation, 64–66; and future research, 212; and Mexican Alaska, 166–67; people as, 1, 4–5, 212; and postcards, 182–86, *184*, 236n11, 236n13; and stability, boundedness, and timelessness, 7; and things that travel, 146–47, 154, 157

Palmer AK, 35, *36*, 191
Pan-American Club, Anchorage, 167
Páramo, Michoacán, 169–70
Paredes, Américo, 20
*Pascalian Meditations*, 10, 217n39, 217n42
Pascual, xxvi, 12, 31–33, 38–39
peace and security, 12, 30–31, 38–39, 127, 202–4
Pepe's North of the Border (restaurant), 107, 237n23
permanent residency, U.S.: about, 216n29, 225n25; and border crossing, 114; comparison of, with dual citizenship, 216n29; and consular processing, 62–64, 88–89, 94, 231n43; feelings about, 115–16; and mobility, 9, 115, 216n29; and restriction on time outside United States, 55, 224n9; and transnational lives, 7–8, 200; and travel with things, 148. *See also* citizenship, U.S.

*pinole* (corn meal), 54, 144, 224n8
place and space, 4–7, 10, 146, 154, 166–67, 207–10. *See also* out of place
population, 27–28. *See also* Alaska demographics; Anchorage demographics
*las posadas* (Christmas traditions), 224n10, 238n33
postcards from Mexico in Alaska restaurant, 182–86, *184*, 236n13, 237n22
postsecondary education, 235n1. *See also* education
property ownership: about, 17, 120–22, 146; and deterritorialization, 146; and "getting used to" transnational life, 108, 120–22; mobility needed for, 14; social networks to support, 120; and things that travel, 146, 157
Prudhoe Bay AK, *36*, 80
P'urhépecha people, 32, 221n58

*quinceañera* (fifteenth birthday), 88–89, 97–99, 230n35, 231n49
Quyana Alaska, 180

race and ethnicity: and demographics of Hispanic Alaskans, 37, 229n18; and diversity in Anchorage, 37, 40, 179, 221n74; and diversity in settlement narratives, 226n29; and ethnic enclaves, 229n18; and

members of Mexican dance group, 237n16; and mestizo nationalism, 175, 180, 236n13; and racial categories, 3–4, 26; and systems of inequality, 8–9
*rancho*, term of, 227n37
recreation, 12–13, 39–40, 45, 46, 208, 217n43
Renata Bravo (Gloria's daughter), xxi, 2–3, 11–12, 13, *78*, 202, 231n46
research project: about, 3–4, 10–11, 40–43; and author's background, 54; excluded areas of, 167, 210–12, 222n83; and field site as transnational social field, 40–43; and fieldwork, 40–41, 45, 231nn49–50; findings of, not to be generalized, 28, 211; and future research, 210, 219n31, 238n29; and multigenerational mobility, 10, 16; and multisited ethnography, 42–43, 47; participants, xix, 7–8, 100, 215n1, 217n47; and transnational habitus, 10–11
resident, permanent. *See* permanent residency, U.S.
restaurants, Mexican: about, 180–82, 237n25; in Barrow, 107, 230n40, 237n23; and immigration raids, 222n84; and Mexican Alaska, 166–67, 180–81. *See also specific restaurants*
roads and highways, 64, 70–72. *See also* Alaska Highway; car culture in Alaska; car culture in Mexico; travel by road
Roberts, Bart, 182–86, *184*, 237n22
Rosa (Ana Bravo's sister), xxvi, 143
Rouse, Roger, 10, 47, 228n5, 230n42, 233n18
Rugh, Jacob S., 20–21

salmon, 35–36, 150
Salvador (husband of Inés), xxvii, 62–63
Schmalzbauer, Leah, 21, 215n2, 218n17
schools in Acuitzio: and cultural knowledge, 129, 176–77, 233n18; and postsecondary education, 220n54, 235n1; and relocation of students, 130, 233n18, 235n1, 238n1; and schedules, 130, 233n19. *See also* education
schools in Alaska, 37, 129, 235n1. *See also* education
Schoppert, Jim, 236n11
second generation. *See* multigenerational mobility, second-generation
sedentary space, term of, 216n18
Serefina (Efrén's sister-in-law): about, xxvi, 117–18, 124–25; citizenship of, 117, 125; and dance group, 237n16; and everyday economics, 159; family ties of, in Acuitzio, 95–96, 117; and feeling at home, 11, 13; as hairdresser, 117–18, 232n7; and languages, 117–18, 125; and travel with things, 148, 159
Seward AK, 36
Simpson, Audra, 7, 239n15
soccer, 12–13, 45, 208, 217n43
social and kinship relationships. *See* family and kinship ties; translocal social field
social class. *See* class
sociospatial distance, 39, 56–57, 64–67, 70–71, 72, 102
Soledad (wife of Efrén), xxvii, 128, 176, 202, 237n16
Sophia Bravo (Luis Jr. and Juana's daughter): about, xxi, *78*, 98; citizenship of, xxi, 54, 75–76, 77, 92, 103–4; and clothes, 131–32;

Sophia Bravo (*continued*)
and everyday economics, 158; and feeling at home, 103–4; future plans of, 97, 103–4; homes of, *78*, 98, 103; identity of, 75–76; mobility of, 48–55, *49*, 231n53; and *quinceañera*, 97–98, 158; and service industry, 55; as third generation, xxi, 96–97, 103–4
sourdough, term of, 82, 215n3
*Soy Tu Dueña*, 46
space. *See* place and space
Spanish language. *See* language(s)
sports. *See* recreation
Striffler, Steve, 9, 21, 42, 102
swallows (*golondrinas*), 45–47, 72–73, 227n51

tamales, 51, 144, 147, 223n5
temporary foreign workers, 26, 192
territorialization, 14, 59, 108, 120–22, 146, 157
Texas, 21, 58, 89, 172, 191–92
things that travel: about, 17, 137–38, 151–57, 162–63; in both directions, 137–38, 151–52; buying, selling, or trading of, 17, 138, 160–62; and citizenship status, 138, 148; as deterritorialized from place, 146; and entrepreneurship, 160–62; everyday items as, 151–52; and feeling at home, 17, 137–38; and feeling like yourself, 138; as gifts, 54, 138, 145, 150, 154–55; and home décor, 54, 151–52, 155; and kinship ties, 138; list of, 140–41; and place, 146; and price comparisons, 139, 157–60; roosters as, 136–38, 161–62; and social networks, 154–55; and socioeconomic status, 138; as symbolic markers, 17. *See also* food that travels; material culture
third generation. *See* multigenerational mobility, third-generation
3xI Program, 169, 171, 236n8
Tiripetio, Michoacán, 29, *29*, 32, 66, *67*
Tomás (brother of Ana Bravo), xxvii, 38, 204
Toño. *See* Luis Antonio (Toño) Bravo (son of Luis Jr. and Juana)
Tordrillo Range, 36, 222n76
tortillas, 145
tourism, 35–36
traction, 77, 78, 83, 105. *See also* mobility
Trans-Alaska Pipeline: map and route of, *36*, 80; and migrant workers, 79, 80, 226n29; postcard images of, 183, *184*, 186
translocal social field, 16, 37–38, 47, 208
transnational habitus, 10–11, 47, 217n39, 217n42
transnational lives of Acuitzences: about, 7–14, 77–78, 199–200, 206–12; and barriers to mobility, 8, 205–6; and citizenship status, 7–8, 9, 200; and class mobility, 8; and continuity and fragmentation, 23; and cultural preservation, 176–77; and emotional in-betweenness, 52–53, 72–74; and family and social support, 121–22; and first generation, 104–5; and future plans, 18, 204–5; and mestizo nationalism, 175, 180, 208, 236n13; mobility needed for, 7–10, 15, 47, 77–78, 199–200, 205–6, 213; and North American Dream, 9, 109, 199; places needed

for, 7–14, 77–78, 199–200, 213; and relocations, 204–5; and research project, 40–43, 210; and second generation, 96, 104–5, 201–2; and tension between here and there, 95–97; and third generation, 103–5, 201; and traction and resilience, 77, 78, 83, 105; and transnational social field, 47, 77–78, 207–8, 217n39, 217n42; and travel knowledges, 42, 47; and uneven attachments, 13–14, 77–78, 154–56, 197–99, 213
travel by air, 48–58, *49*
travel by road, 58–61, 64–72
travel knowledges: about, 15, 47–48, *49*, 61; and cell phones, 53–54; and challenges and barriers, 57; and citizenship and mobility, 47, 55, 61–62, 205–6; and consular processing, 62–64; and continent as frame of analysis, 48; and costs, 55, 61; and emotional in-betweenness, 52–53, 72–74; and research project, 42; and seasons for travel, 55, 57, 91; and sociospatial distance, 56–58, 64–67
Trique people, 211, 238n29
Trouillot, Michel-Rolph, 6
Trump, Donald, 222n84, 239n8

uncle, term of, 230n36
undocumented migrants: amnesty for (1986), 79; Cárdenas family's border crossing as, 59–61, 114; and consular services, 62; and demographics in Alaska, 28; desert crossers as, 58, 139; and DREAM Act proposal, 239n8; and immigration raids, 222n84;

mobility goals of, 8–9; protection of privacy of, 171; travel limitations of, 61–62; and travel with things, 148; and U.S.-Mexican land border, 58, 139. *See also* deportation
United States, Lower 48: and children's freedom, 102; demographics of, 27; ethnic enclaves in, 229n18; imperial frontiers of, 22–23; and Mexican Alaska culture, 40; and Mexican consulate services, 191–92; and Mexican cultural preservation, 176–77; and Mexican food, 180–81; Migrant Clubs in, 172; and migration receiving regions, 20–21; and NAFTA, 23, 90, 157; and National Hispanic Heritage Month, 25, 172, 193, 236n10; and spatial categories, 4
Utqiaġvik AK (was Barrow), 36, 107, 230n40, 232n1, 237n23

Valdez AK, 36, 80
Velázquez, Dayra, 26–27, 229n29
Verónica (Vero) Bravo (Luis Jr. and Juana's daughter): about, xxi, *78*, 100; citizenship of, xxi, 54, 75–76, 92, 104; and education, 102; and feeling at home, 104, 133; future plans of, 102–4; and "getting used to" transnational life, 133; homes of, 52, *78*, 102; mobility of, 48–55, *49*, 100–103, 231n53; and *quinceañera*, 98–99, 158; and service industry, 55; as third generation, 96–97, 100–104
visas, 62–64, 88–89, 94, 225n24, 231n43

INDEX  267

Vivaldi, Ana, 227n51

Wasilla AK, 35, 36, 191
weather and climate: in Acuitzio, 40; as factor in future plans, 204; and feeling closed in, 124; and "freezing the people together," 166; and "getting used to" differences, 2–3, 123–24, 126–27; photos of, 154
Whitehorse, Yukon Territory, 69, 71
Wiest, Raymond E., 33–34, 66, 85–86, 226nn33–34
wilderness, 38–40, 88, 153–54, *184*, 185–86
Willis, Roxanne, 71
women and girls: ability of, to drive, 124; careers and gender roles of, 118; educational attainment of, 89, 117; *quinceañeras* of, 88–89, 97–99, 230n35, 231n49; and travel with things, 144, 152–53
work: and feeling at home, 14; and kinship networks, 91; and labor migration, 20–21, 24–25, 101, 213. *See also* entrepreneurship
World War II, 25, 35, 71, 221n74, 229n17

Xochiquetzal-Tiqún dance group: about, 172–80, *174*, 237n16; costumes of, 2, *174*, 178; and images of wilderness and indigeneity, 174–75; members of, 2, 173, 176, 178, 179, 187, 237n16; and mestizo nationalism, 175, 180, 236n13; and Mexican Alaska, 166–67, 176–78; origin of name of, 173–74; as out of place, 2, 3; performances of, 1–2, 172–73, *174*, 179–80, 187–88

Yolanda Bravo (daughter of Luis Sr.), *78*, 105
youth. *See* children and youth
Yukon First Nations, 71–72
Yukon Territory, *49*, 68–69, 71–72

Zacatecas, Mexico, 177, 222n83

In the Anthropology of Contemporary North America series:

*America's Digital Army: Games at Work and War*
Robertson Allen

*Governing Affect: Neoliberalism and Disaster Reconstruction*
Roberto E. Barrios

*White Gold: An Ethnography of Breast Milk Sharing*
Susan Falls

*Mexicans in Alaska: An Ethnography of Mobility, Place, and Transnational Life*
Sara V. Komarnisky

*Holding On: African American Women Surviving HIV/AIDS*
Alyson O'Daniel

*Rebuilding Shattered Worlds: Creating Community by Voicing the Past*
Andrea L. Smith and Anna Eisenstein

*Religious, Feminist, Activist: Cosmologies of Interconnection*
Laurel Zwissler

To order or obtain more information on these or other
University of Nebraska Press titles, visit nebraskapress.unl.edu.

www.ingramcontent.com/pod-product-compliance
Lightning Source LLC
Chambersburg PA
CBHW030233240426
43663CB00035B/247